AMERICAN FOREIGN POLICY
SINCE WORLD WAR II

American Foreign Policy Since World War II

Seventh Edition

JOHN SPANIER

University of Florida

PRAEGER PUBLISHERS

New York

Published in the United States of America in 1977
by Praeger Publishers, Inc.
200 Park Avenue, New York, N.Y. 10017

The original edition of this book was published in 1960, with revised editions
in 1962, 1965, 1968, and 1971. This new edition has been extensively revised
and brought up to date.

Library of Congress Cataloging in Publication Data

Spanier, John W

    American foreign policy since World War II.

    Bibliography: p.
    Includes index.
    1. United States—Foreign relations—1945–
I. Title.
E744.S8   1977   327.73   76-48990
ISBN 0-275-64880-X pbk.
ISBN 0-275-24130-0

Printed in the United States of America

CONTENTS

PREFACE TO
THE SEVENTH EDITION

This edition appears as the Carter Administration begins its first term in office. It is a time of widespread discontent with American foreign policy, and the re-examination of its underlying assumptions, which began during the Vietnam War, continues. It is the purpose of this book to provide the reader with both background and perspective on the role the United States has played in the world since the close of World War II so that he may judge for himself the past efforts of postwar administration and evaluate what America's role should be in the future.

Two particular problems today confront the author of an analytical history of recent and contemporary events. One of these is how to convey to the reader, especially the younger reader who is likely to be a college student, an impression of the past without overwhelming him with a chronological recitation of all the events that together constitute the record of American foreign policy since World War II. The temptation is to concentrate on the more recent past and condense, if not eliminate, accounts of many past occurrences. After all, to most students born during the 1950's, much pre-Vietnam history might as well be ancient Greek history. Precisely because of that, I have made cuts for this edition, but only where I felt this could be done without seriously affecting the outlines of what did happen. Indeed, if the contemporary reader is to gain a perspective on the last three decades of America's active participation in world affairs, past events become more important, and too abbreviated an account of them can only produce a seriously distorted perception of recent and contemporary events.

A knowledge of past events becomes all the more important because of the second problem confronting the political analyst: the current popularity of viewing and seeking to understand the cold war through the prism of Vietnam. This approach suggests that, if the Vietnam war was the end product of our prior policy, the entire record of American foreign policy since 1945 stands condemned. For if Vietnam was allegedly the result of our great power and the instinct of the powerful to extend their control, could not this same "arrogance of power" have been a reason for the eruption of the cold war itself? Or, if Vietnam demonstrated that American capitalism in its never ending search for foreign markets and natural resources would crush any national liberation movement that sought to throw off the imperialist (that is, American) economic chains, then could it not be equally true that this same capitalism after 1945 tried to roll back Russian power in Eastern Europe in order to capture new markets for American products? Indeed, had it not attempted during World War II and immediately thereafter to destroy the Soviet revolution, committed as the latter was to the destruction of world capitalism of which the United States later emerged as the leading exponent? Or, if Vietnam were said to be the product of American leaders' misperceptions of the nature of the Communist threat and the stakes at issue in the small Southeast Asian country, could it not be that a similarly distorted view of Stalin's Russia after 1945 led the U.S. Government to see a threat where none existed (or, at least, to see a vastly exaggerated Soviet threat), and thus led Washington to overreact to Russia's essentially defensive moves in Eastern Europe by launching an anti-Communist crusade to ward off a presumed Communist world revolution?

These and other views, spelled out in great detail, are part of the dogma of contemporary "revisionist" historians. Essentially, their argument is twofold: One, the forces that precipitated the cold war and led to Vietnam exist *within* the

United States; and two, but for America's expansionist and aggressive behavior, the world would be at peace. The "natural" harmony of interests among states and the "normal" condition of peaceful relationship among these states would, presumably, re-emerge if men wedded to old myths were replaced with new men who recognize present realities or if fundamental structural changes, such as replacing capitalism with socialism, took place within the American system.

The framework within which we will recount and analyze postwar American foreign policy is quite different from this one, which focuses solely on domestic factors. We will emphasize not only America's national style, the product of domestic values and experience, but also the nature of the international state system and suggest that the foreign policies of its members are primarily determined by the distribution of power within the state system. The security and independence of each member state are enhanced by a balance of power, whereas an imbalance in its distribution will grant one state a superiority of power that might tempt it to impose its will on a weaker opponent. Thus the balance, by seeking to prevent any state from gaining a predominant power position that enables it to subordinate other states to its control, is the principal "peace strategy" available for states, each of which must be its own protector. This means that a nation's foreign relations—certainly any Great Power's —are largely determined by the requirement of maintaining a balance of power; to neglect this essential task is to risk endangering its security.

If this view is correct, then our postwar foreign policy can most fruitfully be evaluated by analyzing how well the United States, formerly an isolationist nation, adjusted to the state system's "imperatives" after the defeat of Germany and Japan. For there was simply no other nation at the time capable of establishing a balance of power in a new world characterized by the collapse of Europe, Soviet expansion, Chinese resurgence, and the birth of a multitude of new nations in the Third World between East and West. Indeed, we will suggest that the evidence of past events strongly suggests that conflict between Moscow and Washington would have erupted even if both nations had shared the same social and economic system. In any case, given the United States's inexperience, the suddenness with which it was confronted by "reality," the scope and novelty of the challenges of nuclear technology, revolutionary Communism, and the nationalist and social revolutions of the underdeveloped countries, the American response to its new balancing role needs to be judged in a broader perspective than that of Vietnam alone, although this is not to deny the significance of Vietnam.

In the final analysis, the reader must judge for himself how he would evaluate the over-all record of American foreign policy, including the decade since 1962. The United States, current critics assert, is now playing the unnecessary role of "world policeman," a task beyond its capacity. They say that instead of involving itself in all areas of the globe, this country should be more discriminating, decide its priorities, and concentrate its attention and energies on its own hemisphere and Western Europe. Indeed, foreign policy should not receive the preponderance of attention and resources it has, at a time when widespread poverty, urban slums, racial revolution and rioting, and air and water pollution threaten the quality of American life; the United States should not "crusade" for democracy overseas before first ensuring its benefits at home. As former Senator Fulbright, a leading critic, voiced it in early 1968 during the Vietnam War:

> To that school of political thinkers who call themselves "realists" it is irrelevant sentimentalism to question the primacy of power politics in terms of its costs, purposes and human rewards. There is—so they tell us—no choice involved. . . .
>
> Power politics is practiced under different names. . . . No empire stood stronger and prouder than the British Empire a hundred years ago; today we are witnessing its sad, final sunset.
>
> Can America escape the same fate? Accepting the gloomy determinism of the "responsibilities of power," in effect our present policymakers tell us that it cannot. They do not, of

course, predict our decline and fall, only the extension of power, the drain of material and human resources, and the neglect of domestic requirements that precede and precipitate the fall of empires.

I do not think we are condemned to this. . . . Nations, like individuals, have some freedom of choice, and America of all nations is equipped to exercise it. . . . If we do not, it will not be because history assigned to us an imperial role. It will be because we *chose* to believe such pompous nonsense, because power went to our heads like a superdose of LSD, leading us to betray our history and the purposes for which this nation was founded.

Foreign policy, then, is a corrupting influence.

Yet, is the Senator correct? One supporter of American foreign policy, a Canadian, Lionel Gelber, thinks not. Writing in the *Yale Review* in the fall of 1967, at the height of the debate over what policies the United States should pursue in Vietnam and, more broadly, in the world as a whole, he said:

I have yet to hear of any viable alternative to what the United States has been doing on the world stage. Even if free countries wished to reject American leadership in theory they could not do so in practice; the United States herself cannot throw it off. For the American role is shaped by the nature of the world in which we live. And the nature of that world is ignored when there is talk about the American role as that of a self-appointed global gendarme. Such a gibe appears to suggest that no custodian of world order is needed. . . . But what it tends to suggest, above all, is that the militancy of others has not been the danger in our time. Caprice in leadership by the United States —that, presumably, is the source of trouble.

[Yet,] under altered conditions, the United States, as leader of the West, has only been taking a leaf out of the British book. Britain's own role, after all, was a "self-appointed" one when free communities (including the United States) developed overseas under the shelter of British sea power; when ideas of freedom took root among people not yet free; when, too, Britain stood alone between civilized society and its debasement by the Nazis. It is odd that in this day and age such truths have to be restated. They would not have to be restated if, at the heart of the West, a woeful incomprehension of the forces in play did not exist.

Which view of the contemporary role of the United States in world affairs is the right one? Is it a curse or a blessing? The reader will have to decided that for himself.

Gainesville, Florida
Winter, 1976

AMERICAN FOREIGN POLICY
SINCE WORLD WAR II

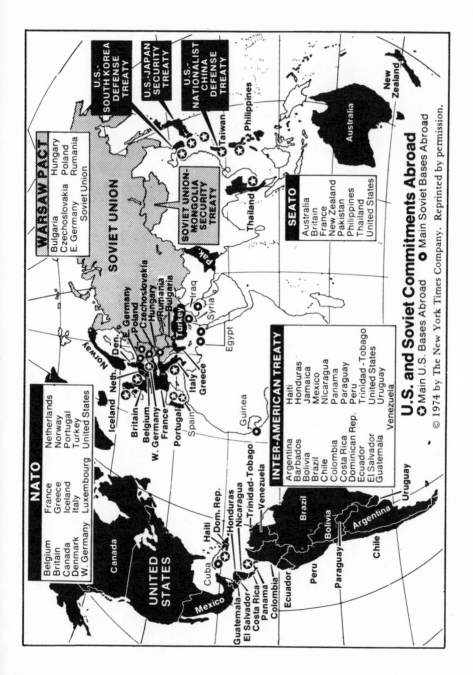

U.S. and Soviet Commitments Abroad

✪ Main U.S. Bases Abroad   ○ Main Soviet Bases Abroad

© 1974 by The New York Times Company. Reprinted by permission.

NATO

Belgium	Netherlands
Britain	Norway
Canada	Portugal
Denmark	Turkey
W. Germany	United States
France	
Greece	
Iceland	
Italy	
Luxembourg	

WARSAW PACT

Bulgaria	Hungary
Czechoslovakia	Poland
E. Germany	Rumania
	Soviet Union

SOVIET UNION MONGOLIA SECURITY TREATY

SEATO

Australia
Britain
France
New Zealand
Pakistan
Philippines
Thailand
United States

INTER-AMERICAN TREATY

Argentina	Haiti
Barbados	Honduras
Bolivia	Jamaica
Brazil	Mexico
Chile	Nicaragua
Colombia	Panama
Costa Rica	Paraguay
Dominican Rep.	Peru
Ecuador	Trinidad-Tobago
El Salvador	United States
Guatemala	Uruguay
	Venezuela

U.S.-SOUTH KOREA DEFENSE TREATY

U.S.-JAPAN SECURITY TREATY

U.S.-NATIONALIST CHINA DEFENSE TREATY

1

THE AMERICAN APPROACH
TO FOREIGN POLICY

The State System

American foreign policy since World War II is the story of the interaction between the state system and the American style of conducting foreign policy. In this state system, each member—especially the Great Powers, its principal actors— tends to feel a high degree of insecurity. In the absence of a world government which could govern and safeguard it, each state knows that it can depend on no one but itself for its own preservation and safety. Self-protection is the only protection in an essentially anarchical system; understandably, states tend to regard one another as potential adversaries, menaces to each other's territorial integrity and political independence. In short, the very nature of the state system breeds feelings of insecurity, distrust, suspicion, and fear.

It is this atmosphere that produces a constant scramble for power. Enhancing one's power relative to that of a possible foe becomes a principal means of reducing one's own insecurity. When a state perceives its neighbor as a potential enemy, it will try to deter a possible attack by becoming a little stronger than its neighbor; the latter, in its turn, will also fear an attack and, therefore, will perceive its own best interest to lie in sufficient strength to forestall such a contingency, or, failing that, to win the resulting war. Thus, it is not man's alleged aggressive instinct as a "naked ape" or man's presumed desire for acquiring ever greater power that accounts for what is popularly called "power politics"; rather, power politics stems from each state's continuous concern with its

3

security. Because the external environment is perceived by states as menacing to their security—the prerequisite for the enjoyment by each one of them of its particular way of life— they are naturally prone to react fearfully against what they believe to be threats. And in such a context it does not take much to arouse and confirm another state's apprehensions and thereby stimulate reciprocal images of hostility, which each state will find it easy to substantiate by the opponent's behavior. Indeed, this enmity will in most instances be maintained despite contradictory evidence and even avowedly friendly acts. Conciliatory behavior is likely to be dismissed as an indicator of weakness or as a trick to relax one's guard and, therefore, not to be accepted at face value but exploited or guarded against.

In any event, it is easy to understand why in these circumstances states pursue a "balance of power" policy. A balance or equilibrium would make victory in a war less probable for an opponent and certainly very costly in comparison to any possible gains. Logically, therefore, a balance is presumed to be that distribution of power most likely to deter an attack. By contrast, possession of disproportionate power might tempt a state to undertake aggression by making it far less costly to gain a predominant position and impose its will upon other states. In other words, the fundamental assumption underlying the state system is that its members cannot be trusted with power, since they will be tempted to abuse it. Unrestrained power in the system constitutes a threat to all states; power is, therefore, the best antidote to power. As one close observer of international politics, Arnold Wolfers, has noted:

> Under these conditions of anarchy the expectation of violence and even of annihilation is ever-present. To forget this and thus fail in the concern for enhanced power spells the doom of a state. This does not mean open constant warfare; expansion of power at the expense of others will not take place if there is enough counterpower to deter or to stop states from undertaking it. Although no state is interested in a mere balance of power, the efforts of all states to maximize power may lead to

equilibrium. If and when that happens, there is "peace" or, more exactly, a condition of stalemate or truce. Under the conditions described here, this balancing of power process is the only available "peace" strategy.

Power thus elicits countervailing power. The basic rule of the "international game" is to resist attempts by any state to expand and seek a predominant position in the international system. Therefore, when the balance is disturbed, equilibrium will tend to be restored by the emergence of counterpower. States ignore at their peril this rule to maintain a balance of power; policy-makers need to be equally careful that they judge correctly the necessary countervailing power.

What all this means is that we can to a very significant degree explain any state's behavior in terms of the ever changing distribution of power. As that distribution changes, so does a state's foreign policy. For example, the impact of a shift in the distribution of power is evident in America's involvements in the two world wars of this century. During most of the nineteenth century and early twentieth century the United States was able to preserve its historical isolation from "power politics" thanks to the balance of power on the European continent maintained by Britain to protect its own security. No one state or coalition of states was able to conquer most of Europe, organize its vast resources in manpower and industrial strength, and then use these to menace the United States. England's opposition to any state's seeking such hegemony therefore made it possible for the United States to remain was today is called "nonaligned."

However, after 1870, when Germany was unified and launched a massive program of industrialization, British power declined relative to Germany's growing capability. The early years of World War I showed clearly that even British and French power together could not contain Germany. With the collapse of Tsarist Russia in the East and the transfer of almost 2 million German soldiers to the Western Front, a German victory became a distinct possibility. It was at that point that Germany's unrestricted submarine warfare, which included attacks on American shipping, precipitated

U.S. intervention, and this was what made it possible to contain the German spring offensive of 1918 and led to Germany's defeat.

After victory America retreated into isolationism again, only to be compelled just over two decades later once more to concern itself with the European balance of power. The unexpected German defeat of France in 1940 again confronted the United States with the specter of an invasion and defeat of England. President Franklin D. Roosevelt therefore undertook a number of measures to strengthen Britain to withstand any Nazi assault. He sent fifty old destroyers to help defend the English Channel, and he set up the Lend Lease program, which made the United States the "arsenal of democracy." The balance of power had made this increasing commitment to Britain necessary, even though such actions increased the risk of war with Germany. In fact, by the time of Pearl Harbor, the United States was already engaged in an undeclared naval war with Germany in the Atlantic, and full-scale war with Germany was merely a matter of time: German submarines would, sooner or later, start sinking American ships carrying war supplies for Britain in order to compel its surrender. The German invasion of Russia in 1941 briefly postponed the Battle of the Atlantic, and when it did take place the United States was already at war. But had Hitler, in 1940–41, given the order to sink all ships bound for England, President Roosevelt, like President Wilson before him, would have had to ask Congress for a declaration of war.

One further point is worth noting about these two examples, namely, that the issue in neither case was whether the American people wished to go to war against Germany. The isolationist mood was still far too strong. Nevertheless, the United States did intervene in both cases; in neither instance, furthermore, was there any existing commitment, legal or moral, which obligated the nation to intervene. The issue in 1917 and in 1941 was not whether the nation preferred peace and domestic preoccupation to foreign involvement, but what self-preservation obliged it to do. The shifting balance of power left the country little choice.

The American National Style

The approach to foreign policy with which America entered World War II was the product of domestic experiences and values developed in isolation from the state system—which meant in effect the European state system. The priority of internal political and economic tasks, all of which were reinforced by the opening of the West and the subsequent transcontinental drive to the Pacific, led to the depreciation of the importance of foreign policy and the role that power plays in protecting the nation's interests. The ability of the United States to live in isolation during the nineteenth century and a good part of the twentieth century was attributed not to the nation's geographic distance from Europe or to the Royal Navy as the protector of the *Pax Britannica,* but to the nature of democracy. The United States was more than just the world's first "new nation"; it was also the world's first democracy and, as such, the first country in history that would devote itself to improving the lot of the common man, granting each individual the opportunity to enrich and ennoble his life. ("Give me your tired, your poor, your huddled masses yearning to breathe free," reads the inscription on the Statue of Liberty.) The more perfect union was to be an egalitarian society. European concepts of social hierarchy, nobility and titles, and bitter class struggles were not to be planted in its democratic soil. "Here the free spirit of mankind, at length, throws its last fetters off," exclaimed one writer. America was to be a "beacon lighting for all the world the paths of human destiny," wrote Emerson. From the very beginning of their national life, Americans believed strongly in their destiny—to spread, *by example,* freedom and social justice to all men and to lead mankind away from its wicked ways to the New Jerusalem on earth. The massive immigration of the nineteenth century—particularly after 1865—was to reinforce this sense of destiny. "Repudiation of Europe," as John Dos Passos once said, "is, after all, America's main excuse for being." Europe stood for war, poverty, and exploitation; America, for peace, opportunity, and democracy. But the United States was not merely to be a beacon of a superior democratic domestic way of life. It was also to be an example of a morally superior democratic pattern of international behavior. The United States would voluntarily reject power politics as unfit for the conduct of its foreign policy. Democratic theory posits that man is a rational and moral creature, and that differences among men can be settled by rational persuasion and moral exhortation. Indeed, granted this assumption about man, the only differences that could arise would simply be misunderstandings, and, since man is endowed with reason and a moral sense, what quarrels could not be settled, given the necessary good will? Peace—the result of harmony among men—was thus considered the natural or normal state.

Conversely, conflict was considered a deviation from this norm, caused primarily by wicked statesmen whose morality and reason had been corrupted by the exercise of uncontrolled authority. Power politics was an instrument of selfish and autocratic rulers—that is, men unrestrained by democratic public opinion—who loved to wield it for their own personal advantage. To them, war was a grand game. They could remain in their palatial homes, continuing to eat well and to enjoy the luxuries of life. They suffered none of the hardships of war. These hardships fell upon the ordinary people; it was they who had to leave their families to fight, to endure the higher taxes made necessary by the costs of war, possibly to see their homes destroyed and their loved ones maimed or killed. It was only the despot who thought of war as a sport, as a sort of "bully" fox hunt; the common man, who had to endure all the cruelties of war, was therefore by his very nature peaceful. The conclusion was clear: Undemocratic states were inherently warlike and evil; democratic nations, in which the people controlled and regularly changed their leaders, were peaceful and moral.

American experience seemed to support this conclusion. The United States was a democracy, and it was at peace. Furthermore, peace seemed to be the normal state of affairs. It was therefore logical that democracy and peaceful behavior and intentions should be thought of as synonymous. Americans never asked themselves whether democracy was really responsible for the peace they enjoyed, or whether this peace they assumed to be a natural condition was the product of other forces. The constant wars of Europe appeared to provide the answer: European politics was power politics, and this was because of the undemocratic nature of European regimes. Americans were therefore relieved that they had long ago, at the time of the Revolutionary War, cut themselves off from Europe and its class conflicts and power politics. America had to guard its democratic purity and abstain from any involvement in the affairs of Europe lest it be soiled and corrupted. Nonalignment was therefore the morally correct policy which allowed the United States to quarantine itself from contact with Europe's hierarchical social structures and immoral international habits. At the same time, by confusing the results of geography and international politics with the supposed consequences of democracy, Americans could smugly enjoy their self-conferred moral superiority as the world's first democracy. It was the Monroe Doctrine, proclaimed in 1823, that first stressed, officially and explicitly, this ideological difference between the New and Old Worlds. It declared specifically that the American political system was "essentially different" from that of Europe, whose nations were constantly engaged in warfare. The implication was very clear: Democratic government equals peace, and aristocratic government—which was identified with despotism—means war.

But this association of peace with democracy was not the only reason for the American depreciation of power politics. Another was that the United States was an overwhelmingly one-class society—one in which most shared a common set of middle-class, capitalistic, and democratic values or beliefs. America was unique among nations in this respect. The European countries were, by contrast, three-class societies. In addition to the middle class, they contained in their bodies politic an aristocratic class, whose energies were devoted either to maintaining itself in power or to recapturing power in order to return to the glorious days of a feudal past. More-over, European urbanization and industrialization during the nineteenth century gave birth to a proletariat, which, because it felt it did not receive a fair share of the national income, became a revolutionary class. The nations of the Old World were, in short, a composite of three elements: a reactionary aristocracy, a democratic middle class, and a revolutionary proletariat. Or, to put it another way, these nations had, in an intellectual as well as a political sense, a right, a center, and a left. The United States had only a center, both intellectu-ally and politically. It had never experienced a feudal past and therefore possessed no large and powerful aristocratic class on the right; and because it was, by and large, an egali-tarian society, it also lacked a genuine left-wing movement of protest, such as socialism or communism. America was, as Tocqueville had said, "born free" as a middle-class, individ-ualistic, capitalistic, and democratic society. It was not di-vided by the kind of deep ideological conflicts that in France, for instance, set one class of Frenchmen against another. No one class was ever so afraid of another that it preferred na-tional defeat to domestic revolution—as in France in the late 1930's, when the *haute bourgeoisie* was so apprehensive of a proletarian upheaval that its slogan became "Better Hitler than Blum [the French Socialist leader]."

Americans in the past have been so in accord on basic values that whenever the nation has been threatened exter-nally the public has become fearful of internal disloyalty. It is one of the great ironies of American society that, while Amer-icans possessed this unity of shared beliefs to a greater degree than any other people, their apprehension of external danger led them, first, to insist upon a general and somewhat dog-matic reaffirmation of loyalty to the "American way of life," and then to hunt for internal groups that might betray this way of life. Disagreement tended to become suspect as dis-loyalty; men were accused of "un-American" thinking and behavior, and labeled "loyalty or security risks." Perhaps only a society so overwhelmingly committed to one set of values could have been so sensitive to internal subversion and so fearful of internal betrayal; perhaps only a society in which two or more ideologies have long since learned to live together can genuinely tolerate diverse opinions. Who has ever heard of "un-British" or "un-French" activities? The United States has often been called a "melting pot" because of the many different nationality groups it comprises, but, before each generation of immigrants has been fully accepted into American society, it has had to be "Americanized." Few Americans have ever accepted diversity as a value. American society has, in fact, taken great pride in destroying diversity through assimilation.

It was precisely this overwhelming agreement on the fundamental values of American society and Europe's intense class struggles that reinforced the American misunderstanding of the nature and functions of power on the international scene. Dissatisfied groups never developed a revolutionary ideology because the growing prosperity spread to them before they could translate their grievances against the capitalist system into political action. (The black American, of course, represents a clear and important exception.) With the exception of the Civil War, America—politically secure and economically prosperous—was able, therefore, to resolve most of its differences peacefully. In sharp contrast, because of their internal class struggles and external conflicts among themselves, the nations of Europe fully appreciated the role of power politics.

Politics did not, in any event, seem very important to Americans. The United States matured during the nineteenth century, the era of *laissez-faire* capitalism whose basic assumption was that man was economically motivated. It was self-interest that governed the behavior of man; it might be referred to as "enlightened self-interest," but it was nevertheless self-interest. Each individual, seeking to maximize his wealth, responded to the demand of the free market. In an effort to increase his profit, he supplied the product the consumers wanted. The laws of supply and demand therefore transformed each person's economic selfishness into socially beneficial results. The entire society would prosper. The free market was thus considered the central institution that provided "the greatest good for the greatest number." Politics mattered little in this self-adjusting economic system based upon individuals whose combined efforts resulted in the general welfare. The best government was the government that governed least. Arbitrary political interference with the economic laws of the market would only upset the results these laws were intended to produce. Private property, profit, and the free market were thus the keys to ensuring the happiness of man by providing him with abundance. Capitalism, in short, reflected the materialism of the age of industrialization.

To state the issue even more bluntly: Economics was good, politics was bad. This simple dichotomy came naturally to the capitalist middle class. Were the benefits of economic freedom not as "self-evident" as the truths stated in the Declaration of Independence? And had this economic freedom not been gained only by a long and bitter struggle of the European middle class to cut down the authority of the powerful monarchical state, and finally to overthrow it by revolution in France? The middle class, as it had grown more prosperous and numerous, had become increasingly resentful of paying taxes from which the aristocracy was usually exempt, of the restrictions placed upon trade and industry, of the absence of institutions in which middle-class economic and political interests were represented, of the class barriers to the social status that came with careers in the army and in the bureaucracy, and of the general lack of freedom of thought and expression. Since the middle class identified the power of the state with its own lack of freedom, its aim was to restrict this power. Only by placing restraints upon the authority of the state could it gain the individual liberty and, above all, the right to private enterprise it sought. Democratic philosophy stated these claims in terms of the individual's "natural rights" against the state. The exercise of political authority was thus equated with the abuse of that authority and the suppression of personal freedoms. The power of the state had therefore to be restricted to the minimum to ensure the individual's maximum political and economic liberties. It was with this purpose in mind that the American Constitution

divided authority between the states and the federal government, and, within the latter, among the executive, legislative,
and judicial branches. Federalism and the separation of powers were deliberately designed to keep all governments—and
especially the national government—weak. Man's secular
problems would be resolved not by the state's political actions
but by the individual's own economic actions in society.

Again, both man's economic motivation and the benefits of
a government that acts least were considered to be reflected in
the American experience. Millions came to the United States
from other lands to seek a better way of life. America was the
earthly paradise where all men, no matter how poor or hum-
ble they had been in the old country, could earn a respectable
living. A virgin and underdeveloped land, America presented
magnificent opportunities for individual enterprise. First,
there was the Western frontier with its rich soil; later, during
the Industrial Revolution, the country's bountiful natural resources were exploited. The environment, technology, individual enterprise, and helpful governmental policies enabled
the American people to become the "people of plenty." But
to earn money was not only economically necessary in order
to attain a comfortable standard of living; it was also psychologically necessary in order to gain social status and to earn
the respect of one's fellow citizens.

It follows logically that, if material gain confers social respect and position upon men, everyone will preoccupy himself with the pursuit and accumulation of the "almighty
dollar." If men in an egalitarian society are judged primarily
by their economic achievements, they will concentrate on
"getting ahead." It is not surprising, therefore, that money
comes closer to being the common standard of value in the
United States than in any other country. For money is the
symbol of power and prestige; it is the sign of success, just as
failure to earn enough money is a token of personal failure.
It has been said, not without some justice, that the American
prefers two cars to two mistresses.

It was hardly surprising that in these circumstances the
solution to international problems should be thought of in

economic terms. Economics was identified with social harmony and the welfare of all men; politics was equated with conflict and war and death. Just as the "good society" was to be the product of free competition, so the peaceful international society would be created by free trade. An international *laissez-faire* policy would benefit all states just as a national *laissez-faire* policy benefited each individual within these states. Consequently, people all over the world had a vested interest in peace in order to carry on their economic relations. Trade and war were incompatible. Trade depended upon mutual prosperity (the poor do not buy much from one another). War impoverishes and destroys and creates ill will among nations. Commerce benefits all the participating states; the more trade, the greater the number of individual interests involved. Commerce was consequently nationally and individually profitable and created a vested interest in peace. War, by contrast, was economically unprofitable and therefore obsolete. Free trade and peace, in short, were one and the same cause.

Thus the United States entered the twentieth century with a relative unawareness of the role that power plays in the relations among nations, even though as a highly industrialized and powerful nation it was, at the turn of the century, increasingly exerting a dominating influence in the Western Hemisphere. At no time was this attitude more vividly demonstrated than at the point of its entry into World War I and during the interwar period. It was Germany's unrestricted submarine warfare in early 1917 that brought the United States into that conflict; it was thus the German High Command's fatal decision that propelled it into the war. Yet American security demanded this entry. The balance of power in the European battlefield was about to collapse; Britain and France were nearing financial exhaustion; Britain's food supply had reached near-starvation level because of the effectiveness of the German submarine campaign; the French Army had suffered such enormous casualties during a series of offensives that it had mutinied; and above all, the Tsarist empire was about to collapse. If the Western Allies had then been defeated, as seemed quite likely, the United States would have had to confront a Germany astride the whole continent, dominating European Russia and, in alliance with Austria-Hungary and the Ottoman Empire, extending its influence over the Balkans and the Middle East as far as the Persian Gulf. This would have posed a grave threat to American security. The United States, therefore, had good reason to ally itself with Britain and France to safeguard its own security before this menacing situation matured. But it did not—and would not have, if Germany had not launched its unrestricted submarine warfare in the spring of 1917.

The United States thus entered the war in a political vacuum. The American people were never aware of the power realities and security interests that made American participation in the war absolutely necessary. Rather, they believed they were fighting a war for freedom and democracy, conducting a crusade to destroy German despotism and militarism and to banish power politics forever. It is hardly surprising, therefore, that, once the war had burned out this crusading spirit, the American public, still blissfully unaware of the relationship between American independence and the balance of power, should again wish to retire into its prewar isolationist state. The United States thus refused to help protect itself, although Britain and France had been exhausted by the four years of fighting and Germany remained second only to the United States as potentially the most powerful country in the world. Americans refused to face the responsibility that attended the possession of great power. Instead of playing their proper role in world affairs and attempting to preserve the international balance, thereby heading off the next war, they buried their heads in the sand for more than twenty years. The result was that a renascent Germany—allied this time with Italy and Japan (plus the Soviet Union from 1939 to 1941)—once again sought to dominate the world. In December, 1941, Japan's attack on Pearl Harbor precipitated the American entry into World War II. America's ostrich policy had not prevented the waves of world politics from once more lapping its shores.

This American depreciation of power, so evident in these events, has meant that the United States draws a clear-cut distinction between war and peace in its approach to foreign policy. Peace is characterized by a state of harmony among nations; power politics, or war, is considered abnormal. In peacetime, one need pay little or no attention to foreign problems; indeed, to do so would divert men from their individual, materialistic concerns and upset the whole scale of social values. The effect of this attitude is clear: Americans turn their attention toward the outside world only with the greatest reluctance and only when they feel provoked—that is, when the foreign menace has become so clear that it can no longer be ignored. Or, to state it somewhat differently, the United States rarely initiates policy; the stimuli that are responsible for the formulation of American foreign policy come from beyond America's frontiers.

Once Americans are provoked, however, and the United States has to resort to force, the employment of this force can be justified only in terms of the universal moral principles with which the United States, as a democratic country, identifies itself. Resort to the evil instrument of war can be justified only by presuming noble purposes and completely destroying the immoral enemy who threatens the integrity, if not the existence, of these principles. American power must be "righteous" power; only its full exercise can ensure salvation or the absolution of sin. The national aversion to violence thus becomes transformed into a national glorification of violence, and wars become ideological crusades to make the world safe for democracy—by democratizing it or by converting the authoritarian or totalitarian states into peaceful, democratic states and thereby banishing power politics for all time. Once that aim has been achieved, the United States can again withdraw into itself, secure in the knowledge that American works have again proved to be "good works." In this context, foreign affairs are an annoying diversion from more important domestic matters. But such diversions are only temporary, since maximum force is applied to the aggressor or warmonger to punish him for his provocation and

to teach him that aggression is immoral and will not be rewarded. As a result, American wars are total wars—that is,
wars aimed at the total destruction of the enemy.

Not only does the American approach to international
politics consider peace and war as two mutually exclusive
states of affairs; it also divorces force from diplomacy. In
peacetime, diplomacy unsupported by force is supposed to
preserve the harmony among states. But, in wartime, political
considerations are subordinated to force. Once the diplomats
have failed to keep the peace with appeals to morality and
reason, military considerations become primary. During war,
the soldier is placed in charge. Just as the professional medical man has the responsibility for curing his patients of their
several maladies, so the military "doctor" must control the
curative treatment of the international society when it is in-
fected with the disease of power politics. General Douglas
MacArthur aptly summed up this attitude: When diplomacy
has failed to preserve the peace, he said, "you then go to
force; and when you do that, the balance of control . . . is
the control of the military. A theater commander, in any
campaign, is not merely limited to the handling of his troops;
he commands the whole area politically, economically, and
militarily. . . . when politics fail, and the military take over,
you must trust the military."

The United States, then, has traditionally rejected the concept of war as a political instrument and the Clausewitzian
definition of war as the continuation of politics by other
means. Instead, it has regarded war as a politically neutral
operation which should be guided by its own professional
rules and imperatives. The military officer is a nonpolitical
man who conducts his campaign in a strictly military, technically efficient manner. And war is a purely military instrument whose sole aim is the destruction of the enemy's forces
and of his despotic regime so that his people can be democ-
ratized.

War is thus a means employed to abolish power politics;
war is conducted to end all wars. This same moralistic attitude, which is responsible for the Americans' all-or-nothing

approach to war—either to abstain from the dirty game of power politics or to crusade for its complete elimination—also militates against the use of diplomacy in its classical sense: to compromise interests, to conciliate differences, and to moderate and isolate conflicts. While, on the one hand, Americans regard diplomacy as a rational process for straightening out misunderstandings between nations, they are, on the other hand, extremely suspicious of diplomacy. If the United States is by definition moral, it obviously cannot compromise; for a nation endowed with a moral mission can hardly violate its own principles. That would constitute appeasement and national humiliation. The nation's principles would be transgressed, the nation's interests improperly defended, the national honor stained. For to compromise with the immoral enemy is to be contaminated with evil. Moreover, to reach a settlement with him, rather than wiping him out in order to safeguard those principles, would be an acknowledgment of American weakness. This attitude toward diplomacy, which, in effect, makes its use as an instrument of compromise so difficult, thus reinforces the predilection for violence as a means of settling international problems. For war allows the nation to destroy its evil opponent, while permitting it to keep its moral mission intact and unsullied by any compromises which could infect its purity.

Thus, on the eve of the cold war the American approach to foreign policy contrasted sharply in a number of important respects with the conduct required by the state system. For example, having historically given precedence to domestic affairs, the United States, not surprisingly, has found it difficult to attain and maintain a balance between foreign and domestic priorities. On the whole, American foreign policy has tended to swing from an isolationist position in which the country served as an example of democratic brotherhood and social justice on earth to a posture of massive and violent intervention once provoked. Level-headed, consistent participation in the international system has been difficult; all-or-nothing swings have been the more common pattern.

Furthermore, the American perception of an international

harmony of interests stands in stark contrast to the state system's emphasis on the inevitability of conflict and differences of interests among states. The former view regards conflict as an abnormal condition, the latter perceives harmony as an illusion. The United States, long isolated from Europe and therefore not socialized into the state system, did not accept the reality and permanence of conflicts among its members. Differences between states were not considered natural, and certainly not deep and long-range; rather, they were attributed to wicked leaders (who could be eliminated), authoritarian political systems (which could be reformed), or misunderstandings (which could be straightened out if the adversaries approached each other with sincerity and empathy). Once these obstacles had been removed, peace, harmony, and goodwill would reign supreme.

Above all, America has always considered itself a morally and politically superior society due to its democratic culture. This has meant that its attitude toward the use of power internationally has been dominated by the belief that the struggle for power did not exist or could be avoided by isolating oneself from it or could be eliminated by crusading against those countries indulging in power politics. Moralism in foreign policy proscribed the use of power in peacetime lest one became tainted; it could be employed only in confrontations with unambiguous aggression, transformed then into an obligation to fight on behalf of righteous causes. In short, power, internationally just as domestically, can be legitimated only by democratic purposes; otherwise, its exercise would be evil and would necessarily arouse guilt feelings.

The great American compulsion to feel moral internationally reinforced the cyclical swings from isolationism to crusading and back again. The perception of power as simply the raw material of international politics—its use as an instrument of compromise, conciliation, and moderation of interstate politics, its discriminating application toward achievement of specific and less-than-total objectives—was clearly antithetical to the American understanding of power.

Perhaps the most telling symptom of America's national

style in conducting foreign policy is that after every major war the reasons for the country's participation in struggle and bloodshed have been reinterpreted. These revisionist histories have certain common themes: the conflicts in which the nation had become entangled did not in fact threaten its security interests; it became involved because the politicians saw a menace where none existed, and this illusion had been promoted by propagandists who aroused and manipulated public opinion, by soldiers with bureaucratic motives, and, above all else, by bankers and industrialists—the "merchants of death" of the 1930's, the "military industrial complex" of the 1960's—whose economic interests benefited from the struggle. America's engagements in the two world wars of this century (as in the cold war later) were mistakes; they were really unnecessary or immoral, if not both. The evil enemy yesterday identified as the aggressor and *provocateur* thus apparently did not represent a threat to American security at all; to the contrary, the threat turns out to have been from within, not from without. In brief, but for certain *domestic forces,* the United States could have continued to isolate itself from international politics.

The fundamental revisionist assumption, then, is that the nation has had a choice whether it wants to employ "power politics." Conversely, revisionism rejects the idea that the distribution of power in the state system leaves the United States —or any other country, for that matter—with a choice only of whether it will help maintain the balance of power. Power is equated with its abuse. Abstention from its use and creating a truly just society at home are considered wiser and more moral policies. Crusading, allegedly for the reform of the world, risks corrupting America's very soul, since it diverts attention and resources from reform at home to military preparation and war.

The United States after World War II, therefore, confronted a world with attitudes and a behavior pattern inherited from its long period of isolationism from Europe. But the situation that faced the United States in 1945 no longer allowed it to abstain from this struggle. The need to contain the Soviet Union by establishing and maintaining the balance of power required long-range policies that would effectively combine the political, military, and economic factors of power. American security interests demanded no less. It remained to be seen whether a nation, inwardly oriented and temperamentally impatient, with little experience in international politics, could adjust to the sudden demands of "power politics," switching from isolationism to involvement first in the eastern Mediterranean, then Western Europe, and finally Asia.

2

THE BEGINNING OF
THE COLD WAR

American Wartime Illusions

Before one of the wartime conferences between Prime Minister Winston Churchill and President Franklin Roosevelt, an American Intelligence forecast of Russia's postwar position in Europe concluded that the Soviet Union would be the dominant power on the continent of Europe: "With Germany crushed, there is no power in Europe to oppose her tremendous military forces. . . . The conclusions from the foregoing are obvious. Since Russia is the decisive factor in the war, she must be given every assistance, and every effort must be made to obtain her friendship. Likewise, since without question she will dominate Europe on the defeat of the Axis, it is even more essential to develop and maintain the most friendly relations with Russia."

The importance of this estimate lies less in its prediction of the Soviet Union's postwar position—which was, after all, fairly obvious—than in its reflection of American expectations about future Russo-American relations. American policymakers were apparently unable to conceive of the Soviet Union, the acknowledged new dominant power in Europe, replacing Nazi Germany as a grave threat to the European and global balance of power. Yet the United States had already twice in this century been propelled into Europe's wars at exactly those moments when Germany became so powerful that it menaced—indeed, almost destroyed—this balance. The lessons of history—specifically, the impact of any nation's domination of Europe upon American security—had not yet been absorbed. President Roosevelt and the American Government did not aim at re-establishing a balance of power in Europe to safeguard the United States; they expected this security to stem from mutual Russo-American goodwill, unsupported by any power considerations. This reliance upon mere goodwill and mutual esteem was to prove foolish at best and, at worst, might have been fatal.

Indeed, the expectation of a postwar "era of good feeling" between the Soviet Union and the United States was characteristic of the unsuspecting and utopian nature of American wartime thinking, which held that war was an interruption of the normal state of harmony among nations, that military force was an instrument for punishing the aggressor or war criminals, that those who cooperated with their country in its ideological crusade were equally moral and selfless, and that, once the war was finished, the natural harmony would be restored and the struggle for power ended. The implication was clear: The United States need take no precautionary steps against its noble wartime allies in anticipation of a possible disintegration of the alliance and potential hostility among its partners. Instead, it was hoped that the friendly relations and mutual respect which American leaders believed had matured during the war would preserve the common outlook and purposes and guarantee an enduring peace.

These optimistic expectations of future Russo-American relations made it necessary, however, to explain away continuing signs of Soviet hostility and suspicion. Throughout the war, the Russians constantly suspected the United States and Britain of devious intentions. This was particularly true with regard to the Western delay in opening up a second front. When the front was postponed from 1942 to 1943 to 1944, Stalin, Russia's dictator, became very bitter. He brusquely rejected Allied explanations that sufficient invasion barges for such an enormous undertaking were not available, and he especially denounced Prime Minister Churchill for declaring that there would be no invasion until the Germans were so weakened that Allied forces would not have to suffer forbiddingly high losses. To Stalin, this was no explanation, for the

Russians accepted huge losses of men as a matter of course. "When we come to a minefield," Marshall Zhukov explained to General Eisenhower after the war, "our infantry attacks exactly as if it were not there. The losses we get from personnel mines we consider only equal to those we would have gotten from machine guns and artillery if the Germans had chosen to defend that particular area with strong bodies of troops instead of with minefields." It was no wonder, then, that the Russians should dismiss these Allied explanations and fasten instead upon a more reasonable interpretation which, to them, would account for American and British behavior. From the Marxist viewpoint, the Allies were doing exactly what they should be doing—namely, postponing the second front until the Soviet Union and Germany had exhausted each other. Then the two Western powers could land in France, march bloodlessly into Germany, and dictate the peace to both Germany and Russia. The Western delay was, in short, apparently seen as a deliberate attempt by the world's two leading capitalist powers to destroy both of their two major ideological opponents at one and the same time. Throughout the war, the Russians displayed again and again this almost paranoid fear of hostile Western intentions.

American leaders found a ready explanation for these repeated indications of Soviet suspicion. They thought of Soviet foreign policy not in terms of the internal dynamics of the regime and its enmity toward all non-Communist nations, but solely in terms of Russian reactions to Western policies. The Soviet attitude was viewed against the pattern of prewar anti-Soviet Western acts: the Allied intervention in Russia at the end of World War I in order to overthrow the Soviet regime and, after the failure of that attempt, the establishment by France of the *cordon sanitaire* in Eastern Europe to keep the Soviet virus from infecting Europe; the West's rejection of Soviet efforts in the mid- and late 1930's to build an alliance against Hitler; and especially, the Munich agreement in 1938, which, by destroying Czechoslovakia, in effect opened Hitler's gateway to the East. In short, Western efforts to ostracize and ultimately destroy the Soviet Union, as well as attempts to turn the Hitlerian threat away from the West and toward Russia, were considered the primary reasons for the existence of Soviet hostility. To overcome this attitude, the West had only to demonstrate its good intentions and prove its friendliness. The question was not *whether* Soviet cooperation could be won for the postwar world, only *how* it could be gained. And if Western efforts did bear fruit and create goodwill, what conflicts of interest could not be settled peacefully in the future? Various Soviet policies and acts during the war—the disbanding of the Comintern (the instrument of international Communism), the toning down of Communist ideology and new emphasis placed on Russian nationalism, the relaxation of restrictions upon the Church, the praise of the United States and Britain for also being democratic, and, above all, the statement of Russian war aims in the same language of peace, democracy, and freedom used by the West—all seemed to prove that if the Western powers demonstrated their friendship they could convert the Russians into friends.

President Roosevelt and his advisers certainly believed that they had firmly established such amicable relations with the Soviet Union at the Yalta Conference in February, 1945. Stalin had made concessions on a number of vital issues and promised goodwill for the future. He had accepted the United Nations on the basis of the American formula that the veto in the Security Council should be applied only to enforcement action, and not to peaceful attempts at the settlement of disputes. Moreover, in the "Declaration on Liberated Europe," he had promised to support self-government and allow free elections in Eastern Europe. And regarding the Far East, he had responded to the wishes of the American military and promised to enter the war against Japan. Finally, he had repeatedly expressed his hope for fifty years of peace and "big power" cooperation.

It is little wonder that at the end of the conference the American delegation felt a mood of "supreme exultation." The new era of goodwill was to be embodied in the United Nations. Here the peoples of the world could exercise vigilance over the statesmen in their dealings with one another and prevent them from striking any wicked bargains that might erupt into another global war. The United Nations was regarded as an example of democracy on an international scale: Just as the people within democratic states could constantly watch their representatives and prevent them from effecting compromises injurious to their interests, so the people of all countries would now be able to keep an eye on their statesmen, making it impossible for them to arrange any secret deals which would betray the people's interests and shatter the peace of the world. Peace-loving world public opinion, expressing itself across national boundaries, would maintain a constant guard over the diplomats and hold them accountable. Covenants were to be open, and "openly arrived at," as President Wilson had once expressed it. Power politics would then be banned once and for all. In the words of Secretary of State Cordell Hull: "There will no longer be need for spheres of influence, for alliances, balance of power, or any other of the special arrangements through which, in the unhappy past, the nations strove to safeguard their security or promote their interests." Reliance would instead be placed upon sound principles and good fellowship. Again, in Hull's words: "All these principles and policies [of international cooperation] are so beneficial and appealing to the sense of justice, of right and of the well-being of free peoples everywhere that in the course of a few years the entire international machinery should be working fairly satisfactorily." The Advisory Commission on Postwar Foreign Policy had been even more emphatic in its stress on the subordination of power politics to principles: "International security was regarded as the supreme objective, but at the same time the subcommittee held that the attainment of security must square with principles of justice in order to be actual and enduring . . . the vital interests of the United States lay in following a 'diplomacy of principle'—of moral disinterestedness instead of power politics." No comment could more aptly have summed up the American habit of viewing international politics in terms of abstract moral principles instead of clashes of interest and power.

Soviet Postwar Expansion

The American dream of postwar peace and Big Three co-operation was to be shattered as the Soviet Union expanded into Eastern and Central Europe, imposing its control upon Poland, Hungary, Bulgaria, Romania, and Albania. (Yugo-slavia was already under the Communist control of Marshal Tito, and Czechoslovakia was living under the shadow of the Red Army.) In each of these nations of Eastern Europe where the Russians had their troops, they unilaterally established pro-Soviet coalition governments. The key post in these re-gimes—the ministry of the interior, which usually controlled the police—was in the hands of the Communists. With this de-cisive lever of power in their grasp, it was an easy matter to extend their domination and subvert the independence of these countries. Thus, as the war drew to a close, it became clear that the words of the Yalta Declaration, in which the Russians had committed themselves to free elections and democratic governments in Eastern Europe, meant quite dif-ferent things to the Russians and to Americans. For the Soviet Union, control of Eastern Europe, and especially Poland, was essential. This area constituted a vital link in its security belt. After two German invasions in less than thirty years, with no natural barriers to protect it, Russia would as a matter of course try to establish "friendly" governments throughout the area. To the Russians, however, "democratic governments" meant Communist governments, and "free elections" meant elections from which parties not favorable to the Communists were barred. The peace treaties with the former German sat-ellite states (Hungary, Bulgaria, Romania), which were pain-fully negotiated by the victors in a series of foreign ministers' conferences during 1945 and 1946, could not loosen the tight Soviet grip on what were by now Russian satellite states. In terms of the state system, this Soviet behavior is understand-able. Each state must act as its own guardian against potential adversaries in a system characterized by conflict among states and a sense of insecurity and fear on the part of its members. Thus, as the alliance against the common enemy came to an end, Soviet Russia would predictably strengthen itself against the power most likely to be its new opponent. As Russia, with a long history of invasions from the West, it had learned the basic rules of the international game through bitter experience; as *Soviet* Russia, its sense of peril had been intensified by an ideology that posited capitalist states as implacable enemies, merely waiting for the opportunity to strike; hence, the establishment of anti-Communist regimes in Eastern Europe would have been intolerable, and the American insistence upon free elections was seen as an attempt to push the Soviet Union out of Europe. In any event, as a state that had no natural protective barriers, such as the English Channel or the Atlantic Ocean, the Soviet Union not unnaturally pushed outward to keep enemies as far away as possible; "defensive expansionism," as it has been called, became mingled with expansionism for offensive motives, such as extending the sphere of Communist control.

President Roosevelt during the war had been all too aware of the consequences of a possible Russian-American clash in the wake of Germany's defeat. As the leader of a nation that had *not* been socialized by the state system, he accurately represented American attitudes and expectations when he so single-mindedly pursued his policy of friendship toward the Soviet Union to reduce its suspicions of the West and lay a foundation of mutual trust and goodwill upon which the postwar peace could be built. Roosevelt, as we have seen, explained Soviet behavior almost exclusively as a reaction to such interwar Western steps as the establishment of the *cordon sanitaire* in Eastern Europe. Thus, he did not view free elections in that area in terms of the creation of a new anti-Soviet belt. For him, free elections, non-Communist coalition governments in which Communists might participate if they gained a sizable vote, and a friendly attitude toward both the West *and* the East were quite compatible. The model he had in mind was Czechoslovakia, a democracy that had ties to the West but had become friendly to Russia, especially in view of the West's failure to come to its rescue before Munich. But this model was not feasible, if only because the Soviet Union was unwilling to tolerate even an independent Czechoslovakia in which the Communist Party received the largest vote of any party in a postwar free election and thus held key posts in the government. To share power in a coalition government was to share power with class enemies. A "friendly" state, to the Soviets, was a completely Communist state, and a Communist state could not be friendly to the capitalist enemy.

The power vacuum created by Germany's defeat, which permitted Russian power to extend into the center of Europe and which precipitated the cold war, was almost exactly a replay of the struggle that erupted after the end of the war against Napoleon. The Tsar's troops on that occasion entered Paris; his alliance with Prussia and his control over what then constituted Poland presented Russia's allies—Austria-Hungary and England—with the possibility of Russian Continental hegemony. These two states plus the former enemy, France, therefore signed a secret alliance threatening to go to war with Russia if the Tsar remained adamantly opposed to a peace treaty that distributed power in such a manner that all the principal states could feel reasonably secure. When the news of this secret arrangement was leaked, the Tsar became more compliant. In brief, the post–World War II conflict—with Stalin taking Tsar Alexander's place and the United States playing the role of England in rearranging the new balance of power—was not fundamentally due to the personalities of leaders or to the principal contestants' domestic political or economic systems; it was essentially due to the nature of the state system and the emergent bipolar distribution of power, which led each state to see the other as the principal threat to its security and to take the appropriate steps. There was one further element of continuity. As in the two world wars, in which England had led the effort to contain Germany, London—not Washington—took the first steps in opposing Russia after 1945. Indeed, the United States attempted initially to play the role of mediator between Russia and England! Only as English power proved to be insufficient did the United States, as before but more quickly, take over the task of balancing Russian power.

American initiative came about gradually in the 1946–47 period and was precipitated mainly when Stalin turned from consolidating his grip in Eastern Europe to seeking to extend Soviet influence beyond the lines drawn by allied armies during the war. The United States had accommodated itself to Russian control over Eastern Europe, especially Poland, the corridor through which German armies had marched on Russia twice in a quarter-century. Moscow's security interests were understandable, and Washington, despite, for instance, its disappointments over the Soviet non-fulfillment of its Yalta obligations in Poland, quickly recognized the new Polish government. Only when the Russians attempted to effect a major breakthrough into the Middle East did American opposition become genuinely aroused. Greece, Turkey, and Iran were the first states beyond the confines of the Red Army to feel the pressure of the Soviet Union.

The pressure on Iran began in early 1946, when the Russians refused to withdraw their troops from that country. These troops had been there since late 1941, when Russia and Britain had invaded Iran in order to forestall increased Nazi influence and to use Iran as a corridor for the transportation of military aid shipped by the West to the Persian Gulf for transit to Russia. The Russians had occupied northern Iran, the British the central and southern sections. When the latter withdrew their troops after the war, the Soviets sought to convert Iran into a Soviet satellite.

During this period, the Soviet Union also put pressure on Turkey. Indeed, the Russians had begun to do this as early as June, 1945, when they suddenly demanded the cession of several Turkish districts lying on the Turkish-Russian frontier, the revision of the Montreux Convention governing the Dardenelles Straits in favor of a joint Russo-Turkish administration, Turkey's severance of ties with Britain and the conclusion of a treaty with the Soviet Union similar to those which Russia had concluded with its Balkan satellites, and finally, the leasing to the Soviet Union of bases for naval and land forces in the Dardenelles for its "joint defense." In August, 1946, the Soviet Union renewed its demand, in a note to the United States and Britain, for a new administration of the straits. In effect, this would have turned Turkey into a Soviet satellite.

In Greece, too, Communist pressure was exerted on the government through wide-scale guerrilla warfare, which began in the fall of 1946. Civil war in Greece was actually nothing new. During the war, the Communist and anti-Communist guerrillas fighting the Germans had spent much of their energy battling each other. When the British landed in Greece and the Germans withdrew from the country, the Communists had attempted to take over the capital city of Athens. Only after several weeks of bitter street fighting and the landing of British reinforcements was the Communist control of Athens dislodged and a truce signed in January, 1945. Just over a year later—in March, 1946—the Greeks held a general election in which right-wing forces captured the majority of votes.

The Greek situation did not improve, however. The country was exhausted from the Italian and German invasions, the four years of occupation, and the Germans' scorched-earth policy as they retreated. Moreover, Greece had always been dependent upon imports that were paid for by exports, but its traditional market in Central Europe was now closed. While the masses lived at a bare subsistence level, the black market flourished. The inability of any government to deal with this situation aroused a good deal of social discontent. And the large, 100,000-man army which Greece needed to protect itself from its Communist neighbors (Albania, Yugoslavia, and Bulgaria) had brought the country to near-bankruptcy. If Britain had not helped finance—as well as train and equip—the army and kept troops in the country to stabilize the situation, Greece would in all probability have collapsed. It was in these circumstances that in August, 1946, the Communist forces began to squeeze Greece by renewing the guerrilla warfare in the north, where the guerrillas could be kept well supplied by Greece's Communist neighbors.

In all these situations, the American Government was suddenly confronted with the need for action to support Britain, the traditional guardian of this area against encroachment. In the case of Iran, the United States and Britain delivered firm statements which strongly implied that the two countries would use force to defend Iran. The Soviet response in late March, 1946, was the announcement that the Red Army would be withdrawn during the next five to six weeks. In the Turkish case, the United States sent a naval task force into the Mediterranean immediately after the receipt of the Soviet note on August 7. Twelve days later, the United States replied to the note by rejecting the Russian demand to share exclusive responsibility for the defense of the straits with Turkey. Britain sent a similar reply. The Greek situation had not yet come to a head, and the need for American action could be postponed for a while longer. But it should be pointed out that the Truman Administration's actions in Iran and Turkey were merely swift reactions to immediate crises. They were not the product of an over-all American strategy. Such a coherent strategy came only after a new assessment of Soviet foreign policy had occurred.

The Strategy of Containment

A period of eighteen months passed before the United States undertook that reassessment—from the surrender of Japan on September 2, 1945, until the announcement of the Truman Doctrine on March 12, 1947. Perhaps such a reevaluation could not have been made any more quickly. Public opinion in a democratic country does not normally shift drastically overnight. It would have been too much to expect the American public to change suddenly from an attitude of friendliness toward the Soviet Union—inspired largely by the picture of Russian wartime bravery and endurance and by hopes for peaceful postwar cooperation—to a hostile mood. The American "reservoir of goodwill" for the Soviet Union could not be emptied that quickly. Moreover, the desire for peace was too strong. The United States wished only to be left alone to preoccupy itself once more with domestic affairs. The end of the war signaled the end of power politics and the restoration of normal peacetime harmony among nations. In response to this expectation, the public demanded a speedy demobilization. The armed forces were thus reduced to completely inadequate levels of strength. In May, 1945, at the end of the war with Germany, the United States had an army of 3.5 million men organized into 68 divisions in Europe, supported by 149 air groups. Its allies supplied another 47 divisions. By March, 1946, only ten months later, the United States had only 400,000 troops left, mainly new recruits; the homeland reserve was six battalion's. Further reductions in army strength followed. Air force and navy cuts duplicated this same pattern.

This deliberate reduction of armaments could not have failed to encourage Russian intransigence in Europe and increased Soviet pressure in the southeast of Europe and the Middle East. As this pressure increased in intensity and scope, however, American policy toward the Soviet Union began to be re-evaluated.

Three positions became clear during this period. At one extreme stood that old realist Winston Churchill. At the end of the European war, he had counseled against the withdrawal of American troops. He had insisted that they stay, together with British troops, in order to force the Soviet Union to live up to its Yalta obligations regarding free elections in Eastern Europe and the withdrawal of the Red Army from eastern Germany. The United States had rejected Churchill's plea. In early 1946, at Fulton, Missouri, Churchill took his case directly to the American public. The Soviet Union, he asserted, was an expansionist state. "From Stettin in the Baltic to Trieste in the Adriatic, an iron curtain has descended across the continent. Behind that line lie all the capitals of the ancient states of Central and Eastern Europe. Warsaw, Berlin, Prague, Vienna, Budapest, Belgrade, Bucharest, and Sofia, all the famous cities and populations around them lie in the Soviet sphere and all are subject in one form or another, not only to Soviet influence but to a very high and increasing measure of control from Moscow." Churchill did not believe that the Russians wanted war: "What they desire is the fruits

of war and the indefinite expansion of their power and doc-
trines." This could be prevented only by the opposing power
of the British Commonwealth and the United States. Churchill, in short, said bluntly that the cold war had begun, that
Americans must recognize this fact and give up their dreams
of Big Three unity in the United Nations. International organization was no substitute for the balance of power. "Our
difficulties and dangers will not be removed by closing our
eyes to them. They will not be removed by mere waiting to
see what happens; nor will they be relieved by a policy of appeasement." An alliance of the English-speaking peoples was
the prerequisite for American and British security and world
peace.

At the other extreme stood Secretary of Commerce Henry
Wallace, who felt it was precisely the kind of aggressive attitude expressed by Churchill that was to blame for Soviet hostility. The United States and Britain had no more business in
Eastern Europe than had the Soviet Union in Latin America;
to each, the respective area was vital for national security.
Western interference in nations bordering on Russia was
bound to arouse Soviet suspicion, just as Soviet intervention
in countries neighboring on the United States would. "We
may not like what Russia does in Eastern Europe," said Wallace. "Her type of land reform, industrial expropriation, and
suspension of basic liberties offends the great majority of the
people of the United States. But whether we like it or not, the
Russians will try to socialize their sphere of influence just as
we try to democratize our sphere of influence (including
Japan and Western Germany)." The tough attitude that
Churchill and other "reactionaries" at home and abroad demanded was precisely the wrong policy; it would only increase international tension. "We must not let British balance-of-power manipulations determine whether and when
the United States gets into a war . . . 'getting tough' never
bought anything real and lasting—whether for schoolyard
bullies or world powers. The tougher we get, the tougher the
Russians will get." Only mutual trust would allow the United

States and Russia to live together peacefully, and such trust could not be created by an unfriendly American attitude and policy.

The American Government and public wavered between these two positions. The Administration recognized that Big Three cooperation had ended, and it realized that the time when the United States needed to demonstrate goodwill toward the Soviet Union in order to overcome the latter's suspicions had passed. No further concessions would be made to preserve the surface friendship with the Soviet Union. America had tried to gain Russia's amity by being a friend; it was now up to its leaders to demonstrate a similarly friendly attitude toward America as well. Paper agreements, written in such general terms that they actually hid divergent purposes, were no longer regarded as demonstrating such friendship. Something more than paper agreements was needed: Russian words would have to be matched by Russian deeds.

The American Secretary of State, James Byrnes, called this new line the "policy of firmness and patience." This phrase meant that the United States would take a firm position whenever the Soviet Union became intransigent, and that it would not compromise simply in order to reach a quick agreement. This change in official American attitude toward the Soviet Union was not, however, a fundamental one. A firm line was to be followed only on concrete issues. The assumption was that if the United States took a tougher bargaining position and no longer seemed in a hurry to resolve particular points of tension, the Soviet rulers would see the pointlessness of their obduracy and agree to fair compromise solutions of their differences with the United States and the West. In short, American firmness would make the Russians "reasonable." For they were regarded as "unreasonable" merely on particular issues. The new American position, as one political analyst has aptly summed it up, "meant to most of its exponents that the Soviet Union had to be induced by firmness to play the game in the American way. There was no consistent official suggestion that the United States should begin to play a different game." The prerequisite for such a suggestion was that American policy-makers recognize the revolutionary nature of the Soviet regime.

This recognition came with increasing speed as the Greek crisis reached a peak. By early 1947, it was obvious that the United States would have to play a different game. It was George Kennan, the Foreign Service's foremost expert on the Soviet Union, who first presented the basis of what was to be a new American policy. Kennan's analysis focused on the Communist outlook on world affairs. In the Soviet leaders' pattern of thought, he said, Russia had no community of interest with the capitalist states; indeed, they saw their relationship with the Western powers in terms of an innate antagonism. Communist ideology had taught them "that the outside world was hostile and that it was their duty eventually to overthrow the political forces beyond their borders. The powerful hands of Russian history and tradition reached up to sustain them in this feeling. Finally, their own aggressive intransigence with respect to the outside world began to find its own reaction. . . . It is an undeniable privilege for every man to prove himself right in the thesis that the world is his enemy; for if he reiterates it frequently enough and makes it the background for his conduct, he is bound to be right." According to Kennan, this Soviet hostility was a constant factor; it would continue until the capitalist world had been destroyed: "Basically, the antagonism remains. It is postulated. And from it flow many of the phenomena which we find disturbing in the Kremlin's conduct of foreign policy: the secretiveness, the lack of frankness, the duplicity, the war suspiciousness, and the basic unfriendliness of purpose. . . . These characteristics of the Soviet policy, like the postulates from which they flow, are basic to the *internal* nature of Soviet power, and will be with us . . . until the nature of Soviet power is changed [italics added]." Until that moment, he said, Soviet strategy and objectives would remain the same.

The struggle would thus be a long one. Kennan stressed that Soviet hostility did not mean the Russians would embark upon a do-or-die program to overthrow capitalism by a fixed date. They had no timetable for conquest. In a brilliant passage, Kennan outlined the Soviet concept of the struggle:

The Kremlin is under no ideological compulsion to accomplish its purposes in a hurry. Like the Church, it is dealing in ideological concepts which are of a long-term validity, and it can afford to be patient. It has no right to risk the existing achievements of the revolution for the sake of vain baubles of the future. The very teachings of Lenin himself require great caution and flexibility in the pursuit of Communist purposes. Again, these precepts are fortified by the lessons of Russian history: of centuries of obscure battles between nomadic forces over the stretches of a vast unfortified plain. Here caution, circumspection, flexibility, and deception are the valuable qualities; and their value finds natural appreciation in the Russian, or the Oriental mind. Thus the Kremlin has no compunction about retreating in the face of superior force. And being under the compulsion of no timetable, it does not get panicky under the necessity of such a retreat. Its political action is a fluid stream which moves constantly, wherever it is permitted to move, toward a given goal. Its main concern is to make sure that it has filled every nook and cranny available to it in the basin of world power. But if it finds unassailable barriers in its path, it accepts these philosophically and accommodates itself to them. The main thing is that there should always be pressure, increasing constant pressure, toward the desired goal. There is no trace of any feeling in Soviet psychology that the goal must be reached at any given time.

How could the United States counter such a policy—a policy that was always pushing, seeking weak spots, attempting to fill power vacuums? Kennan's answer was that American policy would have to be one of "long-term, patient, but firm and vigilant containment." The United States would find Soviet diplomacy both easier and more difficult to deal with than that of dictators such as Napoleon or Hitler. "On the one hand, it [Soviet policy] is more sensitive to contrary force, more ready to yield oa individual sectors of the diplomatic front when that force is felt to be too strong, and thus more rational in the logic and rhetoric of power. On the other hand, it cannot be easily defeated or discouraged by a single victory on the part of its opponents. And the patient persistence by which it is animated means that it can be effectively countered not by sporadic acts which represent the momentary whims of democratic opinion, but only by intelligent long-range policies on the part of Russia's adversaries—policies no less steady in their purpose, and no less variegated and resourceful in their application, than those of the Soviet Union itself." Hence, George Kennan was envisaging containment as a test of American democracy to conduct an effective and responsible foreign policy *and* contribute to changes within the Soviet Union which might bring about a moderation of its revolutionary aims. The United States, he emphasized, "has it in its power to increase enormously the strains under which Soviet policy must operate, to force upon the Kremlin a far greater degree of moderation and circumspection than it has had to observe in recent years, and in this way to promote tendencies which must eventually find their outlet in either the breakup or the gradual mellowing of Soviet power. For no mystical, messianic movement—and particularly not that of the Kremlin—can face frustration indefinitely without eventually adjusting itself in one way or another to the logic of that state of affairs." Kennan was, in effect, asserting the thesis that within an authoritarian or totalitarian society there are certain strains and stresses, and that these give rise to frustrations which can only be relieved by being channeled into an aggressive and expansionist foreign policy. Kennan's remedy was to prevent this expansion, thereby aggravating the internal tensions in such a way that they would either destroy the Soviet system or force the Soviet leaders to placate the domestic dissatisfaction. Assuming that the Soviet leaders preferred to remain in power and that they would therefore be compelled to adopt the second course, they would have no alternative but to moderate their foreign policy. For a relaxation of international tensions was the prerequisite for coping with their domestic problems. Thus, the Kremlin would have no choice but to surrender its revolutionary aims and arrange a *modus vivendi* with the Western powers—above all, with the United States.

The Truman Doctrine

Whether the United States could meet this Soviet challenge became a pressing question when, on the afternoon of February 21, 1947, the First Secretary of the British Embassy in Washington visited the State Department and handed American officials two notes from His Majesty's Government. One concerned Greece, the other Turkey. In effect, they both stated the same thing: that Britain could no longer meet its traditional responsibilities in those two countries. Since both were on the verge of collapse, the import of the British notes was clear: that a Russian breakthrough could be prevented only by an all-out American commitment.

February 21 was thus a historic day. On that day, Great Britain, the only remaining power in Europe, acknowledged its exhaustion. It had fought Philip II of Spain, Louis XIV and Napoleon of France, Kaiser Wilhelm II and Adolf Hitler of Germany. It had preserved the balance of power which protected the United States for so long that it seemed almost natural for it to continue to do so. But its ability to protect that balance had steadily declined in the twentieth century. Twice it had needed American help. Each time, however, it had fought the longer battle; on neither occasion had the United States entered the war until it became clear that Germany and its allies were too strong for Great Britain and that America would have to help in safeguarding its own security. Now, all of a sudden, there was no power to protect the United States but the United States itself; no one stood between that country and the present threat to its security. All the other major powers of the world had collapsed—except the Soviet Union. A bipolar world suddenly faced the United States.

The immediate crisis suddenly confronting the United States had its locale in the eastern Mediterranean. Direct Soviet pressure on Iran and Turkey had temporarily been successfully resisted. The Russians had now turned to outflanking these two nations by concentrating their attention on Greece. If Greece collapsed—and all reports from that hapless country indicated that it would fall within a few weeks—it was thought in Washington that it would only be a question of time until Turkey and Iran would crumble before Soviet power. But the fall of Greece would not only affect its neighbors to the east; it would also lead to an increase of Communist pressure on Italy. Italy would then be faced with two Communist states to its east—Yugoslavia and Greece—and with the largest Communist party in Western Europe in its own midst. And to the northwest of Italy lay France, with the second largest Communist party in the West. Thus, the security of all of Western Europe would be endangered as well. The immediate danger, however, remained in the eastern Mediterranean; and the Soviet desire for control over this area was underlined by its demands that the city of Trieste at the head of the Adriatic be yielded to Yugoslavia and that Italy's former colonies of Tripolitania and Eritrea in North Africa be placed under Soviet trusteeship.

The United States had no choice but to act in this situation. The results of inaction were only too clear: the collapse of Europe's flank in the eastern Mediterranean, the establishment of Communist dominance in the Middle East, and a Soviet breakthrough into South Asia and North Africa. The psychological impact upon Europe of such a tremendous Soviet victory over the West would have been disastrous. For Europeans already psychologically demoralized by their sufferings and fall from power and prestige, this would have been the final blow. In short, what was felt to be at stake in Greece was America's security.

President Truman's reaction was to go before a joint session of Congress on March 12, 1947, and deliver a speech that must rank as one of the most important in American history. The President first outlined the situation in Greece: the lack of natural resources; the cruel German occupation, resulting in widespread destruction; its inability to import the goods it needed for bare subsistence, let alone reconstruction; the Communist efforts to exploit these conditions by spreading political chaos and hindering any economic recovery; and the guerrilla warfare in northern Greece, where the Communist forces were receiving aid from Yugoslavia, Albania, and Bulgaria.

Then Truman came to the heart of his speech. Here he spelled out what was to become known as the Truman Doctrine. The United States, he emphasized, could survive only in a world in which freedom flourished. And it would not realize this objective

> . . . unless we are willing to help free peoples to maintain their institutions and their national integrity against aggressive movements that seek to impose upon them totalitarian regimes. *This is no more than a frank recognition that totalitarian regimes imposed on free peoples, by direct or indirect aggression, undermine the foundations of international peace and hence the security of the United States* [italics added].
>
> The peoples of a number of countries of the world have recently had totalitarian regimes forced upon them against their will. The Government of the United States has made frequent protests against coercion and intimidation, in violation of the Yalta agreement, in Poland, Romania, and Bulgaria. I must also state that in a number of other countries there have been similar developments.
>
> At the present moment in world history nearly every nation must choose between alternative ways of life. The choice is often not a free one.
>
> One way of life is based upon the will of the majority, and is distinguished by free institutions, representative government, free elections, guarantees of individual liberty, freedom of speech and religion, and freedom from political oppression.
>
> The second way of life is based upon the will of a minority forcibly imposed upon the majority. It relies upon terror and oppression, a controlled press and radio, fixed elections, and the suppression of personal freedoms.
>
> I believe it must be the policy of the United States to support free peoples who are resisting attempted subjugations by armed minorities or by outside pressure.

I believe that we must assist free peoples to work out their own destinies in their own way.

I believe that our help should be primarily through economic and financial aid which is essential to economic stability and orderly political processes.

Stressing the impact of Greece's collapse upon Turkey and the Middle East, as well as upon Europe, the President asked Congress to appropriate $400 million for economic aid and military supplies for both countries and to authorize the dispatch of American civilian and military personnel in order to help the two nations in their tasks of reconstruction and provide their armies with appropriate instruction and training.

Thus the United States began the policy of containment. A number of points about this initial commitment need special emphasis. First, the Soviet threat to the balance of power left the United States no choice but to adopt a countervailing policy. With the war over, the United States would have much preferred to concentrate on domestic affairs; the massive postwar demobilization clearly demonstrated this preference. But the external environment intervened: the bipolar distribution of power molded the nation's policy course. Such a distribution of power is the most sensitive of all because the two states are bound to be alert to the slightest shift in the balance lest one adversary gain the power he needs to assert and impose his will upon the other. For a gain of power and security by one tends to be seen as a loss of power and security for the other. A bipolar balance is therefore very dangerous, for it produces, among its effects, constant confrontations and crises which could spark a military clash. Yet they are also an indication that the balance is being kept. As one side pushes, his opponent pushes him back.

The second point to stress is that anti-Communism was not a major ingredient of American policy during and immediately after World War II. During the war, the United States had constantly sought to overcome the Kremlin's suspicions of the West in order to lay the foundation for postwar harmony and peace. And as the war drew to its conclusion, the principal concern of American policy-makers was not to eliminate the self-proclaimed bastion of world revolution and enemy of Western capitalism, nor to push Russia out of Eastern Europe and convert that area into a market for American corporations (even had that desire existed, poverty-stricken Eastern Europe would not have been a very profitable market for American goods), but to forestall a complete return to the historic position of isolationism. The public mood was all too evident in the hasty military demobilization, the riots of some overseas units that felt that their demobilization was not rapid enough, and the cries of America's children heard both in Congress and the White House: "We want our daddies." (One group of servicemen sent the President, whose hometown was Independence, Missouri, a telegram with the memorable line: "Give us our independence or you'll go back to yours.") For the United States to have pursued the assertive foreign policy complete with atomic threats that the revisionists have claimed it did, would have required a dictatorial disregard for the widespread demands of public opinion.

It was not until a year and a half after World War II ended that the Truman Doctrine was enunciated. Only after further attempts to reconcile differences with Moscow, after continued Soviet pressure, denunciations, and vilifications, was containment launched. Hostile Soviet behavior was the reason for the gradual shift of American policy and public opinion from amity to enmity; American policy was not the product of a virulent and pre-existing anti-Communist ideology, and therefore not comparable to Soviet policy, which, in addition to its historical roots, reflected an anticapitalist animus that predated both the Bolshevik Revolution of 1917 and subsequent Western anti-Soviet behavior. Even before the Bolshevik leaders seized power, they had already judged capitalists states as hostile simply because they *were* capitalist.

Third, the role of anti-Communism in American policy was essentially to mobilize Congressional and public support for the policy once it had been decided upon. A nation that had historically condemned power politics as immoral and as a corruption of the democratic ideal needed a moral basis for its new use of power. Anti-Communism fitted into the familiar dichotomy of a peaceful and democratic New World confronted by a warlike and dictatorial Old Europe. For a people weary after four years of war, who identified the termination of war with the end of power politics, who were used to isolation from Europe's wicked affairs, and who were preoccupied with the pursuit of happiness, success, and the dollar at home, anti-Communism was like the cavalry's bugle call to charge; it fitted neatly into the traditional American dichotomy of the world into extremes of evil and morality, thereby arousing the nation for yet another foreign policy mission. Until Vietnam, anti-Communism served the policy-makers' purposes; the policy of containment received long and widespread public and Congressional support from both Democrats and Republicans. (Asian policy was to be the major exception to this rule, as we shall see.)

The fourth point worth noting is that, despite the universalism of the Truman Doctrine, its application was intended to be specific and limited, not global. American policy-makers were well aware that the United States, though a Great Power, was not omnipotent; therefore, national priorities—which interests were vital and which were not—had to be decided carefully and power applied discriminately. American responses would depend, then, both on where the external challenges occurred and on how Washington defined the relationship of such challenges to the nation's security.

CONTAINMENT IN EUROPE

The Marshall Plan

The commitment to Greece and Turkey was only the first act under the new American policy of containing Soviet expansion. Britain's state of near-collapse, which had left the United States no alternative but to become involved in the eastern Mediterranean, was symptomatic of all of Europe's collapse. Basically, Britain's crisis was an economic one. As an island-nation, it was dependent for its livelihood—indeed, its survival—upon international trade. It had to export or die, for the Industrial Revolution it had undergone during the nineteenth century had almost completely urbanized it. Less than 5 per cent of Britain's population was engaged in agriculture. This meant that it had to import much of its food. Before World War II, for instance, it bought 55 per cent of its meat, 75 per cent of its wheat, 85 per cent of its butter, all its tea, cocoa, and coffee, and 75 per cent of its sugar. Except for coal, Britain also had to import most of the raw materials needed by its industries: cotton, rubber, wool, iron ore, timber, and the oil on which it was becoming increasingly dependent upon for the fueling of its factories.

Before 1939, Britain had paid for these foods and raw materials by one of three means: services such as shipping, income from foreign investments, and manufactured exports. But the war had crippled its merchant marine, liquidated most of its investments, and destroyed many of its factories. With the first two means of financing its imports all but gone, it had to increase its export drive. Just to maintain the 1939 standard of living, it had to raise its exports by 75 per cent. By December, 1946, despite an American loan and a severe austerity program which included the rationing of bread, Britain had only reached its prewar level of production. It was in these circumstances that nature delivered what almost proved to be a knockout blow. In the winter of 1946–47, Europe suffered one of its severest cold periods in history; temperatures went below zero. In Britain, the transportation system came to a virtual standstill; trucks and trains could not move, barges were frozen in rivers, and ships could not leave their moorings. Industries could not be supplied with the fuel to keep them running, and factories were closed. By February, 1947, more than half of Britain's factories lay idle. Coal was not even mined any longer, and gas and electricity were in short supply. Electricity to industrial consumers was cut off for several days; and domestic consumers had to do without electricity for three hours every day. When the thaw finally arrived, Britain was beset by floods. It would take months to recover.

In the meantime, the export drive had completely collapsed, and Britain had come to the end of its rope. The financial editor of Reuter's saw the true measure of the winter disaster: "The biggest crash since the fall of Constantinople— the collapse of the heart of an Empire—impends. This is not the story of a couple of snowstorms. It is the story of the awful debility in which a couple of snowstorms could have such effects." The future looked bleak and ominous: millions of Britons were unemployed, cold and hungry, worn out by the long years of war and the determined postwar efforts to recover. Despite all the personal and uncomplaining sacrifices they had made, their efforts had come to nothing. Britain's fate could have been worse only if it had lost the war.

In Germany, postwar conditions were truly horrible. The war had been carried into the heart of Germany. Few German cities or towns had escaped Allied bombing, street fighting, or willful destruction by the Nazis themselves as they retreated. Old cities like Cologne, Essen, Mannheim, and Nuremberg lay in ruins; others like Berlin, Frankfort, Hamburg, and Munich were almost as badly damaged. Much of Germany was just a mass of broken stones, and people found shelter among this rubble as best they could. To aggravate this situation, 10 million additional Germans came into these ruins from former German territory annexed by Poland; they settled mostly in West Germany, adding further discomfort to the inhabitants already hard-pressed for survival. There was only one word to describe Germany in 1945—chaos. Millions upon millions of people were faced with the basic necessity of finding food, shelter, and work.

The measure of Germany's collapse was indicated by the fact that the cigarette had replaced money as the prevailing unit of exchange. Cigarettes could buy almost anything. The black market flourished. Even as late as 1947, a package of cigarettes was equivalent to a working man's entire wages for a month; one cigarette had twice the purchasing power of the salary a man could earn in Berlin after a hard day's work clearing away rubble. The Allied target ration of 1,550 calories per day, which was hardly sufficient to sustain a healthy human being, was rarely reached. In March, 1946, the British were forced to cut their rations to 1,040 daily calories, and in April the Americans cut theirs to 1,275 calories. Everywhere people were hungry; the few who found jobs to earn a little money often fainted from sheer exhaustion. It was a desperate situation. Respectable girls sold their bodies for one or two cigarettes, a pair of nylons, or an army ration; dishonor was preferable to death. Illegitimate births rose sharply, and so did divorce petitions. Juvenile delinquency increased 400 per cent over the prewar level; stealing became as respectable a way of earning a living for boys as did prostitution for girls. Along with this economic, social, political, and moral breakdown came the cold weather. There was no fuel for heating. During the severe winter of 1946–47, 200 people froze to death in Berlin alone. Three-quarters of the factories still standing in the American and British zones of occupation were closed. In January, 1947, production fell to 31 per cent of the 1936 level, Germany's best year; by February, it had declined to 29 per cent. Even before this industrial shutdown, German steel production during 1946 had reached only 2 million tons—approximately only one-third of Allied authorization.

Allied policy was certainly not designed to help matters.

The Allies were still primarily engaged with Germany's disarmament and demilitarization, and with the elimination of all industries whose output could be used for military production. America and Britain were not particularly anxious to rebuild Germany's industrial power. They recalled only too vividly that it had taken the combined efforts of three world powers to bring the Nazi war machine to a halt and defeat it. And they believed that many of Germany's industrialists had been ardent supporters of the Nazi regime. Nor were the Allies especially concerned with the lot of the German people during the immediate postwar days. After six years of war, such concern could hardly have been expected. The memories of Nazi atrocities and crimes, of wanton destruction, and of millions of innocent people slaughtered in concentration camps were still very much alive. These could not soon be forgotten. The hatred the Nazis had engendered in their opponents could not be erased overnight. After six years of brutal warfare, the Allies were unlikely to display much forgiveness and chivalry toward the Germans.

The French, above all others, were not likely to forget the Nazis. Though their economy had been badly damaged during the war, by late 1946 the French had made a remarkable recovery. But iron and steel production had reached only half the prewar total. Here, too, coal was the key factor, since the iron and steel industry was dependent upon imported coal. But European coal production was still well below the pre-1939 annual average. German production was low, and Britain needed for itself all the coal it mined. Therefore, scarce dollars had to be spent for the purchase of high-cost American coal. The result was a vivid demonstration of the division of labor in the modern economy. France's industry was unable to produce sufficient goods to exchange for food. The farmer thereupon withdrew fields from crop cultivation and used them for grazing. He kept more food for himself and his family, and also fed his livestock more grain. Meanwhile, the urban population was short of food, and the government had to spend its few remaining dollars—which it needed for reconstruction—to buy food from abroad. The winter of 1946–47 aggravated this situation even further by destroying an estimated 3 to 4 million acres of wheat.

This situation was made to order for the large and well-organized French Communist Party. One-quarter of France's electorate—practically the entire working class—voted for the Party. (In Italy, the figure was one-third of the electorate.) The reason for this was simple: Capitalism had alienated these people. The workers were, in effect, internal *émigrés* who voted Communist in protest against a system they felt had long mistreated them; unlike workers in Britain and in the United States, they had suffered all the hardships of capitalism while enjoying few of its benefits, such as good wages and social opportunities. As a result, the Communist Party in France was placed in a powerful position in political and trade union life. The Party was the largest in France and in a key position to prevent any improvement in the workers' conditions. It represented the workers; there was therefore no democratic left-wing alternative. This benefited the conservative forces. Since these would not be challenged by a strong left-center opposition at the polls, they felt no need to pass any reform legislation. This further strengthened the Communist claim that democracy and capitalism would not and could not help the worker, and that his lot would not be bettered while the bourgeoisie remained in power. France was thus caught not only in a vicious economic circle but also in a political one: The social and economic conditions gave rise to the Communist Party, and the Party in turn could prevent any reforms from being adopted, thereby preserving its *raison d'être*. The Party also controlled the Confédération Générale du Travail, the largest French trade union, which had a membership of 80 per cent of the workers in the immediate postwar years. In 1947, as United States–Soviet tensions increased, the Party used this control to initiate or exploit strikes in order to paralyze the entire economy and bring the Republic to its knees.

With Europe on the verge of collapse, everything seemed to force it into dependence upon America. Most of the items needed for reconstruction—wheat, cotton, sulphur, sugar, machinery, trucks, and coal—could be obtained in sufficient quantities only from the United States. Yet, Europe, with a stagnating economy, was in no position to earn the dollars needed to pay for these goods. Moreover, the United States was so well supplied with everything that it did not have to buy much from abroad. Thus, the European countries were unable to obtain enough dollars for the purchase of the commodities required for their recovery. The result was the ominous "dollar gap"—a term that frightened the Europeans as much as the "cold war."

Europe's collapse thus posed a fundamental question to the United States: Is Europe vital to American security? The answer was never in doubt: American independence and security required that the United States establish a balance of power in the interior of Europe. This was necessary to check any nation with designs on the sea-bordering states as a prerequisite to the elimination of England and eventual world conquest. During most of the nineteenth century, this balance had been maintained by the English Navy. Now that Britain's power had declined drastically, the United States would have to carry out the task alone. Western Europe possessed the largest aggregation of skilled workers, technicians, and managers outside the United States. It maintained the second greatest concentration of industrial power in the world. A healthy and strong Europe could help shore up the balance of power.

The role of the United States toward Europe, therefore, had to be that of a doctor toward an ill patient—and the prescribed cure was a massive injection of dollars. A large-scale program of economic aid was to be administered in the form of grants rather than loans, which would only intensify Europe's dollar problems. Only such a program could restore and surpass Europe's prewar agricultural and industrial production, close the dollar gap, and lead Europe to the recovery of its *élan vital,* political stability, and economic prosperity, thereby possibly allowing France and Italy to reintegrate their working classes into their bodies politic.

American aid was made conditional, however, upon eco-

nomic cooperation among the European states. In this respect, the United States clearly held itself up as a model for
the Europeans. The Economic Cooperation Act of 1948 called
specifically for European economic integration. America, it
stated, was "mindful of the advantage which the United
States has enjoyed through the existence of a large-scale domestic market with no internal trade barriers and [believed]
that similar advantages can accrue to the countries of Europe." Thus, in official American opinion, European integration became both the prerequisite for Europe's recovery and
the necessary basis for Europe's long-range economic prosperity. It is not difficult to see why American policy-makers, with
their belief in low-cost mass production, should have felt that
Europe's economic recovery and health were dependent upon
the creation of a mass market. For decades, the European nations living together on a continent one-fourth the size of the
United States had shut their markets off from one another
with tariff walls, quota systems, and import and export li-
censes. By this means, national manufacturers assured themselves of the lion's share of their national markets. Sheltered
from external competition, they had little incentive to modernize their equipment or techniques, for they minimized domestic competition by dividing their relatively small domestic
markets among themselves. The American aim was to modernize this machinery, to overcome the cartelization of industry
and the inefficiency of small family enterprises (as in France),
and to destroy the artificial national divisions. Europe's industries were to be compelled to become large-scale and competitive by the creation of a "united states" of Europe.

The economic cooperation required by the United States
was first stressed by Secretary of State George C. Marshall's
call upon the European states to present his country with a
plan for their *common* needs and *common* recovery. The result was the Organization for European Economic Cooperation, whose seventeen members (plus the free state of Trieste)
pledged themselves to "cooperate with one another and with
other like-minded countries in reducing tariffs and other barriers to trade" and "to promote with vigor the development

of productivity through [the] efficient use of the resources at their command." The OEEC's estimate of the cost of Europe's recovery over a four-year period was $22 billion. Congress was to cut this figure down to $17 billion, and the amount actually used by the Economic Cooperation Administration (ECA) between 1948 and 1952 was just over $12 billion. Britain, France, and West Germany received more than half of this amount.

The original invitation by the United States to the nations of Europe to plan their joint recovery was deliberately extended to *all* European countries, including the Soviet Union and the nations of Eastern Europe. If the United States had invited only the nations of Western Europe, it would have placed itself in a politically disadvantageous position in which it would have been blamed for the division of Europe and the intensification of the cold war. Actually, if the Russians had participated, it seems unlikely that Congress would have supported the Marshall Plan: first, because the costs of the plan would have risen astronomically as a result of the very heavy and extensive damage suffered by Russia during the war; and second, because of the growing anti-Soviet feeling which the Soviet Union had engendered. The risk had to be accepted, however; it had to be the Russians who, by their rejection of Marshall Plan aid, would be responsible for the division of Europe. And the chances that the Russians would do precisely that were very good. For European cooperation would mean that Russia would have to disclose full information about its economy and allow the United States to have some control in its economic planning, as well as in that of its satellites. This was unthinkable to a totalitarian state; a Communist state could hardly permit capitalists to have a voice in its economic development. Soviet participation would also require the Soviet Union and its satellites to contribute toward Europe's recovery with food and raw materials, in return for the help they were receiving from the United States. Thus, the Russians would actually be helping to stabilize the European situation. But if they did not participate—preferring to exploit Europe's misery—they would be blamed for continuing and aggravating the cold war. In either case, the United States could not lose by invoking Marx's slogan, "From each according to his ability, to each according to his need." Actually, Soviet Foreign Minister Molotov did arrive in Paris with a large delegation of experts, and he gave American policy-makers a scare. But only for a moment. Molotov soon denounced the plan as an attempt to interfere with Soviet sovereignty and withdrew. Western Europe could now plan the use of America's dollars for its recovery.

Was the Marshall Plan a success? The results tell their own story. By 1950—when the Korean War broke out—Europe was already exceeding its prewar production by 25 per cent; two years later, this figure was 200 per cent higher. English exports were doing well, the French inflation was being slowed down, and German production had reached Germany's 1936 level. The dollar gap had been reduced from $12 billion to $2 billion. The Marshall Plan had indeed been a massive success, and at a cost that represented only a tiny fraction of the U.S. national income over the same four-year period and was smaller than America's liquor bill for these same years! Far from bankrupting the economy, as some of the Marshall Plan's critics claimed it would, the plan helped the country enjoy an economic boom.

This is not to suggest that there were not grave shortcomings, for there were. The first of these was that the growing economic prosperity was not equitably distributed. One of the purposes of the Marshall Plan had been to gain the political allegiance of the Continent's working classes and to render them immune to the blandishments of Communism. In France and Italy, however, the workers continued to vote Communist. The reason was simple: They continued to live in relative poverty. In France, for instance, real wages throughout this period were lower than in the prewar days. As expressed by Theodore White: "It was pointless to explain to the workers that without the Marshall Plan they would have been entirely unemployed, that they might have starved or died, that the Plan had saved them. The workers could see only that what had been saved was the *status quo,* that the recovery had preserved their discomfort and given its fruits to the privileged. In the slums the Communists held on to their votes even through the happiest days of the Plan." The working classes remained "a nation within a nation," alienated from the national society and hostile to the social and economic system that they felt had mistreated them for so long. Still, the Marshall Plan had laid an economic basis from which future progress and social reform could spring.

The second handicap was that the rate of integration was far slower than the Americans had expected. The belief that one could wipe out the national divisions of a century overnight and reform the business habits formed by decades of experience in a few years proved false. American businessmen in ECA soon discovered that their European counterparts did not like competition and much preferred their monopolistic practices. Ironically enough, the real impetus toward European integration came from quite a different direction—the military situation.

The North Atlantic Treaty Organization

Soon after the Marshall Plan was launched, it became clear that the plan by itself would not suffice. For in February, 1948, the Russians engineered a *coup d'état* in Prague, and—ten years after Munich and Hitler's subsequent seizure of that hapless nation—Czechoslovakia disappeared behind the iron curtain. A few months later, in June, the Russians imposed their blockade on Berlin in an effort to dislodge the Western powers from that city. It is hardly surprising that the Europeans, who lived closer to these events than Americans, felt extremely jittery at these overt signs of Russian hostility and aggressive intent. In this atmosphere of tension and insecurity, in which comparisons of Stalin's Russia with Hitler's Germany seemed all too valid, it became obvious that Europe's economic recovery was impossible; people do not make the necessary sacrifices and work hard to recuperate today if they feel that tomorrow they will be conquered and that their efforts will all have been in vain. In short, it suddenly became crystal clear that a prerequisite for Europe's recovery was military security.

The Europeans had already made some moves in this direction. In March, 1947, France and England had signed the Treaty of Dunkirk to provide for their mutual defense against a threat to their security. Exactly a year later, in March, 1948, Great Britain, France, the Netherlands, Belgium, and Luxembourg signed the Brussels Pact of collective self-defense. This Brussels Pact was established as a military counterpart to OEEC. Just as OEEC represented an organization dedicated to economic cooperation, the Brussels Pact represented one dedicated to military cooperation. And just as the vitality of OEEC had depended upon American capital for its success, the Brussels Pact members expected their alliance to attract American military support.

They were not to be disappointed. In April, 1949, Belgium, Canada, Denmark, France, Great Britain, Iceland, Italy, Luxembourg, the Netherlands, Norway, Portugal, and the United States signed the North Atlantic Treaty. The U.S. Senate ratified the treaty in July after extended hearings and debates, and the other ratifications were completed by August, 1949. For the United States, this NATO commitment set a precedent: For the first time in its history, the country had committed itself to an alliance in peacetime. Europe had become "our first line of defense." It was precisely this knowledge that the United States would fight to preserve Europe's freedom that was supposed to prevent a Soviet attack. Two world wars had proved Europe's vital importance to American security. Instead of again allowing the balance of power to be upset and thereby once more becoming drawn into war, the United States now expected to eliminate this contingency by committing itself to the preservation of the European balance in peacetime—that is, *before* the enemy attack took place. The presumption was that the fear of meeting American resistance and fighting an all-out war with the United States would deter the potential aggressor from launching his attack.

This strategy of deterrence relied almost exclusively upon

American strategic air power—that is, upon the ability of the Strategic Air Command (SAC) to destroy completely the Soviet Union with atomic bombs. This strategy was based upon two assumptions: first, that the only form of future war would be a total war, which would be precipitated by a direct Soviet attack upon the United States or Western Europe, and second, that deterrence could be achieved by air power and its ability to inflict such heavy damage upon an enemy that he would, in effect, be committing suicide if he launched an attack.

Two events were to change this reliance upon air power alone to deter or destroy the enemy. The first was the explosion of the first Soviet atomic bomb in late 1949. This foreshadowed a time when the Soviet Union, too, would possess an atomic stockpile; in short, it portended a significant increase in Soviet capability. The second event was the North Korean attack upon South Korea in June, 1950. Since it was presumed that this attack could not have occurred without Soviet permission, the North Korean aggression suggested a change in Soviet intentions. And this possibility received further support from Communist China's intervention in North Korea in late November; perhaps the Soviet Union was ready, or would soon be ready, for war. The Western response was large-scale rearmament.

This involved three tasks for NATO: the establishment of a command structure, the formulation of a strategy by which to defend Europe on the ground, and the rebuilding of its ground forces. These efforts received their initial impetus when, in the dark days after Communist China's entry into the Korean War, President Truman appointed General Eisenhower to serve as Supreme Allied Commander in Europe. Eisenhower, in turn, strove to make his command operational. His first move was to establish three commands under him: a Central Europe Command, a Northern Europe Command, and a Southern Europe Command. The first of these commands presided over the most important front—militarily because here was the plane upon which the Red Army could apply its full force and be met with full counterforce, and politically because Germany, France, and Great Britain lay on this axis.

The strategy NATO adopted was known as the "forward strategy"—that is, a defense at the Elbe. Politically, the Europeans wanted no part of a strategy that called for a withdrawal and would bring the Red Army to their borders, and most probably into their countries. They had no desire to provide battlefields again; they wanted the Red Army to be kept far from their frontiers. And liberation in a war in which atomic bombs would be dropped was no liberation at all: One could not liberate a corpse. Indeed, if the first Soviet onslaught were to drive the Allies completely out of Europe, the continent would fall permanently under Soviet control. The atomic bomb forbade a Normandy-type landing. Thus, from a political standpoint, Allied forces could not retreat. Europe would have to be defended as far east in Western Germany as possible.

Such a defense required troops and proper logistical support. When Eisenhower arrived in Europe, he found only twelve divisions—including the American ones—none of which was at full strength, properly trained, or fully equipped with the latest weapons. Nor were there any effective reserves to back them up. Perhaps neither of these facts was surprising: The European powers had greater needs and more important things to do in the immediate postwar days than to maintain or rebuild sizable military forces. In addition, because of America's atomic monopoly, it had seemed quite safe to rely solely upon SAC for deterrence and to use the troops in Germany solely for occupation duties.

But Eisenhower needed more ground forces for two purposes: The first would be to act as a "tripwire." In case the Russians had any delusion that the United States would not go to war to defend Europe, the tripwire troops were to remove this belief. An attack by the Red Army would be bound to run into American troops, some of whom would obviously be killed. This would ensure American retaliation against the Soviet Union. The second function of the NATO army was to act as a "shield" by holding the Red Army at the point of attack, the Elbe River, while SAC laid waste the Soviet Union. Military planners believed that such shield forces would have to be quite large because of the size of the Red Army.

But the need for an ample number of divisions faced the European states with a dreadful dilemma. They were unable and unwilling to mobilize the necessary troops. They were still in the midst of economic recovery and unprepared to make the necessary sacrifices to raise large national armies. Unlike the United States, which was rich enough to produce both guns *and* butter, the Europeans had to choose guns *or* butter. While the Soviet threat made it necessary to have a minimal military protection, the task of economic reconstruction made it undesirable to devote too large a share of national budgets to rearmament. The American answer was the rearmament of Germany. If France and Britain could not supply the necessary troops, Germany would serve to supply them. Moreover, this decision seemed an eminently correct one. For the forward strategy meant that NATO would try to hold West Germany. It was only fitting that the Germans should contribute to their own defense. In turn, of course, German rearmament reinforced the need for a forward strategy. For the West Germans could hardly be persuaded to rearm if they could not be assured that West Germany would not be turned into a battlefield and that German troops would not be used merely for the defense of France and England. Thus, the German question once more raised its head. It was not a new question—but this time it received new answers.

German Recovery and Rearmament

Ever since the middle of the nineteenth century—if not since the Congress of Vienna in 1815—Germany has held the key to the European balance of power. This was true of Germany even in defeat in 1945. Almost from the cessation of hostilities, the Soviet Union and the United States began their contest over Germany. East Germany had fallen into Russian hands; West Germany was occupied by the Western powers. Actually, the Allies were lucky, for West Germany contained the great majority of Germany's population and held the heart of its industrial power. West Germany, in short, was—and still remains—the chief prize in Europe.

During the war, Stalin, Churchill, and Roosevelt had decided to govern Germany through a four-power Allied Control Commission (with France as the fourth power), which would administer the entire country as a single economic unit. In practice, this task proved impossible. The Russians, the British, and the French, as well as the smaller European nations, had been promised reparations payments in compensation for the widespread destruction the Germans had caused in their countries. The Russian sum was to consist of all the industrial equipment in the Soviet zone, plus one-quarter of the far greater industrial complex in West Germany (it was assumed during the war that Germany's industrial power would be intact at the end of the war). But—and these were to be the decisive points—the United States and Great Britain had insisted upon two restrictions on these reparations payments. First, Germany was to be left enough of its nonmilitary industries to maintain its standard of living at the same level as the rest of Europe (but definitely not higher); and second, no reparations were to be paid out of current production until Germany had earned enough money with its exports to pay for the imports it needed. Germany was to support itself. The Allies had no desire—to put it mildly—to spend their money supporting their former enemy.

The Russians quickly began demolishing the industry in their zone with great gusto—never, of course, informing the Western powers how much they were taking. The Russians also cut off the regular food supply from East Germany, which had traditionally been Germany's breadbasket; under the original agreement, they were to furnish this food in return for the three-fifths of capital equipment they were allowed to remove from the Western zones. These Soviet actions were bound to lead to trouble, and they did. Almost exactly a year after V-E Day, the United States announced that it was suspending all further West German reparations payments to the Soviet Union. They were not to be resumed until the Soviet Union operated its zone as part of Germany under the original terms of agreement. The reason for this American action was clear: If East Germany no longer furnished the supplies of food which West Germany needed, West Germany would have to increase its exports to buy food from abroad; and if it had to increase exports, it had to increase production. The British agreed; they were unwilling to spend their few remaining dollars buying food for the Germans. Thus, the wartime agreement to hold German industrial production down for fear that Germany would again use its heavy industry in a secret rearmament program—as it had during the years between the two world wars—collapsed. The American and British purpose was to make Germany pay for its own needs.

But the two powers also had another and more important aim in mind: As Europe's economic collapse became clearer and the cold war intensified, it became necessary to lift Germany out of its economic stagnation and make its industry contribute to the general economic recovery of Europe. In July, 1946, the United States offered to merge its zone with those of Britain and France; Germany was to be decompartmentalized in order to speed up its industrial recovery. The French, fearing Germany's reviving strength, refused to participate. The result was that in January, 1947, an embryonic German state known as Bizonia (France was to join later) formally emerged. But this fusion would not by itself suffice to achieve Germany's economic recovery. The willing cooperation of the Germans themselves was needed. America and Britain therefore decided to let the Germans begin to take a more active part in running their own country; this, in effect, foreshadowed the eventual establishment of a West German government. Lastly, Germany needed a sound currency; without it, its economy could not recover. The subsequent currency reform carried out by the U.S. Military Government became the basis of West Germany's amazing economic recovery.

The Russians reacted by blockading Berlin. The issue at stake was more than just Berlin. The issue was Germany itself. Berlin, as the old capital of Germany, was the symbol of the conflict: *Quo vadis Germania?* The Russians certainly did not want to see West Germany become a partner of the West. Germany and Russia had fought two wars in forty years. Germany had beaten Russia the first time and almost defeated it again on the second occasion. Moreover, Germany was not a *status quo* power but a revisionist state eyeing territory now controlled by the Soviet Union and Poland. Whether these defensive reasons, springing from Russia's fear of Germany, were primary in precipitating the Berlin crisis, however, is rather doubtful. For if Russia's fear of Germany was so deep, it is difficult to understand why the Russians did not accept the American proposal, offered them by Secretary Byrnes, of an alliance of twenty-five or even forty years to neutralize Germany. In any case, whereas Russia had been much weaker than Germany before World War II, it emerged from that conflict far stronger—a superpower, in fact—while Germany, in spite of its potential strength, was now only a second-class power. The Russo-German balance of power had decisively changed in Russia's favor, and an independent German attack upon Russia was unlikely in these circumstances. For in any war, whether it acted unilaterally or as an ally of the United States, Germany would be the battlefield and therefore the first country to be destroyed. Fear of this consequence was a sufficient deterrent. The real danger to the Soviet Union of a revived Germany came from the fact that, once Germany's power had been added to that of the United States and its allies, the American position in Europe would obviously be greatly consolidated. This, in turn, stood in the way of two Russian objectives: one, the immediate withdrawal of American forces and the liquidation of American bases on the Continent; and two, the long-term aim of winning Germany's participation in a subservient partnership. Germany's recovery, in short, blocked Russia's expansionist purposes in Europe.

In order to forestall Germany's revival, therefore, the Russians resorted to a test of strength. If the Allies could be forced out of Berlin, German confidence in American strength would be undermined. The Germans would hardly attach themselves to a friend too weak to protect them. Indeed, if American will power would crumble under Soviet pressure, France and Britain also might reconsider their adherence to NATO. The Berlin crisis, then, if it were not met, would disintegrate the entire American position in Europe and nullify America's postwar efforts to rebuild Europe as a partner in the struggle against the Soviet Union.

The method of conflict was decided at the outset by the unwillingness of either the United States or the Soviet Union to risk a total war. Thus, the Western powers ruled out almost at the start an attempt to reopen the corridor to Berlin by sending troops and tanks to challenge the Red Army. Instead, they limited themselves to an airlift to supply the city with all its needs. The Russians did not challenge this effort, for they were aware that in doing so they would leave the West no alternative but to fight a total war. Instead, they decided to wait and see whether the Western powers could take care of the needs of Berlin's 2.5 million citizens. It would take a minimum of 4,000 tons of food and fuel daily—an enormous amount of tonnage to ship in by air. After 324 days of waiting, the Russians were convinced that the Americans and the British were more than equal to the task. While the total supplies did not immediately attain the 4,000-ton target, Allied planes were eventually to fly in as much as 13,000 tons daily. Planes landing at three-minute intervals flew in 60 per cent more than the 8,000 tons that had previously been sent each day by ground transport. By the spring of 1949, West Berliners were eating more than at the beginning of the blockade—and considerably more than the East Berliners! Faced with this colossal Allied achievement, the Russians called off the blockade in May.

America's determination to hold Europe and not to allow further Soviet expansion had been demonstrated. The West Germans clearly saw that they could count on America to protect them. Just as NATO had been the prerequisite for Europe's economic recovery, the Berlin airlift was the final

American act which led to Germany's resurgence. America had laid the basis for Germany's economic recovery through Marshall Plan funds and the currency reforms; and now, it had given Germany the sense of military security without which its economic reconstruction could not have been completed.

European Integration

Ironically, it was the fear of Germany's rising strength that was now, in turn, to stimulate further efforts toward European integration. The specter of a fully revived Germany struck fear into most of Germany's neighbors. The French, with their memories of 1870, 1914, and 1940, were particularly alarmed. Germany's recovery—stimulated by America's response to the cold war—thus posed a serious problem for Germany's partners: How could they hold Germany, potentially the strongest nation in Europe outside of Russia, in check? Ever since Germany's unification in the late nineteenth century, France had attempted to deal with the inherently greater strength of its aggressive and militaristic neighbor by forming alliances which could balance Germany's power. Since Britain had usually preferred to retain a free hand, and since its interests were also at times opposed to those of France, the French had relied primarily upon Continental allies. Before World War I, they discovered such an ally in Russia, and between the two wars they found partners in Poland, Czechoslovakia, Romania, and Yugoslavia. None of these alliances had saved France, however; in both wars, British power and especially American power had been the decisive factors in defeating Germany (aided by Russian power, of course, in World War II). But once saved, the French again responded in terms of their traditional reflex—despite the extension of Soviet power into the heart of Europe. For France, Germany was still *the* enemy, and in December, 1944, the French signed a Treaty of Mutual Assistance with the Russians, thus making an alliance which they considered necessary for their security. Soviet hostility soon disillusioned the French and deprived the treaty of any meaning, however, and in fact made it necessary to add Germany's power to that of the West.

The failure of the traditional balance-of-power technique, by which an inferior power had always sought to balance a stronger nation, led France to seek a new way of exerting some control over Germany's growing power. French statesmen found an imaginative means in European integration. It was through the creation of a supranational community, to which Germany could transfer certain sovereign rights, that German power could be controlled. Only in this manner could German strength be prevented from again causing harm to all of Europe, and at the same time be employed instead for Europe's welfare and security.

France made its first move in this direction of a united Europe in May, 1950, when Foreign Minister Robert Schuman proposed the plan that has since borne his name: a European Coal and Steel Community (ECSC) composed of "Little Europe" (France, Germany, Italy, and the Benelux countries of Belgium, the Netherlands, and Luxembourg). The Schuman Plan was to interweave German and French heavy industry to such an extent that it would become impossible ever to separate them again. Germany would never again be able to use its coal and steel industries for nationalistic and militaristic purposes. The political and military power of the Ruhr, for purely German purposes, was to be destroyed for all time. War between Germany and France would become not only unthinkable but impossible under these circumstances.

But the new French technique of restraining Germany did not consist merely of fusing Germany's superior strength with France's own lesser strength and thereby subjecting Germany's power to a certain degree of French control. "Europeanization" was also a means for France to achieve a balance with Germany. The combination of the French and German coal and steel industries would strengthen French heavy industry and create a Franco-German equilibrium within ECSC. Economic integration would thus allow France to overcome its inferior industrial strength, which had been imposed upon it in large part by the division of Europe into separate national markets. One of the main reasons for France's industrial lag has been its lack of energy sources. It possessed Europe's largest iron ore deposits, in Lorraine—resources which during Germany's annexation of Alsace-Lorraine from 1871 to 1918 had added in considerable measure to making Germany the second greatest industrial power in the world before 1914. But even when it had regained Alsace-Lorraine after World War I, France still lacked the coal to heat the furnaces. Europe's largest coal deposits lay in the Ruhr, and to a lesser extent in the Saar—that is, in Germany. The Schuman Plan now, in effect, held out a bargain to West Germany. France was to receive coal from Germany at the same price paid by German manufacturers—and not at the previously much higher prices that made French products more expensive than German ones. In return, France was to abandon its opposition to raising German production, and prevail upon Britain and the United States to lift *all* controls from Germany's heavy industry—which would mean that Germany could once more compete on the international market. Even more important for Germany, entry into ECSC would be the first step toward regaining equal status with its former Western enemies, recovering its sovereignty, and strengthening its ties with the Western powers so that they would eventually include Germany in NATO. Thus, the Schuman Plan had both an economic and a political appeal for the Germans as well as the French.

The French Plan was not, however, devised only to control Germany's resurgent power or to give France a strength equal to that of Germany. It had a third and more ambitious goal in mind: a united Europe under French leadership. For only by creating Little Europe could France again play a major role in world affairs. France alone was too weak to pursue an active part in a world dominated by two superpowers. Even in the Western coalition, the most influential European nation was Britain, not France; and, with Germany's recovery, it was very likely that Bonn's voice and opinions would also outweigh those of Paris in Washington. By itself, France would remain dependent upon its American protector—a "satellite" state, powerless to affect major Western policy decisions. A united Europe, with Franco-German unity at its core, was therefore France's alternative to remaining subservient to the United States and without influence either in NATO or on the world stage. Only through a united Europe could France gain an equal voice with what De Gaulle was later to call the "Anglo-Saxons" in NATO, and possibly even exert independent pressure upon the Soviet Union.

These, then, were the benefits the French expected to gain from the Schuman Plan, and their approach was a highly realistic one. For they clearly saw that the nucleus of a united Europe would have to be a Franco-German union. The antagonism between these two states, born of their traditional enmity, would first have to be healed. Moreover, the French scheme did more than just evoke the dream of a united Europe, hoping that its vision would so fire people's imagination that they would suddenly discard their narrow nationalistic loyalties for a wider European allegiance. Europe could not be created by sentiment alone. The French determined to erect the new Europe upon a solid foundation, building from the bottom upward. Europe, they knew, could be forged only by tying together the interests of politically powerful and economically important groups in the various nations *across* national boundaries. For instance, the removal of all trade barriers in the coal and steel sector of the economy would encourage the modernization of mines and plants, as well as the elimination of those mines and plants that continued to operate inefficiently. And once the efficient producers had adjusted to the wider market and witnessed its opportunities, they would want to remove national barriers in other areas. Further, as production increased, Europe's standard of living would rise, and as French and Italian workers received more of what they believed to be their share, labor would see that its goal of a welfare state could be achieved only at the European level. The French also showed great political astuteness in their selection of heavy industry as the first to be integrated. Coal and steel form the basis of the entire industrial structure—they represent a sector that cannot possibly be separated from the over-all economy. Since the separation created by ECSC was to be an artificial one to begin with, this would create a "spillover" effect. Or to put it another way: This would exert pressure on the unintegrated sectors of the economy: and as the benefits of the pooling of heavy industry became clearly observable, these sectors would follow suit. The Coal and Steel Community was thus seen as the first stage of an attempt to create a wider market in one particular area of the economy; and it was expected that this approach would be gradually extended to other areas of the economy, such as agriculture, transportation, and electricity, eventually leading to the creation of a "united states" of Europe with a huge market and a mass-production system.

This was a quite different approach to Europe from that of the OEEC and its multilateral clearing house, the European Payments Union. It also differed greatly from the Council of Europe, which has achieved few tangible results and apparently has little or no influence on the individual European governments. These other organizations, which included Britain and therefore represented "Big Europe," depended upon intergovernmental cooperation. But the functional approach stressed supranational cooperation and institutions within a limited functional sphere and the creation of common interests within that particular area of activity before extending it to other functional fields. The Schuman Plan took this supranational approach, for it intended to remove national control over the coal and steel industries.

The ECSC institutions, then, were the embryo of a united Europe. They were soon to be applied to an area that their initial planners had not expected to include—the military forces of the different nationalities. The French originated this idea, too. American insistence on German rearmament made it unavoidable. To the French, the rearmament of their old enemy was both distasteful and dangerous. But France was faced with the inevitable, since German rearmament was made necessary primarily by France's own inability to supply more troops itself. Yet the French remained determined that the world would never see another *German* army, *German* general staff, *German* war ministry, or *German* ministry of armaments. The solution they proposed was the formation of a European army. Just as the French had conceived of ECSC as a means for controlling Germany's growing economic strength and harnessing it to Europe's welfare, so they now proposed a European army, composed of army corps in which no more than two divisions could be of one nationality, as an instrument for checking Germany's rising military power and using it for Europe's defense. The EDC Treaty was signed in May, 1952. NATO, of course, remained the supreme command. EDC and NATO were, however, formally linked. Since all EDC members except Germany were members of NATO, this link ensured that Germany was obligated to come to NATO's defense and vice versa.

For Germany, entry into EDC was another step toward regaining full equality with the other Western powers and asserting its political prestige. Most important, in return for providing EDC with 500,000 men organized into twelve divisions, Germany would recover its sovereignty, with certain limitations. The Allies would reserve their authority to take the necessary measures to protect the security of their forces in Germany (not only against external aggression, but also against possible attempts by the extreme left or right to subvert West Germany from within), to continue governing Berlin, and—in order to prevent any Russo-German deal—to preserve their exclusive right to negotiate with the Soviet Union on the question of German reunification. The kind of Germany they would seek—the United States, Britain, and France declared—would be "a unified Germany enjoying a liberal-democratic constitution, like that of the Federal Republic, and integrated within the European community."

The likelihood of attaining this objective was very small indeed. Western proposals to unite Germany constantly included terms which the Soviet Union could not possibly accept. These terms included reunification via free elections in both halves of Germany and insistence upon allowing the government of this reunified Germany freedom to conduct its own foreign policy. The former would have meant the end of the Soviet-imposed Communist regime in East Germany; and the latter condition would have allied a unified Germany, probably headed by the pro-Western government of Konrad Adenauer, with the West. NATO would thus be extended to the Polish frontier and the Eastern satellite belt. The Russians were hardly likely to accept such a restriction of their sphere of influence or permit willingly such an advance of Western power. Allied terms thus ensured a continuation of a divided Germany—which was precisely what they wanted. France did not wish to integrate with a united Germany—only with a split Germany. A reunited Germany would tend to dominate Little Europe, for it would certainly be more powerful than France or Italy. These nations were therefore opposed to Germany's reunification; and they, together with the United States, paid verbal allegiance to this goal only to keep the West German Government of Chancellor Adenauer in power. For the German people, reunification was of course a vital concern, and Adenauer's claim was that through the alliance with America, Britain, and France, West Germany and the Western powers would be placed in such a strong position that one day they could negotiate Russia's exit from East Germany. Yet it must also be noted that the Federal Republic between the Elbe and the Rhine is a Germany without Prussia, that South Germany has long been hostile to Protestant Prussia, and the Rhineland has been much influenced by Western (especially French) democratic thought. A reunified Germany would undoubtedly stimulate a movement to resurrect Prussia. It might therefore be said that, if Germany had to be divided, the present division which cuts Prussia off from the Western part of Germany could not have been more aptly drawn. It is this latter half which is integrating with the West in defense against the Soviet pressure from the East.

The Soviet Shift to Asia

It seems a cruel twist of fate that this very success of American foreign policy in Europe should have brought about a shift of Communist pressure from Europe to Asia—a shift which in June, 1950, led to the outbreak of the Korean War. The Truman Doctrine had prevented a Russian break- through into Southeast Europe and the Middle East and established Western Europe's flank in the eastern Mediterra- nean. The Marshall Plan had set Europe on the path to eco- nomic recovery and health. NATO had guaranteed Europe its security. The lessons of two world wars had been absorbed, and the NATO commitment was the proof of this.

The United States had transformed a position of great weakness and vulnerability into one of relative strength. It had drawn a clear line between the American and Russian spheres of influence and had demonstrated, in both Greece and Berlin, that it was in Europe to stay. (The Greek crisis had passed when Yugoslavia was ejected from the Soviet bloc in 1948; the Yugoslavs no longer provided aid to the Greek guerrillas.) What all this meant was that Europe was no longer a profitable field for guerrilla warfare, *coups d'état,* or subversive attempts.

Opportunities for immediate expansion had disappeared. To cross the line drawn by the United States was to risk total war, and this risk was hardly one the Soviet Union was will- ing to assume during a period in which the United States held atomic superiority. The Russian leaders, as George Ken- nan had said, did not believe in pursuing an "adventuristic" policy which gambled with the very existence of the Soviet state.

So they turned their attention to the Far East. Here was a much more attractive field for political and military exploita- tion. Most countries in this area had only recently emerged from Western colonialism, and their nationalistic and anti- Western feelings were very strong. Nationalist China's col- lapse and the establishment of a Communist government on the mainland in late 1949 had even further weakened the Western position in Asia, for it had gravely shifted the bal- ance of power in the Far East against the United States. The United States no longer confronted only Russia; it was now faced with the challenge of the combined power of the Sino- Soviet bloc. Moreover, whereas pressure in Europe united the

Western powers, pressure in Asia divided them, because they were fundamentally split over the character and nature of the new Chinese regime. And finally, no expansionist move in the Far East would entail the risk of total war. In the American pattern of defense, Europe held strategic priority; Asia was of secondary interest. Europe was so vital to American defense that any Soviet move in Western Europe entailed the risk of an all-out clash with the United States; no single area in Asia was so immediately vital to American security that it was worth the cost of total war. The recovery of Europe and China's collapse, then, created a vacuum in the East and turned Russian pressure toward Asia. It was here that the dramatic clashes of the cold war were to occur during the next four years. And it was these clashes that were to lead to a reaction within the United States itself against American foreign policy.

4

CONTAINMENT IN
THE FAR EAST

The Fall of China

During World War II, the United States had a twofold purpose in the Pacific: to defeat Japan and to create a powerful and friendly China in its place. It was hoped that a strong and democratic China would play a leading role in protecting the postwar peace in the Far East. The United States took several actions to confer upon China the status of a great power. It renounced its extraterritorial rights in China, repealed the Chinese exclusion laws, established an annual Chinese immigration quota, and made it possible for legally admitted Chinese to become American citizens. At Cairo in 1943, together with Great Britain, the United States promised to return "all the territories Japan had stolen from the Chinese, such as Manchuria, Formosa, and the Pescadores." It also awarded to China one of the five permanent seats on the United Nations Security Council; China was thus granted equal status with the Soviet Union, Great Britain, France, and the United States.

The belief of American statesmen that the mere pronouncement of China as a Great Power could actually convert it into one was typically American: One need only believe strongly enough in the desirability of an event for it to happen. Perhaps American policy-makers also hoped that if China were admitted into the Great-Power club, it would behave like one. But American faith without Chinese works was insufficient to accomplish the task. It would have taken a miracle to do that; and while statesmen at times delude themselves into thinking that they can perform miracles, such things happen only in storybooks.

The first obstacle to creating a strong China was the sharp division within the country. Quite apart from the Japanese occupation of large areas of the country during the war, the Chinese were deeply split among themselves. There was not one China; there were two Chinas—a Communist China and a Nationalist China. The Communists were not scattered throughout the whole population, as in Europe; already in control of large segments of northwest China, they extended their sphere during the war by infiltrating into north-central China. In this area, the Japanese held the cities and the major lines of communication, while the Communists organized the countryside. By 1945, they controlled 116 million people, one-fourth of China's entire population, within an area that constituted 15 per cent of China's territory, exclusive of Manchuria. Communist China was, in short, a nation within a nation.

Thus, if the United States wanted to create a united China, it would have to end this internal split. The American aim was to achieve this objective by establishing a coalition government in which all parties would be represented. The desirability of such a government was not questioned. What possible harm could there be in uniting the Nationalists and the Communists? The United States and the Soviet Union were cooperating against the common enemy, and most leaders and officials of the American Government looked forward to friendly postwar relations. If these two nations, each representing a totally different way of life, could overcome past differences and get along together, why should the two Chinese parties not be able to settle their conflict? There was also another and more immediate reason why the United States wished to end China's division as quickly as possible. A China torn apart by internal strife could not make an effective contribution to the winning of the war. Both the Nationalists and the Communists were concerned more with fighting each other than with fighting the Japanese. But the American attitude is that once war breaks out, the total effort must be directed toward the single goal of military victory; any diversion of strength—particularly for "extraneous" political purposes—is considered unjustifiable. The war had to be won in the quickest possible time and with the minimum number of casualties. This attitude, then, reinforced the American desire to establish a coalition government in China.

All efforts aimed at achieving this goal, both during the war and afterward, were, however, in vain. Neither the Nationalists nor the Communists trusted one another. Both sought a monopoly of power, and both were constantly aware of the important role their armies played in the struggle for power: The Nationalists recognized that they would have to deprive their enemy of his army in order to ensure their own survival; and the Communists were realists enough to know that they needed their army to defeat Chiang. At the end of the war, both parties—and particularly the Nationalists—believed that they had the capabilities to defeat their opponent; compromise was therefore unnecessary.

China was not, however, divided only between two irreconcilable parties. Its pro-American Nationalist government was losing popular support and disintegrating. Perhaps the Nationalists were merely the victims of fate. Except for the two years from 1929 to 1931, the government was constantly engaged in fighting for its very survival—against the Japanese (who attacked Manchuria in 1931, Shanghai in 1932, and China itself in 1937), as well as the Communists. Faced with both external and internal danger, Chiang Kai-shek had neither the time nor the resources to concern himself with formulating and implementing the political, social, and economic reforms China needed. His principal concern was military: to stem the Japanese advance and maintain himself in power. The problem of modernizing China—above all, of meeting peasant aspirations—was strictly a subsidiary problem. Moreover, Japanese successes during the war changed the basis of Chiang's support and thereby rendered any agrarian reform impossible. By 1939, the Japanese had occupied the entire coastal area of China and had driven the Nationalists inland. This meant that Chiang's Kuomintang Party, which controlled the government, had lost the main pillar of its support, the progressive commercial and financial interests in the coastal cities. Instead, it was forced to rely upon the conservative landlord class.

No government ever likes to commit suicide, and the Nationalist government proved no exception. A government whose principal social and economic support came from the landlords was unlikely to carry out any land reforms. Probably a majority of peasants were independent landowners, but many of China's peasants were tenants. Both groups were, at any rate, profoundly dissatisfied. Those who rented their land had to pay excessive sums; after the war, these sometimes amounted to 50 to 90 per cent of the peasant's crops. Those who owned their own land were handicapped by the small size of their holding and the lack of capital. The government's taxation policies further impoverished the peasant, who bore the main burden of the taxes. Since the peasant's crops were visible and easily appraisable, corrupt officials usually took more of the crops than the peasant could afford to spare. The result was that the peasant lived in a constant state of impoverishment and indebtedness. In order to survive, he had to seek funds from a money-lender, usually the local landlord, who charged him an extremely high rate of interest, often from 20 to 30 per cent. Consequently, the peasant got himself deeper and deeper into debt.

The fact that the peasants constituted four-fifths of China's population also meant that they had to provide most of the conscripts for the Nationalist army. But the able-bodied and eligible sons of the rich avoided military service; there were always enough corrupt officials who could be bribed. In the same way, the rich tended to avoid paying taxes. Chiang, in short, seemed to be doing his best to earn the peasants' hatred.

After the war, the Nationalists even managed to alienate the business circles which had formerly supported them. As the Nationalists returned to the coastal cities, they took over all Japanese-owned industries and ran them as state enterprises. This incensed the business community. Some of the Japanese property had formerly belonged to the Chinese, but the government simply neglected to return such property to its owners. Even worse was the fact that private enterprise now found itself faced with the powerful competition of state industries, which were controlled by relatives and close friends of Chiang. Naturally, the American aid funds with which the government supported its enterprises provided great profits for these people. As the American commander in China during the war, General Wedemeyer, observed in 1947 upon his return on a fact-finding mission for the American Government: "Certain rich families, some of whom have relatives in high positions of the Government, have been greatly increasing their fortunes. Nepotism is rife . . . sons, nephews, and brothers of government officials have been put into positions within the government-sponsored firms or in private firms to enable them to make huge profits at the expense of their government and their people."

The Nationalist position deteriorated even further because of China's unchecked inflation. The government had no fixed budget, and its accounting system did not function. When the government needed money, it simply printed it, thereby further inflating the currency. Prices doubled sixty-seven times in the two and a half years from early 1946 to late 1948. No one seemed willing or able to control this spiral. The most devastating impact of this hyperinflation was upon government officials at the lower level; it provided them with a massive incentive for corruption. Their salaries were wholly inadequate, and they had to find means of supplementing their meager incomes. Honesty in these circumstances simply did not pay. Corruption became rife throughout the government.

As Chiang's government lost popularity, it began to resort increasingly to force to hold its position. The resulting police and military measures only further alienated the people. Wedemeyer found this situation: "Secret police operate widely, very much as they do in Russia and as they did in Germany. People disappear . . . No trials and no sentences . . . Everyone lives with a feeling of fear and loses confidence in the government." This was particularly true of the intellectuals, who together with the peasantry have been the traditional supporters of China's governments. Professors were dismissed, even arrested, when they began to criticize the government for its policies. Students similarly inclined were also thrown into jail.

The behavior of the army also spread hatred of the government. The Manchurian episode was typical. In Manchuria, according to Wedemeyer,

the Central Government armies were [at the end of the war with Japan] welcomed enthusiastically by the people as deliverers from Japanese oppression. Today, after several months of experience with the Central Government armies, the people experience a feeling of hatred and distrust because the officers and enlisted men were arrogant and rude. Also, they stole and looted freely; their general attitude was that of conquerors instead of liberators.

To sum up the position of the Nationalists: The government had alienated important segments of the politically articulate minority, especially the businessmen and intellectuals. The more inarticulate and passive peasants were tired of the constant fighting, the high rents and taxes. All three groups had either lost confidence in the ability of the government to take care of the problems of postwar China, or felt that the government was not interested in their welfare. But only minorities in each group turned to the Communists. The majority simply disengaged themselves from the Nationalists and became indifferent to the outcome of the civil war. They did not rise up against the government in a "popular revolution." If the Communists won the civil war—and the military conflict would play the decisive role in determining this issue—they did so because most Chinese were willing to give the Communists the benefit of the doubt and allow them to demonstrate that they could give China a more effective government.

One reason for this lack of popular hostility and suspicion toward the Communists was, of course, the reverse side of the widespread anti-Nationalist sentiment. But another was the favorable picture the Communists presented of themselves to the Chinese population. The policies they pursued in the areas under their control were responsible for this. They did not destroy the traditional tenure system and expropriate or eliminate the landlords and money-lenders. They only reduced the rents to a fixed maximum and lowered the interest rates that could be charged on borrowed money. They permitted private enterprise and allowed all factions to participate in local government. Though they did assure Communist control by retaining the power to approve all candidates, their activities nevertheless seemed to support their claim that they stood for democracy, freedom, and individual liberty. Certainly, their economic and political practices demonstrated little Marxist bias. They appeared, instead, in the guise of genuine democrats; and their pose as agrarian reformers was widely accepted—precisely because, as an agrarian-based party, they actually did act as agrarian reformers.

If the Communists acted as if their only wish was to reform China along democratic and capitalistic lines, this was, of course, a tactical device. But the point remains that it was effective and achieved its purposes: It attracted minority support among the various strata of China's population disaffected by Nationalist policies, and it gained extensive acquiescence among the rest of the population. Chiang had alienated most of his popular support. The Communists, by cleverly hiding their real intentions, exploited this feeling of neutrality. For their purposes, a large neutral public was almost as beneficial as positive majority support; the only thing that really mattered was that this support had been withdrawn from Chiang.

The Communist position for the final military struggle was further strengthened when, near the end of the Pacific war, the Russian Army marched into Manchuria. Once established, the Russians did two things that badly hurt China. First, they dismantled Manchuria's industry and transported the machinery back to Russia to help restore their own badly destroyed industry; as a result, Manchuria, China's industrial heartland, was unable to contribute to the country's economic recovery. Second, the Russians allowed the Chinese Communists to infiltrate the countryside and handed them large stocks of Japanese arms and ammunition. Conversely, the Russians delayed the return of Nationalist troops, who had to launch a major offensive to establish their control over Manchuria. The government forces did capture the cities, but the Communists remained in control of the countryside. The Soviet invasion of Manchuria thus was a serious blow to the Nationalists.

The blame for these events has often been attributed to President Roosevelt and the Yalta "betrayal," which granted Russia, among other things, a restoration of the rights Russia had held in Manchuria before its defeat by Japan in 1904–5: the lease of Port Arthur as a Soviet naval base; the internationalization of the commercial port Dairen, which, unlike Russia's own Siberian port of Vladivostok, was not icebound part of the year; and the joint Sino-Soviet operation of the Chinese-Eastern and South-Manchurian Railroads, which served these three cities. To take this charge seriously, though, one has to deny certain clear facts of wartime military strategy: namely, that American military men were unsure that the atomic bomb would be a success; that they believed an invasion of Japan would be necessary to bring about Japan's surrender; that they expected to suffer at least 1 million casualties, and feared even more if the Japanese reinforced the home-island garrison with troops from Manchuria and northern China; and that they therefore wanted the Red Army to tackle these mainland forces before their invasion. The American Government was willing to pay the Russians the price they demanded if this would help save the lives of American soldiers, and this willingness was further increased by its suspicion that the Russians planned to restore their Tsarist position in Manchuria by declaring war on Japan at the moment when the United States seemed on the verge of victory. The Russian takeover would then be a practically bloodless operation, with a minimal contribution to Japan's defeat. American officials wanted Russia to pay some kind of price, at least, for what it could actually take for nothing. Finally, they wanted to secure a promise from the Russians that they would sign a treaty of alliance and friendship with the Nationalist government. The purpose of this treaty was to secure the Soviet Union's support for Chiang Kai-shek and to isolate his Communist opponents; this would enable Chiang to consolidate his grip on China and perhaps allow him to defeat his domestic enemy. The Russians did, in fact, sign such a treaty, but then proceeded to violate it by aiding their Chinese comrades. However, Stalin apparently did not believe that this help strengthened the Chinese Communists sufficiently to defeat the Nationalists. He is reported to have counseled Mao Tse-tung to join Chiang in a coalition government and accept Chiang's supremacy; in this respect, Stalin's policy seemed to have been the same as Truman's. Mao is said to have nodded his assent to Stalin's advice and then disregarded it; he was more confident than Stalin in a final victory.

So was Chiang, as the decisive stage of the civil war began in 1947. The Nationalist army had a strength of approximately 2.7 million troops, while the Communists had 1.1 million men, including 400,000 guerrillas; the Nationalists held a superiority of rifle firepower of more than three to one. However, the Nationalists should not have been so confident. In the first place, Chiang tended to choose his top generals for their personal loyalty rather than their ability. He constantly interfered in the chain of command. He would send orders to officers in the field countermanding those of the local commanders, or change generals in the middle of a battle or campaign. This lack of continuity in the field command and Chiang's own interventions caused uncertainty, confusion, and resentment. In the second place, Nationalist strategy was unsound and could not have been better selected to ensure defeat. Chiang and his commanders were imbued with the "wall" psychology: Their military strategy was to employ their forces only to capture cities and then to hold these cities. Instead of conducting a war of maneuver in order to find the Communist armies and destroy them in battle, the Nationalist forces immobilized their strength by walling themselves up in the cities. Consequently, they failed either to hurt the Communists' strength or to weaken their hold on the countryside. At the same time, however, their armies in the cities degenerated from the status of field armies capable of offensive operations to that of garrison troops; this sapped them of any aggressive spirit.

Throughout 1946 and 1947, the Communists limited their operations largely to raiding supply depots and communication lines, ambushing Nationalist forces, engaging in skirmishes, and attacking isolated garrisons. These local tactical successes heightened the Communist forces' confidence and morale just as they added to their opponents' demoralization. By 1948, the Communists had so increased the strength of their forces and firepower that they no longer had to rely solely upon hit-and-run tactics; they now sought out the Nationalist forces in order to completely annihilate them by concentrating superior masses of troops against them and attacking without respite. Throughout the whole campaign, the Communists kept the initiative; it was they who constantly chose the time and place of attack. By February 1, 1949, they controlled Manchuria. Nationalist strength had by then declined to 1.5 million men, including 500,000 service troops. Up until mid-September, 1948, the Nationalists had been able to replace their combat losses and thereby maintain their army at a strength of 2.7 million men. In other words, in only four and a half months, the Nationalists had lost 45 per cent of their troops. Meanwhile, Communist strength had risen to 1.6 million regular troops—partly as the result of defections from the Nationalist armies. Eighty per cent of the American equipment furnished to the government forces during and after the war had been lost, with an estimated 75 per cent of it falling into the Communists' hands. General Barr, the head of the American military mission in China, summed up the situation succinctly: "No battle has been lost since my arrival due to lack of ammunition or equipment. Their [the Nationalists'] military debacle, in my opinion, can all be attributed to the world's worst leadership and many other morale-destroying factors that led to a complete loss of the will to fight." Nowhere was this more clearly demonstrated than in Chiang's failure, after his loss of northern China, even to attempt a defense of south China by making a stand along the Yangtze River. Chiang thereby forfeited the mainland, and he withdrew to Formosa, an island lying 100 miles off the mainland coast. In the fall of 1949, Mao Tse-tung proclaimed the People's Republic of China.

One question about Nationalist China's defeat remains: Could the United States have prevented it? The answer is "Probably"—*if* American officers had taken over the command of the Nationalist armies; *if* the United States had been willing to commit large-scale land, air, and sea forces to fight in China; and *if* the United States had been willing to commit even greater financial aid than the approximate $2 billion it had already given in grants and credits since V-J Day. But these conditions could not have been met. America's helter-skelter demobilization left it with insufficient forces either for supplying the officers for the direction of the Nationalist forces or for intervention in China. The United States had only one and one-third divisions at home. Nor did the American people seem to be in any mood to rearm in 1947–48, particularly to fight a war in China.

The problem of extending further economic aid to Chiang was equally vexing. His corrupt, inefficient, and reactionary government did not provide a politically effective instrument through which to carry out the social and economic reforms China needed. Aiding Chiang seemed to be "pouring money down the drain." In contrast, U.S. economic aid to Europe, which the Administration considered the area most vital to American security, had a good chance of achieving its objective—political and economic recovery for Britain and the Continent. It would probably have been unwise in these circumstances to divert a very large slice of the government's not unlimited dollar funds to attempt to restore a government that had lost the confidence of its own people. The power of the United States was, after all, not unlimited; it would have to be applied selectively. Hence, those areas of vital interest in which its use would be most effective were to be the prime focus. As Secretary Acheson stated it: "Nothing that this country did or could have done within the reasonable limits of its capabilities could have changed that result; nothing that was left undone by this country has contributed to it. It was the product of internal Chinese forces, forces which this country tried to influence but could not. A decision was arrived at within China, if only a decision by default."

Re-evaluation of American Far Eastern Policy

Despite Chiang's debacle and the disintegration of the Far Eastern balance of power, the U.S. Government took an optimistic view of developments. Shortly after the Nationalist collapse, Secretary Acheson expressed his belief that despite the common ideological points of view of the Chinese and Russian regimes, they would eventually clash with one another. Acheson predicted that Russia's appetite for a sphere of influence in Manchuria and northern China would alienate Chinese nationalism. The implications of this point of view are clear. The first is that if the Chinese Communists were genuinely concerned with the preservation of China's national interest, they would resist Soviet penetration. Mao Tse-tung might, therefore, be a potential Tito. On the other hand, if Mao proved himself to be subservient to Russia, he would lose the support of the Chinese people. Since he would have shown that he served not the interests of China but those of another power, his regime would be identified with foreign rule. Given time, Acheson declared, the Chinese people would throw off this "foreign yoke." Thus, whichever of these two developments occurred, the United States could only gain from the antithesis between Communism and Chinese nationalism.

This analysis of Sino-Soviet relations indicated that the United States must first disentangle itself from Chiang Kai-shek. Until this disassociation had been completed, the United States would remain identified with the government rejected by the Chinese people. This could only foster the growth of anti-American sentiment in China. It was precisely this that had to be avoided, for the attention of the Chinese people should not be diverted from the Soviet Union's actions. Under no circumstances, Acheson emphasized, must America "seize the unenviable position which the Russians have carved out for themselves. We must not undertake to deflect from the Russians to ourselves the righteous anger, and the wrath, and the hatred of the Chinese people which must develop." Only by disengaging itself from Chiang Kai-shek could the United States exploit the alleged clash of interests between China and Russia.

The first step taken by the Truman Administration to implement this policy was the release of a White Paper which argued that the Nationalists had lost control of the mainland despite adequate American economic and military aid. The clear implication was that Chiang was no longer worthy of American support; hence, American recognition of Chiang's government as the official government of China should be withdrawn. Conversely, it was suggested that the Communists should be recognized as the official government of China, both as a matter of fact and as a gesture of friendship. A second act was an announcement that American forces would not be used to defend Formosa, and that the Administration would no longer provide the Nationalists with military aid or advice: "The United States Government will not pursue a course which will lead to involvement in the civil conflict in China." This opened the way for the Chinese Communists to take Formosa—an event that was expected before the end of 1950. The Communist government would then be the only claimant to represent China, and the United States could extend it recognition. Chiang, through whom containment had been impossible because he had been not a container but a sieve, would have been eliminated; containment of Russia could then be implemented through "Mao Tse-tito." But before this could happen, war had broken out in another area in the Far East—Korea.

The Korean War and the Truman-MacArthur
Controversy

Korea had been a divided nation since 1945. Soviet forces had entered Korea two days after Japan surrendered. The nearest American troops at the time were in Okinawa, 600 miles away, and in the Philippines, 1,500 to 2,000 miles away. Consequently, the two powers decided to divide the country temporarily at the 38th parallel; the Russians would disarm the Japanese above the parallel, the United States below. With the beginning of the cold war, this division became permanent. All American attempts to negotiate an end to the division and establish a democratic and united Korea failed.

As a result, the United States took the problem to the United Nations in late 1947 and called upon that organization to sponsor a free election throughout all of Korea. The General Assembly thereupon established a Temporary Commission in Korea and charged it with the responsibility of holding and supervising such an election. The Russians, however, refused to grant the Commission access to North Korea, and the election was thus limited to South Korea. Afterward, the United States recognized South Korea as the official republic and the government of Syngman Rhee as its legitimate representative. The American Government also extended to Rhee economic, technical, and military aid to bolster his non-Communist government and help Korea establish a democratic society. Thus, while South Korea was not an ally of the United States, there could be little doubt that the young republic was America's protégé.

It was this country which the North Korean Communists attacked in late June, 1950. The Communist aggression took the American Government by complete surprise. American policy-makers had believed that the Soviet leaders, like themselves, thought only in terms of all-out war. It was precisely this single-minded American preoccupation with total war that had accounted for Korea's being left outside the American Pacific defense perimeter, which ran from the Aleutians to Japan, through the Ryukyus (Okinawa) to the Philippines. This made Korea militarily dispensable within the pattern of American security, for in a global war its fate would be decided in other theaters of war. A Soviet occupation of Korea would not raise Korea's strategic significance, since the peninsula could be neutralized by American air and sea power.

American troops had therefore been withdrawn from Korea, because in a major war they would be vulnerable to Russian land power and would probably be trapped. The resulting absence of pledged American military support to resist North Korean aggression rendered South Korea highly vulnerable; indeed, it left South Korea as an attractive vacuum inviting Communist expansion. On June 25, the North Korean Army struck.

Overnight, the survival of South Korea became identified with the survival of the United States itself. For North Korea's aggression, which in Washington's opinion could hardly have been launched without Soviet encouragement and support, altered the basis upon which Korea's strategic significance had been calculated. Korea's value could no longer be assessed in terms of its relative importance during a total war. The cold war focused attention upon the wider political and military implications of a Communist occupation of South Korea and upon the threat such an occupation would pose for the entire containment policy. If the principal purpose of containment was to prevent further Soviet expansion, American inaction in the face of Soviet aggression could only encourage further aggressive acts in the future. The appetites of dictators—as both Hitler and Stalin had presumably amply demonstrated—are insatiable. And if containment was possible only through an alignment of the United States' power with that of its allies, then failure to respond to South Korea's pleas for help must result in the disintegration of the alliance system and the isolation of the United States. If the United States merely stood by while South Korea fell, it would demonstrate to the world that it was either afraid of Russian power or unconcerned with the safety of its allies. American guarantees to help preserve their national integrity and political independence would thereafter be regarded as valueless; and this would leave nations whose security depended upon U.S. willingness to live up to its commitments with no alternative but to turn to neutralism for protection—a state in which they would be subject to increasing Soviet pressure and possibly eventual domination.

This reasoning applied particularly to Japan. With the demise of Nationalist China and the disintegration of the Far Eastern balance of power, the United States was about to turn Japan into an ally and rearm it in an effort to recreate some semblance of strength in the Pacific. This reasoning applied equally to the NATO countries in Europe. If NATO collapsed, the balance of power would shift drastically in favor of Russia. In these circumstances, the consequences of American inaction would be extremely grave. In fact, the United States had no choice in a bipolar world but to oppose force with force—if it wished to prevent an upset of the global balance of power and its own strategic isolation.

Nevertheless, the limited Soviet aggression did not fit American strategic doctrine, based on a one-sided concentration upon air-atomic striking power. The Russians had cleverly faced the United States with the dilemma of either risking a total war for a limited objective or taking no action at all and thus surrendering South Korea. American policy was prepared to deal only with an all-out Soviet surprise attack upon the United States or Western Europe; such an attack would be met by the power of SAC. But American strategy was completely unprepared to deal with the kind of less than total challenge which the Russians had now posed in Asia. The North Korean aggression, in effect, meant that massive retaliation outside of Europe was not an effective policy. For the deterrent effect of U.S. retaliatory power depended upon whether an enemy believed that the country would actually "unleash" this power if he committed aggression. The limited attack in Korea clearly demonstrated that the Soviet leaders were not deterred by the policy of massive retaliation, despite America's far greater atomic stockpile and ability to deliver it. They did not believe that the United States would risk all-out war to save Korea. For the Korean type of challenge could be met only by local response and primarily through the commitment of American ground forces. Containment depended not just upon the capacity to deter total war with strategic air power; it required, in addition, an army to meet precisely this kind of limited incursion.

But it was the army forces that the Administration had been cutting since the end of World War II. General Marshall recalled in 1951 that the army had been so small in the years preceding the Korean War that there had been only one and one-third divisions in the United States. The Chiefs of Staff had had so few troops at their command that they had even been worried about obtaining enough men to guard airstrips at Fairbanks, Alaska. According to Marshall, "We had literally almost no military forces outside of our Navy and outside of an effective but not too large Air Force, except the occupation garrisons, and . . . even in Japan they were only at about 60 per cent strength."

Yet, if the United States was to escape the dilemma of total war or surrender, the Japanese-occupation divisions—undermanned and undertrained but luckily near the scene of battle—had to be committed. For two days, on June 27 and 28, the United States tried to stem the North Korean advance with air and sea forces alone. But on June 29, General MacArthur, the Commander-in-Chief in the Far East, reported that Korea would be lost unless ground forces were employed to halt the enemy army. These forces were then sent in under the aegis of the United Nations. This was done for two reasons. First, because by virtue of the free election it had sponsored in South Korea, the United Nations had been intimately concerned with the birth of the young state. Second, one of the aims of American foreign policy was to associate its cold war policies with the symbolic, humanitarian values of the United Nations. Though it is traditional for nations to attempt to justify their policies in such a manner, the United States has shown a marked propensity for doing so. American depreciation of power and reluctance to recognize it as a factor in human affairs makes it psychologically neccessary to rationalize actions in the international arena in terms of ideological objectives and universal moral principles. American power must be "righteous" power used not for purposes of power politics and selfish national advantage but for the peace and welfare of all mankind. Inherent in this public self-image of the United States as a noble and unselfish crusader on behalf of moral principles was an extreme danger, however—namely, that if the enemy were not properly punished through total defeat, the reaction to the war would be one of frustration and disillusionment, which could only jeopardize the containment policy itself.

This was precisely what was to happen, although, after initial setbacks, the war went well for a while. In a daring operation on September 15, General MacArthur, now U.N. Supreme Commander, landed an army at the west coast port of Inchon, 150 miles behind the North Korean lines. These forces then drove northward, thereby trapping more than half the enemy army. The rest of the shattered Communist army was in flight. On September 30, the U.N. forces reached the 38th parallel.

The question now confronting the United States was whether to cross the parallel. The war had been fought to restore South Korea; this implied a negotiated settlement on the parallel. This goal was now abandoned. The military situation favored the fulfillment of an American goal of several years' standing: the unification of the whole of Korea. The U.S. Government therefore shifted its emphasis from containing the expansion of Soviet power to the forceful liberation of a Soviet satellite. Inchon, in short, transformed the whole character of the war—from a defensive action seeking only to re-establish the *status quo,* to an offensive one designed to effect a permanent change in the *status quo.*

The U.S. Government believed that it was politically safe to attempt this. The Administration did not believe that the Chinese Communist leaders would consider the U.N. advance a threat to their security, because they were Chinese first and Communists second. Mao and his colleagues were already thought to be so involved in their struggle with the Soviet Union over the detachment of northern China, Manchuria, and Sinkiang that their eyes were fixed on their own northern provinces rather than on North Korea. In short, there was nothing to fear. The new objective of a militarily unified Korea was sanctioned by a U.N. resolution on October 7.

But American policy-makers miscalculated, for the Chinese

sent their armies into North Korea under the guise of "volunteers," and in late November they launched a major offensive which drove the U.N. forces back below the 38th parallel. Throughout December, 1950, and early January, 1951, there was no certainty that U.N. troops could hold the peninsula; but the tired, defeated, and outnumbered troops managed to rally and stem the Chinese offensives. By March, they had once more advanced to the 38th parallel. The Administration was again faced with a decision: whether to seek a militarily unified Korea or to accept a divided Korea.

There was no doubt about what the American field commander wanted to do. MacArthur insisted that the political aim of the war was the establishment of a unified Korea. He maintained that failure to prosecute the military campaign with the vigor necessary to achieve this objective would constitute rank appeasement. Above all, MacArthur felt that the United States should take advantage of China's intervention to counter the latter's growing strength. China was, in his opinion, "a new and dominant power which for its own purposes has allied with Soviet Russia, but which in its own concepts and methods has become aggressively imperialistic with a lust for expansion and increased power normal to this type of imperialism. . . . The aggressiveness now displayed not only in Korea, but in Indo-China, Tibet, and pointing toward the south, reflects predominantly the same lust for power which has animated every would-be conqueror since the beginning of time." He wished, therefore, to "severely cripple and largely neutralize China's capability to wage aggressive war and thus save Asia from the engulfment otherwise facing it." This purpose, MacArthur felt, could be achieved with minimum risk, since the Soviet Union would not dare to resort to war until its atomic and industrial power more nearly matched that of the United States. MacArthur's aim, in short, was not only to unify Korea but to change the entire strategic picture in the Far East while America still held the global balance of power.

The strategy with which MacArthur expected to accomplish these objectives consisted of a naval blockade of the

Chinese coast; air bombardment of China's industrial complex, communication network, supply depots, and troop assembly points; reinforcement of his forces with Chinese Nationalist troops; and "diversionary action possibly leading to counter-invasion" by Chiang against the mainland.

The Truman Administration, however, rejected MacArthur's proposals because they were considered too risky. It was feared that bombing China and inflicting a defeat upon Russia's principal ally would probably precipitate World War III. The Sino-Soviet Treaty of February, 1950, bound the Soviet Union to come to the aid of China if the latter were attacked by Japan "or any other state which should unite with Japan" (an obvious reference to the United States). But even without this treaty, China was the Soviet Union's largest and most important ally. Russian self-interest in the Far East and the necessity of maintaining Russian prestige in the Communist sphere would make it difficult for the Soviet Union to ignore a direct attack upon the Chinese mainland. There were, Secretary Acheson explained, a number of courses the Russians could follow. "They could turn over to the Chinese large numbers of planes and 'volunteer' crews for retaliatory action in Korea and outside. They might participate with the Soviet Air Force and the submarine fleet." Or, the "Kremlin could elect to parallel the action taken by Peiping and intervene with half a million or more ground-force 'volunteers'; or it could go the whole way and launch an all-out war. Singly, or in combination, these reactions contain explosive possibilities, not only for the Far East, but for the rest of the world as well."

But even if the Soviet Union remained a spectator, the United States could not extend the war. A "war of attrition" waged by Chinese manpower in Korea would "bleed dry" and make it impossible to build a strong military defense in Europe. A large-scale diversion of American power to Asia would expose Europe to Soviet armies and might very well incite an attack at a moment of maximum American weakness on the Continent. The United States had to conserve its strength to check its principal enemy, the Soviet Union; the country could not afford to dissipate its power in a peripheral area against a secondary enemy. MacArthur's strategy, in the opinion of General Bradley, Chairman of the Joint Chiefs of Staff, would therefore involve the United States in the wrong war, at the wrong place, at the wrong time, and with the wrong enemy.

This view was shared by Britain and France. America's chief allies were naturally reluctant to see American power diverted to the Far East before Europe was secure against Russian attack; and they had no desire to risk such an early outbreak of World War III for an area that was of minor strategic significance to them. Thus, if the United States decided to carry the war to China, it would have to act unilaterally. But the objective of balancing Soviet might or winning a total war was predicated on NATO's unity and combined strength.

Finally, the Joint Chiefs of Staff rejected MacArthur's proposals because they were judged militarily ineffective. A naval blockade would be of very limited use for two reasons: first, because China was so lacking in industrialization that a blockade would not have sufficient immediate impact; and second, because China's essential supplies came overland from Russia. Air bombardment of China's population and industrial centers would have an equally limited effect, for Communist China's arsenal lay in the Soviet Union. Even with the complete destruction of China's industrial heartland in Manchuria, Russia would still be in a position to supply China with the military equipment and ammunition it required. It was therefore decided to concentrate U.S. air power upon the 200 miles of supply line in North Korea in order to interdict the Chinese logistical system. The employment of Nationalist troops was rejected because they had already demonstrated their ineffectiveness in China. Moreover, the Chinese people were hardly likely to welcome Chiang back.

Inherent in the Administration's rejection of MacArthur's recommendations was the reversal of its position of October 7, that its objective was a militarily unified Korea, and a reassertion of its original attitude that the aim of the war was to restore the *status quo*. The Communists had attempted to erase the 38th parallel and incorporate South Korea into the Communist bloc; neither the North Koreans nor the Chinese Communists had succeeded in achieving this objective. The Communists had also hoped to destroy the Western Alliance and isolate the United States; in this, too, they had failed. NATO had been preserved and greatly strengthened by its rearmament program and the stationing of four new American divisions in Europe. And the primary purpose of U.N. action in Korea, to put the Communists on notice that the Western powers would not tolerate Communist expansion by force, had been achieved. Thus, the wisest course seemed to be to attempt to end the war where it had begun.

However, MacArthur refused to accept this dismissal of his strategy and limitation of the war to the Korean peninsula. He continued to assert that his strategy was both feasible and without great risk. He therefore continued to urge the President and the Joint Chiefs of Staff to lift the restrictions they had imposed upon him; and when they refused, he attempted to force their hand by taking his case into the public arena and appealing over their heads to the opposition party in Congress and to the American people themselves. This produced an intolerable situation. It is the President who is responsible for the formulation of foreign policy; he is the nation's chief diplomat and Commander-in-Chief. No government can allow a field commander to challenge its policies, to appeal to the public and the opposition for a change in these policies, thus undermining its control over the military. The soldier must obey his orders. He is judged not by the nature of the policy he executes—only by how well he executes it. If he cannot accept this policy, he must resign; otherwise, he must be dismissed. In early April, President Truman did precisely that. The resulting furor brought to the surface the public's disillusionment with containment.

The Reaction to Containment

MacArthur's dismissal was met with a storm of disapproval throughout the United States. The President received a flood of vituperous telegrams and letters informing him in no uncertain terms that his decision had been a mistake. In his first public appearance after MacArthur's dismissal, when President Truman attended the first baseball game of the season to throw out the opening ball, he was booed. Several state legislatures condemned him for his "irresponsible and capricious action." Republicans in Congress announced their intention of initiating impeachment proceedings against him and Secretary Acheson. Both Truman and Acheson were burned in effigy in many communities throughout the land. In contrast, MacArthur was received everywhere not as a man who had openly attempted to undermine the cherished American principle of civilian supremacy over the military, but as a great returning hero. In each of the cities he visited—San Francisco, Washington, Chicago, Boston—millions turned out to cheer him. In New York City alone, an estimated 7.5 million people lined the streets to see him—twice the number that had witnessed General Eisenhower's triumphal return from Europe in 1945; 2,850 tons of ticker tape, confetti, and streamers were showered upon MacArthur; New York looked as if it had been hit by a snowstorm in April.

This almost hysterical reception was primarily the result of the nation's frustration with the containment policy, which was psychologically and emotionally in contradiction with American values and experience in foreign affairs. Traditionally, the United States had abstained from involvement in foreign affairs. Attention had, instead, been focused on domestic development. The business of America had been America—not foreign countries. When foreign affairs had occasionally interrupted this preoccupation with domestic concerns, such matters had been quickly settled: If a Latin American state "misbehaved," a few thousand marines soon "corrected" the misdeeds of the offender; or if—as did happen twice in this century—Germany set out to conquer Continental Europe, the United States harnessed all its resources, maximized its military strength, and crushed the enemy in the shortest possible time. Whatever the technique employed, the main point was that the conflict was settled quickly and

completely. Only if the external crisis were solved immediately and totally could the American people return to their
more important tasks—the internal development of their
country and earning their living. In this context, foreign affairs were merely an annoying but temporary diversion.

Containment ran directly contrary to this experience. The
cold war did not draw a clear-cut line between peace and war.
It allowed the United States neither to abstain from foreign
entanglement nor to harness its giant strength for one quick
and all-out military effort to "punish" the enemy who had
forced it to divert its attention from more pressing domestic
matters. The Administration's aim was not the destruction of
Russia and its satellites, but only the creation of a balance of
power to effect the "containment" of further Soviet attempts
to expand. The objective of the government was not to erase
the Soviet Union with a swift blow, but to accept the basic
fact of coexistence. Truman and Acheson sought only to
strengthen the United States and its allies in order to improve
the terms of coexistence and the possibility of survival, not to
end the Soviet threat once and for all.

The frustrations of such a continued defensive and negative policy, which left the initiative to the Soviet Union, were
bad enough; failures made it intolerable. This was especially
the case with China. Americans had long regarded China as
their special ward. Whereas American foreign policy toward
Europe during the last fifty years had been limited to two
short but decisive military interventions occasioned by Germany's threats to the European balance of power, American
involvement in the Far East, and particularly in China, had
been active since the turn of the century. The original interest in China had not been political but commercial: China
was potentially a huge market for American products. But
U.S. policy toward China had contained some elements of al-
truistic intent as well—a genuine interest in the welfare and
Christian salvation of the Chinese people. In fact, the United
States had long regarded itself as the protector of China from
foreign exploitation and invasion. Through the Open-Door
policy—aimed at preventing Great Britain, France, Russia,

Germany, and Japan from shutting American commerce out of China and at obtaining an equal opportunity to sell on the Chinese market—the United States had become politically committed to preserve the territorial integrity and political independence of China. Since the American people had never been prepared to fight for this objective, however, the United States had failed to protect China from external pressures and invasions: The Russians had established a sphere of influence in Manchuria about 1900, and the Japanese had replaced the Russians as the actual rulers of this strategic area after the Russo-Japanese War. During and after World War I, Japan had expanded its influence and control over China, and in 1931 Japan had initiated the Sino-Japanese War to consummate its ambition to turn China into a Japanese vassal or colony. The Open-Door policy, then, had been largely a verbal policy. Indeed, the United States had never been prepared to support this policy militarily; it was a policy in which diplomacy was divorced from force, and what it meant was that the United States usually disregarded its commitment whenever Russia or Japan challenged it. But Americans, even in those days, believed that words were a substitute for an effective policy; out of this arose the illusion that the United States had long been China's protector and friend, extending to the Chinese people the bountiful benefits of Western Christianity, political ideals, science, and medicine.

Americans were, therefore, shocked by Chiang Kai-shek's collapse in 1949 and the establishment of Communist control of the Chinese mainland. Certainly, they were totally unprepared for, and deeply resentful of, the propaganda emanating from Peking accusing the United States of being "the Chinese people's implacable enemy . . . a corrupt imperialistic nation, the world center of reaction and decadence . . . a paper tiger and entirely vulnerable to defeat." They had expected that a "loyal" and fundamentally democratic China, grateful to America for past protection and help, would emerge from World War II as a strong friend of this country and as a powerful and reliable ally in the Far East. The failure of these expectations in late 1949 came as a blow to the American public. Suddenly, the relative security founded on the successful application of containment policies in Europe—the Truman Doctrine, the Marshall Plan, the Berlin airlift, and NATO—seemed to have disintegrated. It appeared that the United States had stemmed the Communist menace in Europe only to allow it to achieve a breakthrough in Asia. The resulting insecurity and anxiety were further heightened by two other events about the same time: the news that Russia had exploded its first atomic bomb and thereby shattered the American monopoly of the weapon widely regarded as the principal deterrent to a Soviet attack, and the conviction in early 1950 of Alger Hiss, followed shortly by the trial of Judith Coplon and the confession of Klaus Fuchs—which suggested continued Soviet espionage in high places. The outbreak of the Korean War and Communist China's subsequent intervention added more fuel to the fires of discontent.

The public did not understand the causes of its frustration; it could not comprehend the reasons for these alleged failures of American foreign policy. Whenever the United States had been drawn into the international arena in the past, its actions had met with quick success. It had beaten the British, the Mexicans, the Spaniards, the Germans, and the Japanese. America had never been invaded, defeated, or occupied as most other nations had been; it had, to be sure, committed mistakes, but with its great power it had always been able to rectify these. To a nation in which one popular slogan expressed confidence in doing "the difficult today, the impossible tomorrow," failure was a new experience. America's history had been a witness to victories only; its unbroken string of successes seemed evidence of national omnipotence.

It was this unquestioned assumption that the United States was omnipotent that suggested the reason for America's political and military failures: treason within its own government! For if America was all-powerful, it could not be its lack of strength that accounted for its defeats. It could not be that there was a limit to its ability to influence events abroad, far away from its shores. America's setbacks must have been the result of its own policies. Ostensibly, the reason China fell was that the "pro-Communist" administrations of Franklin Roosevelt and Harry Truman had either deliberately or unwittingly "sold China down the river." This charge—made primarily by the dominant conservative wing of the Republican Party, and particularly by Senators Taft, Joseph R. McCarthy, and Nixon—was simplicity itself: America's China policy had ended in Communist control of the mainland; the Administration leaders and the State Department were responsible for the formulation and execution of foreign policy; thus, the government must be filled with Communists and Communist sympathizers who "tailored" American policy to advance the global aims of the Soviet Union. In short, disloyal or grossly incompetent American statesmen were responsible for the "loss" of China; it was to them, not to China, that the collapse of Nationalist China was due. Low Nationalist morale, administrative and military ineptness, and repressive policies that had alienated mass support had nothing to do with it; nor did the superior Communist organization, direction, morale, and ability to identify with popular aspirations.

This conspiratorial interpretation thus bridged the gap between the public's illusion of American omnipotence and the limits of America's power. The belief that Communist victories were caused by the treachery or stupidity of American policy-makers made it unnecessary both to recognize this fact and to re-evaluate the traditional American approach to foreign policy. It was also highly flattering to the Americans' chauvinistic sense of pride, for it permitted the public to continue to believe in America's omnipotence—and in its opponent's inferiority. Secretary Acheson had once said: "Our name for problems is significant. We call them headaches. You can take a powder, and they are gone. These pains [brought on by the world situation] are not like that. They . . . will stay with us until death. We have got to understand that all our lives danger, the uncertainty, the need for alertness, for efforts, for discipline will be upon us. This is new to us. It will be hard for us." MacArthur's return demonstrated that it was still very hard for us. The American people were still looking for the aspirin that would dissolve all their foreign-policy problems.

It was precisely because MacArthur identified himself with this illusion of omnipotence that he received such a tumultuous welcome upon his return to the United States. He understood the public's frustration, and he gave voice to it in familiar—one might even say, in "American"—words, words of victory holding forth a view of a quick and successful end to the bloodshed on the battlefield, words of confidence and praise for an America strong enough to accomplish anything it had the mind to do in this world, and words of condemnation for those who, driven by fear of Russia and troublesome allies, chained the proud and invincible American giant to the rock of "weakness" and "appeasement." War, he said, indicated that "you have exhausted all other potentialities of bringing the disagreements to an end," and once engaged, "there is no alternative than to apply every available means to bring it to a swift end. War's very objective is victory—not prolonged indecision. In war there is no substitute for victory." The very term "resisting aggression" indicated "that you can destroy the potentialities of the aggressor to continually hit you" and not "go on indefinitely, neither to win or lose." One cannot fight a "half war." The Administration's policy was based upon the assumption that "when you use force, you can limit that force." This introduced "a new concept into military operations—the concept of appeasement."

Here was the kind of words the public could understand. Once the diplomats had failed to keep the peace and war had erupted, the military expert took over and fought a technically efficient war. As a nonpolitical figure, he should not be burdened with extraneous political considerations. His sole aim was the complete destruction of the enemy's forces—in short, military victory. The enemy needed to be punished for provoking war. Only his total defeat would achieve this aim. Only in this way could the nation's principles be safeguarded. America's full power, if necessary, had to be applied to destroy the aggressor who threatened these principles. Deliberate self-restraint was, in these circumstances, a betrayal of

America's national honor. Evil must be wiped out; to allow its continued existence was intolerable. Such compromise implied weakness or softness. To accept it was "un-American."

The reaction to the Korean War was thus twofold. On the one hand, the public demanded a return to an "American" policy, a "dynamic" or "positive" policy which would brook no compromises with the enemy and would withstand Allied pressure to "appease." Such a "tougher" policy, it was hoped, would restore America's dignity, prestige, and initiative on the world scene. On the other hand, the public wanted relief from the almost constant foreign-policy involvements and costs of the past few years. This indicated a lowering of international tension, ending the Korean War, reducing U.S. commitments, and cutting expenditures. The contradictory nature of these aims was symptomatic of the intense desire to return to the traditional way of conducting foreign policy: either to concentrate on domestic affairs and to abstain from all foreign policy, or to assert America's power without fear or compromise. It was this double and paradoxical legacy that the Eisenhower Administration inherited from the Truman Administration.

5

THE STRATEGY OF

"FRONTIERSMANSHIP"

Eisenhower Liberation

During the Presidential election campaign of 1952, the Republicans cleverly exploited the public's frustration with containment—a frustration grounded in the popular illusion of national omnipotence. America's great insecurity and its present involvement in the Korean War, they asserted, were the result of the "tragic blunders" that Roosevelt and Truman had committed at the Teheran, Yalta, and Potsdam conferences with the Russians. It was there that the Democratic leaders had deliberately and stealthily paved the way for Communism's postwar expansion by selling out Eastern Europe and betraying Chiang Kai-shek. The two Presidents had, according to the Republican Party platform, "flouted our peace-assuring pledges such as the Atlantic Charter, and [they] did so in favor of despots, who, it was well known, consider that murder, terror, slavery, concentration camps, and the ruthless and brutal denial of human rights are legitimate means to their desired ends. Teheran, Yalta, and Potsdam were the scenes of those tragic blunders with others to follow. The leaders of the Administration acted without the knowledge or consent of Congress or the American people. They traded our overwhelming victory for a new enemy and for new oppressions and new wars which were quick to come." In other words, America's wounds were self-inflicted.

Similarly, the Republicans charged that Truman's postwar foreign policy was self-defeating. It underwrote the false premise that American power was limited and committed the United States to continued coexistence and constant involvement in foreign policy. As John Foster Dulles, the chief Republican spokesman on foreign policy, put it: "We are not working, sacrificing, and spending in order to be able to live *without* this peril—but to be able to live *with* it, presumably forever." The Administration's policies were "treadmill policies, which, at best, might perhaps keep us in the same place until we drop exhausted." The failures of containment were many: It was a negative policy; it surrendered the initiative to the enemy; it merely reacted to counter the Communist danger wherever and whenever the latter chose to attack; it was so costly that it would bankrupt the country; and it aimed only at preserving the *status quo*. In short, Dulles condemned the policy of containment as "negative, futile, and immoral."

The aim of American foreign policy, Dulles stressed, should not be to coexist indefinitely with the Communist menace; it should be to eliminate that menace. The purpose of American policy should be a rollback of Soviet power. The United States had only to proclaim its stand for freedom and announce that it would never be a party to any "deal" that confirmed Soviet despotism over alien peoples. Such a declaration would preserve the courage and hope of. the satellite peoples and prevent them from accepting the Soviet regime. In Dulles's words, the United States "should make it publicly known that it wants and expects liberation to occur. The mere statement of that wish and expectation would change, in an electrifying way, the mood of the captive peoples. It would probably put heavy new burdens on the jailers and create new opportunities for liberation."

Never had the illusion of American omnipotence received a greater tribute. America's cause was righteous, and in order to be victorious it need only publicize this cause by launching a moral crusade. Right would then again prevail over might. The Republican program of action apparently envisaged the future Secretary of State, John "Joshua" Dulles, marching around the walls of the Kremlin empire, sounding the call of freedom upon his trumpet. The walls would then come tumbling down, the enslaved peoples would be liberated, and Soviet power would be forced to retreat. The world would once more be safe for democracy.

The Republicans thus appeared not only to promise an eventual end to the cold war—they also pledged themselves to do it at less cost. For they claimed that the Democrats' foreign policy of indefinite coexistence, with its vast outlay for armaments and economic aid, would undermine the nation's economy. The Republicans asserted that it was Russia's aim to destroy America by forcing the country to spend itself into bankruptcy—an aim furthered by Democratic policy. America's defense had to be provided with a healthy economic foundation. This would require a sharp cut in the present huge foreign aid and military expenditures. The Republicans, in brief, promised the nation at one and the same time an offensive strategy, a balanced budget, and reduction of taxes. They pledged a rollback of Soviet power on the one hand and, on the other, a cut in the appropriations for America's defense.

Such goals were not only incompatible; they were unattainable. The mere enunciation of the doctrine of liberation would not free any Soviet satellite; good intentions, unsupported by concrete political and military policies, possess a notorious impotence on the international scene. But perhaps this did not really matter, since the policy of liberation seems to have been devised primarily to roll back the Democrats in the United States, not the Red Army in Eastern Europe. And for this domestic purpose, liberation was a highly effective strategy.

The country desperately wanted a more vigorous and forthright anti-Communist policy that promised an end to the cold war. At the same time, it was unprepared to take the risks involved: That is, a policy that actively sought the liberation of the satellite states would have to accept the very definite risk of all-out war with the Soviet Union. In these circumstances, the only kind of dynamism the country could afford was a verbal dynamism. And this was all the people seemed to want. It allowed them to delude themselves that the United States once again pursued a vigorous and forthright policy that would defeat its opponent. Liberation was the Republican Party's therapy for a public that refused to accept the facts of America's limited power in the world and rejected any changes in its traditional approach to foreign policy. That this policy of liberation was probably never meant to be more than a verbal appeal to the American people was clearly demonstrated at the time of the anti-Communist revolt in East Berlin and other East German cities in June, 1953, and during the national uprising in Hungary in late 1956. In neither case did the Eisenhower Administration act—except to condemn the Soviet Union for its suppression of Germans and Hungarians and to express its sympathy for the victims of Soviet despotism. In Berlin, it substituted food packages to the East Berliners for liberation; and in Hungary, it even reassured the Soviet Union that it had no intention of intervening. The *status quo* was thereby reaffirmed. Liberation had returned to the "womb" of containment.

The Administration did, however, carry out its promises of military and economic retrenchment. This involved three measures. The first of these was to end the Korean War, which would allow the Administration to cut the size of the army and avoid the cost of maintaining large standing ground forces. The second was to draw a clear line, or "frontier," around the entire Sino-Soviet bloc. The Democrats had already drawn such a frontier from Norway to Turkey; the Republicans expected to strengthen and extend it to the Middle and Far East. The third measure was to preserve this global boundary around the Communist world with the deterrent power of the Strategic Air Command. The Russians and Chinese could cross the line only at the risk of total war with the United States; the fear of total destruction was expected to deter them.

This reliance upon strategic air power was also expected to appeal to the American public. In the first place, "massive retaliation" simply sounded more dynamic than containment; at the same time, it made possible a reduction of over-all military expenditures. It was obviously considerably cheaper to concentrate military spending upon a one-weapon system than to build up and maintain large balanced forces to meet any contingency. The second appealing feature of massive retaliation was that it, in fact, rejected the concept of limited war, or "half war," and reasserted the old American doctrine of either abstaining or fighting an all-out war. This return to the more traditional American approach to war was natural in 1952. The Republicans had been elected largely because of the deep popular revulsion against the Korean War; it was clear that the people wanted no more Koreas.

Basically, then, Eisenhower's policy was not to be very different from his predecessor's: containment of Communism by drawing a frontier around the Sino-Soviet periphery and supporting that frontier with nuclear air power. But in one essential aspect the new Administration's policy was different— and this difference was crucial. Truman and Acheson had also relied upon air-atomic striking power to deter a total attack upon either the United States or America's "first line of defense" in Europe. But in Asia, once the Communists had faced them with a limited aggression, they had met this challenge with local ground resistance. The Eisenhower Administration also expected to deter an all-out war with the threat of massive retaliation. But, unlike the Truman Administration, it would not fight local ground wars. It proposed to prevent any future limited attacks by threatening to retaliate against the Soviet Union or Communist China. This basic policy decision reflected Secretary Dulles's own strong conviction that the only effective means of stopping a prospective aggressor was to give him an advance warning that if he committed aggression, he would be subjected to such overwhelming retaliatory blows that his possible gains would be far outweighed by the punishment he would suffer. Dulles believed strongly that Korea would never have been invaded if the Communists had known that their attack would have been met with retaliatory air strikes on Moscow. It was the absence of such a warning that had led the Communists to miscalculate. The Eisenhower Administration did not intend to repeat this mistake. It meant to draw the line so clearly that the enemy could be left in no doubt whatsoever of what would happen to him if he crossed it. The expectation was that by going to the "brink of war," the United States would be able to deter future Koreas. This policy, which later became known as "brinkmanship," was to be applied first in an attempt to bring about a cease-fire in Korea.

Ending the Korean War

Truce talks in Korea had begun in the summer of 1951, but the negotiations had dragged on fruitlessly until they reached a deadlock. When the Eisenhower Administration took office in January, 1953, it decided that if its efforts to gain an armistice failed, it would bomb Chinese bases and supply sources in Manchuria and China, blockade the mainland coast, and possibly use tactical atomic weapons "to provide a tremendous beef-up in the United Nations punch." Dulles conveyed this decision to Prime Minister Nehru of India in late May, 1953, on the assumption that Nehru would pass the message on to the Chinese Communists.

In early June, the deadlocked negotiations were resumed, and in late July the armistice was signed. Whether the Administration's decisions alone were primarily responsible for the Chinese Communists' willingness to conclude the war is difficult to say. Probably other factors did play a significant role. For instance, Stalin had died in 1953, and his successors were proclaiming their belief in "peaceful coexistence" and trying hard to convince the non-Communist world that they wanted to relax international tension. Agreement on an armistice and an end to the war would provide evidence of their earnestness. But in Dulles's own mind, it was his threat to unleash American air power against China that induced the Chinese Communists to agree to end the fighting; in turn, this reinforced his faith in the utility of the advance warning coupled with the threat of heavy punishment.

South Korea's leader, Syngman Rhee, attempted at the last minute to upset the armistice. Rhee wanted to renew the war in the hope of reunifying his country; he had bitterly opposed an end to the fighting which again left Korea divided. But he failed in his purpose.

Thus, the Korean War concluded just about where it had begun—on the 38th parallel (actually, South Korea gained

2,350 square miles north of the parallel and lost 850 square miles to the south). It had taken three years of fighting to decide that this line was to become part of the global line dividing the Communist bloc from the non-Communist bloc. In August, the United States signed a mutual security pact with South Korea designed as a deterrent to another attack. This alliance had already been preceded by a declaration, signed by the fifteen nations that had fought in Korea, warning the Chinese Communists that, in the event of renewed aggression, it would probably be impossible to confine hostilities to Korea. And they added this significant warning: The armistice must not "result in jeopardizing the restoration or the safeguarding of peace in any other part of Asia." Events in Indochina were soon to prove the meaninglessness of this statement.

The Indochinese War and SEATO

After World War II, strong nationalist movements in colonies that had long been ruled by European powers demanded independence for their countries. The British met these demands in India, Burma, and Ceylon. The French did not meet them in Indochina. Returning to Indochina after its years of Japanese occupation, they refused to grant any meaningful concessions to the government which, under Ho Chi Minh, had proclaimed the independence of Vietnam after Japan's collapse. The French, determined to re-establish sovereignty over their colony, recognized Ho's "Democratic Republic of Vietnam" as a free state within the French Union; as a part of the agreement, the French would be allowed to maintain garrisons in Vietnam for five years. But within less than a year, as a result of actions taken by France that the Vietminh considered to be in violation of its agreements, there developed open conflict between the Vietminh and the French, and this soon was transformed into what Bernard Fall called the First Indochina War. When France established an "independent" state of Vietnam in 1949 under Emperor Bao Dai, the Communist-dominated Vietminh became, in effect, "rebels," but with the important difference that they were rebels identified as nationalists fighting for the independence of Vietnam. By contrast, Bao Dai, who spent much of his time on the French Riviera, was seen as a French puppet, and, in fact, he could not have survived one day in office without the presence and support of French arms. The war, therefore, went on unabated. Ho, like Mao Tse-tung in China, conducted a guerrilla operation and met with considerable success, partly because the terrain favored this kind of warfare. The French, who generally held the cities, were at a disadvantage from the beginning, for in the absence of genuine independence, the Vietnamese identified themselves with the Vietminh and saw the French as their colonial rulers. In the long run, France paid a very high price for the war in terms of manpower, material, and morale.

During the first few years of the war, American public opinion was unsympathetic to France's attempt to re-establish its colonial control over Indochina. But two events were to lead to United States involvement in this conflict. The first one was the defeat of Chiang Kai-shek. This was a blow to France, because it meant that the Chinese Communists could now provide assistance to the Vietminh. The second event was the outbreak of the Korean War, which led to an increased awareness of the strategic importance of Indochina as the gateway to the whole of Southeast Asia. In a bipolar world, Indochina could not be allowed to fall.

The Administration began therefore to provide France with economic and military aid. By 1954, the United States was paying about 75 per cent of the costs of the war. The French position continued to deteriorate, however, especially once the Korean armistice was signed. For despite American warnings, Communist China had now shifted its pressure from Korea to Indochina and was rendering increasing assistance to the Vietminh. On March 13, 1954, the entire French position in northern Vietnam suddenly threatened to disintegrate as the Vietminh forces launched an assault upon the French fortress at Dienbienphu. It became painfully clear that the French could not hold the position alone. Only American intervention could save Dienbienphu and the French hold on Vietnam. What was the United States to do?

President Eisenhower had already declared that the fall of Indochina "would be of a most terrible significance to the United States of America," and he had termed Southeast Asia of "transcendent importance" to American security. The Secretary of State had issued several statements that rather strongly suggested that America would not stand idly by while Indochina fell. He had warned the Chinese Communists in the same terms he had used after the armistice in Korea: Any aggression—that is, open intervention—would incur "grave consequences which might not be confined to Indochina." This warning also applied to any indirect Chinese intervention—namely, supplying overt assistance in the form of military advisers, equipment, and training for the Vietminh forces. Of prime importance was the strategic significance of Indochina, not whether the Chinese expanded by direct or indirect means. On March 29, Dulles had explicitly stated:

> Under the conditions of today, the imposition on Southeast Asia of the political system of Communist Russia and its Chinese ally, by *whatever* means, would be a grave threat to the whole free community. The United States feels that that possibility should not be passively accepted, but should be met by united action. This might have serious risks, but these risks are far less than would face us in a few years from now if we dare not be resolute today.

Dienbienphu was for the Administration, therefore, the moment of decision. Eisenhower and Dulles had declared Indochina to be of strategic importance to American security and had cautioned China against direct or indirect intervention by threatening it with massive retaliation. The Chinese had ignored these warnings. The U.S. Government now had to "put up or shut up." It shut up; its threats turned out to have been only bluffs.

The reason for this is fairly clear: Because of the nature of American domestic politics, the Eisenhower Administration was—despite its recognition of Indochina's vital location—unwilling to involve the United States in another Korea. More-over, the Administration was already cutting the size of the army, and apparently there were not sufficient divisions avail-able for fighting in Indochina. The Army Chief of Staff cer-tainly counseled against intervention on this ground. Only two possible courses of action remained. The first was to stop the Communist advance with air power alone. But this was a wholly unfeasible proposition, since air strikes by themselves could not possibly have halted a ground advance. They had failed to do so during the opening days of the Korean War, and it had been this failure that had necessitated the commit-ment of the army. And even if such air strikes had been tried in an attempt to stop the Vietminh, they would have been in-effective; for quite apart from Indochina's topography, the Vietminh were fighting a guerrilla war. Thus, the use of ground troops would have been as mandatory in Indochina as in Korea.

The alternative strategy was, of course, to attack China it-self. Everything indicates that this is what the Administration should have done if it really believed in its own policy of mas-sive retaliation. Its entire strategy was predicated upon two principles of action: first, issuing a clear warning that would allow no doubt of American intentions and no room for Com-munist miscalculation; and second, if the Communists delib-erately ignored the American warnings, punishing the enemy so heavily that he would never again dare challenge the United States. Yet in Indochina the Administration did not follow its warning with such punishment.

Why did this happen? The answer is simple: It is one thing to deliver a threat of massive retaliation to an opponent, and quite another for him to believe it. The Russians had not be-lieved it in Korea; nor did the Chinese in Indochina. Both ap-parently rejected the notion that the United States would risk a total war for anything less than an all-out attack on either the United States or Europe. Thus, the United States was faced for a second time with the terrible dilemma of either doing nothing or risking all-out war (since the Eisenhower Administration shared the Truman Administration's fear that an attack on China would precipitate Russian intervention).

Truman's experience with Korea had clearly shown that containment could not be successful without the willingness and capability to fight a limited war. Reliance upon strategic air power and an all-or-nothing strategy paralyzed American diplomacy. The U.S. ability to drop atom bombs on Moscow or Peking was less than useless to defeat limited incursions in areas which the Americans were unwilling to defend at the risk of total war. Ground forces were absolutely necessary if the United States was to escape either defeat or involvement in a total conflict. (Indochina should also have demonstrated—as Americans were to learn a decade later—that a limited war against guerrilla forces also required political, social, and economic measures to alleviate the popular grievances upon which the guerrillas feed.) The Eisenhower Administration had ignored these lessons of the Korean War. It had persuaded itself that Korea had happened only because the enemy had not received a previous warning that an attack upon South Korea would bring retaliatory strikes. While such warnings were certainly desirable to prevent enemy miscalculation, Indochina now proved that warnings alone were not enough. What it did prove was that containment was incompatible with heavy budget-cutting.

The result of American inaction was the French Government's decision to make the best of the situation by negotiating with the Communists directly for an end to the war. The French people were as weary of the fighting as the American public had been of Korea. Just as the latter had elected Eisenhower to end the war, the French National Assembly had elected Pierre Mendès-France Premier to end the Indochina hostilities. The new Premier announced that he was willing to conclude the war, and on July 20, 1954, an armistice agreement was reached that divided the country at the 17th parallel. The Communists were left in control of northern Indochina; it seemed only a matter of time until they would take over the rest of the country, for the collapse of the Southern rump state seemed imminent.

But the United States prevented this by supporting the new

government of Ngo Dinh Diem, a staunch anti-Communist nationalist appointed by Bao Dai after Dienbienphu (Diem later ousted Bao Dai). The Eisenhower Administration extended him economic and military aid to help him stabilize the situation in Vietnam. The danger of collapse temporarily receded. The 17th parallel, like the 38th parallel in Korea, became part of the international frontier separating the Communist and non-Communist worlds.

The Administration also decided to extend this line to defend the rest of Southeast Asia. Its predecessor had already signed security pacts with the nations lying off the Asian mainland—Japan, the Philippines, Australia, and New Zealand. The collapse of the French position in Indochina and the rising threat of Communist China made it imperative to bring the line inland. In September, 1954, the United States, Britain, France, Australia, New Zealand, the Philippines, Pakistan, and Thailand signed the Southeast Asia Collective Defense Treaty to defend the area of the South Pacific, with the exception of Hong Kong and Formosa. A protocol to the treaty extended SEATO's protection to Vietnam, Laos, and Cambodia. The Manila Pact (as it was also called) provided for joint action to meet aggression; an attack upon any of its members would be considered a danger to the security of all, and each would then act to meet the common danger in accordance with its constitutional processes. In case of subversion, the parties agreed to consult one another immediately and agree on common measures to meet this threat.

SEATO, unlike the NATO alliance, which it resembled, did not possess a unified command or joint forces. The principal force behind the alliance was American sea and air power. The crucial element—land power—would have to be supplied by the member nations if the occasion arose. Moreover—and again unlike NATO—SEATO did not contain within it most of the nations located in the area. India, Burma, Ceylon, and Indonesia would not join. They had just emerged from Western colonialism and were unwilling to be tied again to the West through a military alliance. They preferred to remain neutral in the struggle between the Western powers and the Sino-Soviet bloc. Of the Asian nations that did join the pact, the Philippines did so because of its traditional ties to the United States, and Pakistan because it wished to strengthen itself against India; only Thailand was genuinely concerned with Communist China's expansion, for the French collapse in Indochina had brought Chinese power closer to its borders. But if the Manila Pact was primarily a non-Asian alliance for the defense of an Asian area—a weakness that was to plague the alliance, for the absence of indigenous concern and resistance to Communist expansion could only ensure its eventual failure—its chief purpose was to warn the Communists of the stake America perceived in an area of what it continued to define as a bipolar world. If the United States, therefore, felt its security threatened by direct or indirect Communist aggression, SEATO provided it with the rationale for unilateral intervention to preserve this newly drawn land frontier.

The Formosa Straits and the Offshore Islands

Another critical situation arose in the Formosa Straits. During the summer of 1954, the Chinese Communists openly proclaimed their intention of taking Formosa and began shelling the Nationalist-held offshore islands (Quemoy is only nine miles outside the harbor of Amoy; Matsu lies almost as close, blocking the harbor of Foochow; and the Tachen islands are 200 miles north of Formosa). In December, the United States and the Nationalists signed a Treaty of Mutual Defense, by which the former guaranteed the security of Formosa and the nearby Pescadore islands. The Nationalists also pledged themselves not to attack the mainland or reinforce their offshore garrisons without United States consent.

The offshore islands, however, were not included under the terms of the treaty. But President Eisenhower sent Chiang his personal assurances that the United States would defend Quemoy and Matsu. Moreover, as the situation in the straits grew more tense in January, 1955, the President requested and received from Congress the authority to employ American armed forces to protect Formosa and the Pescadores. This authority extended to the protection of "such related positions and territories" as the President judged necessary. In Dulles's mind, Quemoy and Matsu had to be defended to maintain the Nationalist government's morale. Even more important, the islands had to be guarded since the alternative was to cede them; and this would have been interpreted as a sign of weakness by the Chinese Communists, spurring them on to further aggression. It was this test of wills that was really at stake in the situation, and Dulles's determination to demonstrate American resolution to the Chinese Communists may have been reinforced by the Indochina debacle. It would seem, therefore, that in case of attack, the Administration would have committed American armed forces to the defense of the offshore islands. At least the Communists thought so, and they abstained from any invasion attempts on Quemoy and Matsu. (The Nationalists had, meanwhile, evacuated the Tachens.)

Three years later, in August, 1958, the American position became clear when the Communists again began to shell the offshore islands very heavily. The Seventh Fleet—with orders to retaliate if fired upon—escorted Nationalist supply ships to within three miles of the beleaguered islands and helped them to break the blockade; and the Nationalist air force, equipped by the United States with air-to-air missiles, defeated the Communist air force's attempt to establish air supremacy in the sky between the mainland and Quemoy.

Thus, the line remained where it had been before the two Formosa crises—a few miles off Communist China's coast. Some months later, Dulles reaffirmed this line when he firmly rejected Chiang's calls for the reconquest of the mainland. American policy in the straits was committed to the preservation of the *status quo*. Each side should keep what it had and refrain from attacking the other. The Eisenhower Administration had finally recognized what neither it nor its predecessor had been willing to admit openly before: that the Nationalist expectation of reconquering the mainland was a myth. At the same time, it tacitly acknowledged the Chinese Communist Government as continental China's *de facto* government. It reconciled itself to the Communist conquest of the mainland. Containment had once more replaced liberation. The Administration was, moreover, resolved to back up its "disengagement" policy with force: In the straits, it could support its political position with sea and air power; ground forces were not needed.

For the moment, the situation in the Far East had been stabilized—at the 38th parallel in Korea, in the Formosa Straits, at the 17th parallel in Indochina, and at the line drawn by SEATO. Communist attention now turned to the Middle East.

The Middle East and the Suez War

In 1955, the United States completed its line around the Sino-Soviet periphery. Under its sponsorship, Britain, Turkey, Iraq, Iran, and Pakistan established the Middle East Treaty Organization (METO). Thus, the Baghdad Pact (as this treaty was called) extended the NATO line from Turkey to India. But this "northern tier," drawn—except for Iraq—along 3,000 miles of Russia's southern frontier, drew a sharp reaction from the Soviet Union. Rebuffed in Iran and Turkey, in 1946–57 by America, Russia had not surrendered its ambitions in this area. The Middle East linked Europe, Africa, and Asia. For Britain, the area—and especially the Suez Canal—had traditionally been the lifeline of its old empire and of its present Commonwealth. Above all, Europe's economy was becoming increasingly dependent upon the Middle East for oil; without oil, Europe would collapse. The power that could deny it this oil would be able to dictate its future. Soviet influence in the Arab world might thus allow Moscow to neutralize Europe without firing a shot. In short, for Russia the Middle East was the means to outflank and disintegrate NATO. Its opportunity to attempt to do this came as a result of the bitter Arab-Israeli conflict, the only slightly less bitter Anglo-Egyptian quarrel, and Egypt's own expansionist ambitions.

Arab antagonism toward Israel is understandable. In 1917, Britain had pledged itself in the Balfour Declaration to the establishment of a "national home" for the Jewish people in Palestine, while also promising the Arabs that the civil and religious rights of non-Jews would not be prejudiced. Zionists took this pledge as promising the conversion of Palestine into a Jewish state; they considered Palestine, a British mandate after the collapse of the Ottoman Empire during World War I, as their ancient and traditional homeland.

Britain's troubles became serious after Hitler's assumption of power in Germany—and impossible after World War II. Hitler had slaughtered 6 million Jews in his concentration camps; few of the survivors wished to remain in Europe, with its unhappy memories. Many emigrated to Palestine. The Jews were now determined to establish a Jewish state, while the Arabs feared that the Jewish immigration would crowd them out of what they also regarded as their rightful homeland. British troops were unable to keep the peace between the Arabs and Jews. Under these circumstances, Britain—already gravely weakened by the war, forced to curtail its commitments throughout the world—decided to end its burdensome mandate over Palestine.

In November, 1947, the United Nations decided to partition Palestine into two independent states, one Jewish and the other Arab. The Arabs refused to accept this solution, however; they wanted Palestine to become an Arab state. On May 10, 1948, as Britain ended its mandate, the Jews proclaimed the State of Israel, and the armies of the Arab League (Egypt, Jordan, Syria, Lebanon, and Saudi Arabia) invaded the new state. In the ensuing war, the Israeli Army defeated the larger Arab armies. The state of Israel became a fact of political life.

The Arabs, however, refused to recognize it as such. Though they did sign an armistice in February, 1949, they refused to conclude a peace treaty. They continued to regard the Jews as infidels who had no right to be in Israel. Moreover, they felt deeply humiliated by their defeat. The Arabs awaited their day of revenge; meanwhile, they continued to proclaim their intention to destroy Israel. They conducted constant guerrilla warfare against Israel—sabotaging, pillaging, and murdering (so did the Israeli Army when it intermittently took revenge by launching heavy assaults into Arab territory); they refused to allow Israeli shipping through the Suez Canal and blockaded the Gulf of Aqaba; and they tightened the ring around Israel: In April, 1956, Egypt, Syria, Saudi Arabia, and Yemen formed a joint command against Israel under Egyptian leadership, and in October, 1956, Egypt, Jordan, and Syria announced another joint command "the principal concern of which is the war of destruction against Israel." Earlier (in late September, 1955), Egypt had concluded an arms deal with Czechoslovakia, although the actual agreement was signed with the Soviet Union; under this arrangement, Egypt received a large quantity of arms, including planes and tanks. Egypt now had the tools with which to achieve a decisive military superiority over Israel. This, in turn, raised a very vital question for Israel: Should it strike now or wait until Egypt and its allies were ready for the "second round"? As Egypt solidified the encirclement of Israel, grew increasingly aggressive, and began to absorb the Soviet arms, the Israelis decided to strike before it was too late. All that was needed was the right condition for launching their preventive attack.

This condition, which was to occur in October, 1956, was the product of Anglo-Egyptian antagonism. Britain had controlled Egypt since 1881, when it had established a protectorate over Egypt in order to safeguard its own communications through Suez to India. The 1936 treaty between the two countries had converted this status into an alliance. By its terms, British troops were confined to the Canal Zone, and their presence was declared to be neither an occupation nor an infringement of Egyptian sovereignty. To the Egyptians, however, British soldiers on their soil continued to represent a violation of Egyptian independence, pride, and dignity.

World War II intensified Egyptian nationalism and heightened the demand for a withdrawal of British forces from Egyptian soil. But negotiations on this question broke down, while other postwar events further increased Egypt's anti-British sentiment. The Egyptians resented the Palestine partition plan, for which they blamed Britain as well as the United

States. In late 1951, the Egyptian Parliament abrogated the 1936 Anglo-Egyptian treaty, and in July, 1952, the new military regime that took over the Egyptian Government from King Farouk pressed for the removal of British troops with renewed vigor. The Eisenhower Administration supported this Egyptian demand. Faced with this opposition, and aware of its own unpopularity in Egypt, Britain signed a new Anglo-Egyptian treaty in 1954, by which it agreed to withdraw all its troops from Suez over a twenty-month period. British influence over Egyptian politics had come to an end.

Britain now shifted the focus of its power from Egypt to Iraq, a long-time ally. It therefore joined the Baghdad Pact, of which Iraq was already a member, in order to protect its vital strategic and economic interest in the Middle East. But President Nasser of Egypt did not regard METO merely as a means of containing Russia; he saw it as an instrument to preserve Western domination throughout the area, and, since Iraq had always been Egypt's traditional rival for Arab leadership, he considered it a personal challenge as well. Nasser therefore set out to destroy the Baghdad Pact by forming a counteralliance and undermining pro-Western Arab governments. His means of achieving these objectives was to place himself at the head of the Arab struggle against Israel and Britain. Thereby, he would become the foremost exponent of Arab nationalism and win the allegiance of the Arab masses. Once he had gained this loyalty of the people, no Arab government would dare oppose him, for if it did he would call on the people to overthrow that government. "Revolution in the street" was an accepted Arab method of making and unmaking governments. Moreover, by exerting his influence over the Arab world in this manner, he would gain control over the area's oil resources; this would place him in a position where he could siphon off the oil revenues to help Egypt's economic development. Thus, partly as a reaction to Israel and Britain, but also as a result of his own strong ambitions and the Arab states' domestic condition, Nasser began to use pan-Arabism as an instrument of expanding his own and Egyptian influence. By turning to nationalism, and thereby asserting the Arabs' pride, sovereignty, and dignity, by humiliating those who had in the past humiliated and subjected them, he consolidated his leadership at home, gained the admiration and enthusiasm of the long-suffering masses in other Arab countries, and compelled their rulers to follow him if they did not wish to be overthrown by popular revolutions led by pro-Nasser forces.

Nasser's influence grew quickly. He formed close links with Saudi Arabia, Yemen, Syria, and Jordan (whose pro-Western government he first successfully overthrew). But the act that really endeared Nasser to the Arab masses was his dramatic arms deal with the Soviet Union. This agreement made Nasser the great new hero, the modern Saladin—the staunch opponent of the West and champion of Arab nationalism. At the same time, the Soviet Union became the Arabs' greatest friend. But this Moscow-Cairo axis frightened not only Israel but also Britain; if Russia and Egypt gained control over the Middle East, Britain would be cut off from its oil supplies, which for it were a question not just of profit, but of survival. The situation thus became inflammable.

Only an incendiary incident was needed to start a conflagration. The United States provided this when, on July 19, 1956, it informed the Egyptian Government that it would not help finance Nasser's Aswan Dam, a high dam on the Upper Nile whose purpose was to raise Egypt's low standard of living by irrigating new land and providing electricity for industrial development. The American retraction of its offer to help build this dam was a heavy blow to Egypt's hopes to raise itself by its own "sandal straps." For the American loan had been a prerequisite for further aid from the World Bank and Britain; these offers, too, were now withdrawn. The Eisenhower Administration's action was occasioned by several considerations: Nasser had attempted to blackmail the Administration into providing more money by hinting that the Russians had offered to finance the entire project; Egypt had moved too close to Russia and had recognized Communist China; Nasser had also probably mortgaged the funds he was supposed to provide for Egypt's share of the cost of the dam to buy Russian arms—which, in effect, meant that the entire cost of the dam would fall upon the United States and Britain.

Nasser regarded the American decision as a personal and national humiliation. A few days later, on July 26, he announced that he would nationalize the Suez Canal and use the revenues collected from it to finance the dam. Arab nationalists were ecstatic, and Nasser's stature, already strong, reached new heights.

Unlike the crises in Korea and Formosa, however, the consequences of Secretary Dulles's act fell not on the United States but on its allies—above all, on Britain. And its government reacted sharply to Nasser's seizure of the canal. Prime Minister Eden did not trust the Egyptian dictator; although Nasser guaranteed that all ships, except Israel's, could still pass through the canal, Eden feared that the Egyptian would use the canal as an instrument of political blackmail. Moreover, if Nasser could face the West with such a major act of defiance and go unpunished, Western influence would be destroyed throughout the Middle East. Other Arab governments would expropriate Western oil interests, and all opponents of Nasser would be discouraged and come to terms with him. Western prestige—and especially British prestige, since Britain was the leading Western power in the Middle East—had to be upheld. If it were not, the Cairo-Moscow axis would dominate the entire area and be in a position to strangle Europe. The British were therefore determined to stand up to Nasser, and they insisted upon some form of international control for the canal. But the Egyptians rejected all proposals to wrest their newly won control out of their hands and denounced them as "collective colonialism." All attempts to bridge this gap were therefore doomed to fail.

It was in these circumstances that war broke out. The United States was busily engaged in the last days of its Presidential election campaign, and the Soviet Union was concentrating on crushing the Hungarian uprising. On October 29, only four days after Jordan's Chief of Staff announced that the time had come to launch the Arab assault on Israel, the

Israeli Army marched into Egypt. The Israelis quickly defeated the Egyptian forces in the Sinai peninsula. The British and the French (who sought Nasser's downfall because of his aid to the Algerian rebels who wanted to free Algeria from French control) intervened twenty-four hours later. At this point, the United States saved Nasser. Although the Administration had pressured Britain to sign the Anglo-Egyptian treaty by which all British troops had been removed from Suez and had withdrawn the Aswan Dam offer, thus precipitating Nasser's seizure of the Canal and the British attack, it now opposed the use of force to settle this issue. The reason was that despite its disapproval of Nasser's action and the pro-Soviet direction in which he was leading Egypt, it saw his foreign policy in terms of a reaction against Israel and Western colonialism. If Israel had not existed, and if Egypt and the Arab states had not long been subjected and exploited by the Western powers (especially Britain), Arab nationalism would not be anti-Western and pro-Soviet. The Administration therefore saw the invasion of Egypt as a golden opportunity to win Egyptian and Arab friendship. When the Jews had originally proclaimed the state of Israel, the United States had, because of domestic political considerations, recognized the new state within eleven minutes. Here was a chance to show the Arabs that the United States was not as pro-Jewish as they thought it to be, and that the country could even be pro-Arab. Since Egypt's actions were also the product of her anti-British resentment, it would be beneficial to oppose the British attempt to reassert control over the Suez Canal. By saving Nasser, the United States could align itself with Arab nationalism; supporting Britain, France, and Israel would have left the Soviet Union as the sole champion of Arab aspirations. American opposition to the invasion would, in short, identify the United States with the anticolonialism of the entire underdeveloped world, and particularly with the anti-Israeli and nationalistic sentiments of the Arab world. Since continued evidence of British power in the Middle East only antagonized the Arabs, the destruction of this power and its replacement by American influence would be in the interest not only of the United States but of all the Western powers. In this way, the West's strategic and economic interests could be more adequately safeguarded.

America's opposition to the Suez invasion was the decisive factor in stopping the fighting. Egypt had already blocked the canal, and the Syrians had cut the pipelines running across their country from Iraq. Britain was therefore dependent upon American oil to replace its losses from the Middle East; and the Administration threatened to use this economic sanction if Britain did not cease the attack. Faced with this dire prospect—plus opposition to the invasion within Britain, the Commonwealth (Canada, India, and Pakistan), and the United Nations—the British Government accepted a cease-fire and later withdrew its forces; France and Israel had little choice but to follow suit.

It is ironic, however, in view of America's leading role in halting the attack on Egypt, that it should have been the Soviet Union—and not the United States—that was to reap the benefits from America's opposition. After it had become clear that the United States would not support the British and French invasion, Russia threatened "to crush the aggressor"; it sent notes to the British and French governments warning of possible rocket attacks on their countries, and it bluntly told Israel that its very existence was at stake. It even asked the United States to join forces with it to stop the war. And after the cease-fire, Russia and Communist China threatened to send "volunteers." In short, the Soviet Union risked nothing to deliver these threats, but it was the country that received most of the credit from the Arabs for saving Nasser by its threats to exterminate Israel and attack Britain and France. Suez thus resulted in the collapse of British power in the Middle East, the strengthening of Arab nationalism, and the consolidation of Egyptian-Russian links.

Nasser's great political victory—despite a humiliating military defeat at the hands of Israel—increased his self-confidence. Supported by the Soviet Union—whose aim it was to weaken if not to eliminate all Western power in the Middle East—Nasser continued his expansionist drive. Jordan abrogated the Anglo-Jordan Treaty by which Jordan had received an annual subsidy to maintain its economy; Egypt, Saudi Arabia, and Syria promised to replace the British funds, and Jordan announced that it would seek to establish a federal union with Egypt and Syria. The last two states did, in fact, join together into a union, the United Arab Republic, in early 1958. Attempts to undermine the Iraqi Government continued throughout 1956, and in the spring of 1957, the Egyptians organized riots against the government in Lebanon.

The first step taken by the Eisenhower Administration after the Suez crisis was the formulation of the Eisenhower Doctrine. This joint resolution of Congress in the spring of 1957 declared that the United States considered the preservation of the independence and integrity of the Middle Eastern nations vital to American security, and that it was prepared to use armed force to assist any nation or nations *"requesting* assistance against *armed* aggression from any country controlled by international Communism. [Italics added.]" It was difficult to understand what this doctrine meant. Russia did not border on any Arab state. Iraq, to the south, was already protected by the Baghdad Pact and, through its association with Britain and Turkey, by NATO; so the doctrine could not be directed against Russia. Moreover, the Soviet Union had already leap-frogged the "northern tier" by establishing close relations with Egypt and Syria. And Suez had demonstrated that the United States did not regard such association as turning a country into a Communist-controlled vassal; if it had, it would surely have supported the invasion of Egypt.

But the Administration, viewing Nasser's continued attempts to undermine Western power in the Middle East, his vicious attacks upon all the Western nations, including the United States, and his continued flirtation with Russia, soon reconsidered its views of Nasser. At Suez, it had thought that by demonstrating its friendship, the United States could win his trust. Post-Suez events proved this expectation to have been ill-founded. A reversal of policy was thus in order, and this required a reinterpretation of the Eisenhower Doctrine. First, the term "armed aggression" was no longer to refer only to the direct attack of one nation upon another but also to attempts to overthrow pro-Western governments through internal revolt aided from the outside; and second, "any country controlled by international Communism" was now meant to include nations with close bonds to the Soviet Union.

The doctrine was first applied in Jordan, where King Hussein's dismissal of the pro-Nasser and pro-Communist government led to a general strike, massive street demonstrations, and riots. Jordan's days as an independent state appeared to be numbered. In this crisis, Hussein charged, on April 24, 1957, that international Communism was responsible for the efforts to overthrow him. On the same day, the United States announced that it regarded "the independence and integrity of Jordan as vital." And to prove that it meant what it said, the Administration dispatched the United States Sixth Fleet to the eastern Mediterranean and extended Jordan $10 million for the support of its army and economy. The Hussein government survived.

In the summer of 1958, an even more serious crisis arose when a group of nationalist officers led by General Kassem overthrew the pro-Western government of Iraq and murdered the King and Prime Minister. Although the new regime did not withdraw from the Baghdad Pact until some months later, this revolt, in effect, eliminated Iraq, the pivot on which the alliance had been centered. The United Arab Republic immediately hailed the revolution and recognized the new government; and the two countries quickly signed an alliance. There was little the United States could do but recognize the Kassem government. Arab nationalism seemed to be sweeping everything in front of it. Only Lebanon, Jordan, and Saudi Arabia were still outside the Nasser camp, and the first two were teetering on the verge of revolution. The whole Western position in the Middle East seemed to be on the brink of disintegration.

The Eisenhower Administration now resorted to force. Lebanon had been plagued for some time with civil war between Muslims and Christians. The Muslims wanted close relations, if not union, with the United Arab Republic, and the Christians favored a pro-Western policy and the continued independence of Lebanon. With the Iraqi revolution, men and arms for the pro-Nasser elements began to be smuggled in over Lebanon's Syrian border. In Jordan, too, the situation took a turn for the worse; the Iraqi example was hardly a happy one for King Hussein, who also had his pro-Nasser masses and army officers. Both countries now invoked the Eisenhower Doctrine and asked for military support. The British sent paratroopers into Jordan, and the United States sent 14,000 men into Lebanon. The large size of the American contingent seems to have been deliberate: Apparently, it was meant to warn the new Iraqi Government against nationalizing Western oil resources. Kassem quickly gave the assurance that he had no such intention, and possible American intervention in Iraq was thereby forestalled. Loud Soviet hints of intervention also turned out to be hollow when countered by resolute American action. Both Britain and the United States withdrew their troops in late October.

The Anglo-American action had saved, at least temporarily, Lebanon and Jordan. But it was also intended to have another important effect: to show Nasser and the Arabs that there were limits to Soviet willingness to come to their aid. Nasser's personal ambitions were, by themselves, relatively unimportant; the decisive factor that had reaped success for Egypt's pan-Arab policy was Soviet power. The Western powers, in thinking of counteraction against Egypt, could never eliminate the possibility of Soviet intervention. This, in turn, further encouraged Nasser's expansionist drive. The Anglo-American action in Lebanon and Jordan disabused the Arabs of this notion. Prior to the intervention, the Russians had again threatened to send "volunteers" to oppose the Western "imperialists" and had carried out conspicuous military maneuvers in Soviet Central Asia and Transcaucasia. The firmness of the American position, and the failure of the Soviet Union in the face of Eisenhower's determination to do more than to denounce the intervention and call for a diplomatic settlement, made it very clear that there were limits to Soviet willingness to bail the Arabs out of trouble. This had a dampening effect on Nasser's anti-Western drive.

There was another unexpected turn of events which influenced this situation. The new regime in Iraq, instead of turning out to be pro-Nasser—as almost everyone, including Nasser, had expected—took an anti-Nasser position. It was not long before it began to challenge the Egyptian ruler's leadership of Arab nationalism. Nasser quickly recognized this threat of Egypt's traditional rival and attempted to overthrow the Kassem government. But the revolt by a group of pro-Nasser officers was quickly squashed. At the same time, the Soviet Union gave economic and military support to the Kassem government. Nasser was becoming increasingly isolated in the Arab world: Jordan, Lebanon, and Saudi Arabia had remained independent; Libya and the Sudan had resisted his attempts to subvert them; Syria was restless in the United Arab Republic; and Iraq had become a rival for Arab leadership. Nor was this situation materially changed by the events of the early 1960's: Kassem was overthrown; Syria revolted and quit the United Arab Republic; and the countries between Syria on the one hand and Egypt on the other—Jordan and Saudi Arabia—improved their relations with Nasser. Despite the common pan-Arab aspirations of Egypt, Syria, and Iraq, a real Arab union remained as elusive as ever. Syria and Iraq were unwilling to permit Nasser to dominate them; and Nasser was unwilling to form a union he could not control. The Egyptian leader's new emphasis on domestic reform—or what he called "Arab socialism"—therefore became crucial to his fight for Arab leadership, even though he continued his attempts to overthrow traditional pro-Western regimes and remained generally anti-Western in his policy positions.

Meanwhile, the United States had almost become a full-fledged member of the Baghdad Pact (now renamed the Central Treaty Organization) by joining its economic, military, and countersubversion committees; it was also bound to each of the three Muslim states individually by bilateral defense agreements. But behind these developments remained all the essential problems that had given rise to the turmoil after 1955: the conflicts among the Arab states, the Arab-Israeli quarrel, the overshadowing competition between the United States and the Soviet Union, and, above all, Arab nationalism with its frequent xenophobic overtones. Despite the vast oil wealth, the Arab masses remained very poor and suffered from illiteracy, malnutrition, and disease. Social discontent and political instability were the result. While the area settled down to relative quiescence, the American attempt to fill the vacuum left by the reduction of British power and draw another "frontier" was unsuccessful. Ironically, it was the attempt to do this that drew Russia and Egypt together to destroy the "northern tier," permitting the former to jump over the line that was supposed to contain it.

Western European Union and the Common Market

In Europe, the defense line had already been drawn by NATO. But the strength of this line on the ground depended upon supplementing NATO forces with West German troops. EDC was the means the Allies had chosen to achieve this goal. But in August, 1954, the French National Assembly rejected EDC by a decisive majority. Fear of Germany remained too great, and French nationalists wished to maintain France's identity and honor. This was a real blow to the efforts toward creating a situation of strength in Europe. The whole basis of NATO strategy and European integration was suddenly imperiled.

The response of the Eisenhower Administration was a self-righteous one. Instead of taking the lead in finding a way out of this impasse, it simply withdrew from the problem and waited for the European powers to resolve it. Secretary Dulles only repeated his threat that the United States would make an "agonizing reappraisal" of its NATO commitments if the deadlock were not broken. It was Britain's Prime Minister Eden who took the lead in averting such a reappraisal and seeking a way of rearming West Germany with French approval. He found it in the forgotten Brussels Treaty.

This organization was now to be revised by the inclusion of Germany and Italy. The new alliance, which pledged all its members to come to one another's aid if attacked, would be known as the Western European Union. Yet WEU was not really an alliance, no forces were assigned to it, and it had no responsibility for formulating a strategy to defend its members. These remained within the functions of NATO. WEU's role was to channel West German troops into NATO, while at the same time maintaining a set of controls over West Germany similar to those included in EDC. Furthermore, Britain agreed to keep a minimum number of troops—four divisions and a tactical air force—on the Continent. Britain's pledge was a formalization of its responsibilities under the Dunkirk, Brussels, and NATO treaties. But to the French it seemed an important new commitment; they now felt assured that they would not someday be left to face German troops alone.

These commitments, embodied in the Paris Pact, came into force in May, 1955. Thus, ten years after Germany's defeat, the occupation came to an end, and the Federal Republic regained its sovereignty and entered NATO via WEU. West Germany's military power could now be added to Western strength. Two important declarations were appended to these Paris agreements. In the first, the West German Government subscribed to the principles of the United Nations, undertook "never to have recourse to force to achieve the reunification of Germany or the modification of the present boundaries of the German Federal Republic," and to resolve all disputes between itself and other states by peaceful means. In the second, however, the United States, Britain, and France declared that they recognized the Federal Republic as the only freely and legitimately constituted government entitled to speak for all of Germany—which indicated a policy of nonrecognition of the East German Government. In addition, the Allies would pursue German reunification by peaceful means—which meant that the alliance with West Germany, while revisionist in its political objective, was conceived of as being defensive in nature. Finally, the Western powers stated that they would continue to exercise their responsibilities with regard to the security of West Germany and West Berlin.

With Germany safely enrolled as a member of NATO, the WEU members now took a momentous step toward further economic and political integration. The six states that composed this Little Europe had gained increasing benefits from this movement. On June 1, 1958, they established the European Economic Community, usually referred to as the Common Market, whose objective was to join them together into an economic union. Their plan was to achieve this in a twelve- to fifteen-year period. During this time, all six states would completely eliminate the tariffs and quota systems still hampering trade among them (agriculture was to be the exception—the Market expected to develop a common policy of subsidies and price supports, and eliminate discriminations among farmers within the Community); they would also abolish restrictions on the movement of labor, capital, and services among them, although this commitment was qualified. But these moves, the "Six" realized, would not suffice. A government might abolish a tariff, but it could compensate its producers through subsidies or impose internal taxes that would discriminate against foreign products. Production costs also reflected national regulations on wages, hours, working conditions, and social welfare programs; producers in nations with lower standards would have an obvious advantage against foreign competition. Thus, to ensure maximum free competition in the Common Market, subsidies were forbidden (except for use in developing backward areas); discriminatory taxes, price-fixing, and division of markets by cartel arrangements were not permitted; and the need to equalize hours, wages, and working conditions was recognized as urgent.

What were the chances for the development of this market? The economic benefits suggested that they were excellent. As trade barriers were lowered and then disappeared, the increasing competition would result in the growth of efficient companies and the elimination of the less efficient ones unless they modernized or converted to new lines of production. All members would also gain from the capital funds. Italy would receive capital for the development of its southern area; France and its overseas territories would also receive development capital. While Germany would contribute a large share of these funds that would benefit its partners, it would in re-

turn receive access to their European and African markets—
and Germany was in the strongest competitive position of the
Six. A final factor was that the Community expected to receive advantages against third parties. It would be in a strong
bargaining position to demand reciprocal lowering of tariffs.
All these advantages outweighed the burdens each nation
would suffer as a result of economic dislocation and hardships,
which would, in fact, be minimized by being extended over a
twelve- to fifteen-year period (the plan's initial successes were
to cut this period down by several years) and by being shared
among all members.

Above all, the principal advantage of the Common Market
would be political. For a common market needs common policies; only one set of rules—not six—can govern its competitive
behavior. One nation cannot be allowed to pay its workers
considerably lower wages than its neighbor in order to achieve
a competitive advantage. There would therefore have to be
some standardization of wages, as well as of such related items
as overtime, hours worked per week, and various welfare benefits. In the long run, if the Market developed successfully, it
would therefore also undoubtedly lead to the adoption of
common fiscal policies to control the ups and downs of the
business cycle, a common currency, and a central bank. Thus
the economic "spillover"—from a common market in coal and
steel into a common market for all sectors of the economy—
was expected by the Common Market's founding fathers to
stimulate political unification as economic integration compelled the Inner Six members to harmonize their social and
economic policies. Economic union was expected to encourage increasing political integration. It was precisely this objective to form a political union that had originally inspired
ECSC.

EEC was the culminating act of the movement, initiated by
France and strongly supported by Chancellor Adenauer, to tie
Germany so closely to a European Community that it would
never again be able to use its power for purely national ends.
The formation of the Inner Six was nothing less than the last

link subjecting Germany to European restraints and responsibilities. Its success would make it impossible thereafter for
Germany ever again to pursue a unilateral course. The Common Market was also the end product of France's desire to
supplement its own strength with that of a united Europe, so
that it would gain an equal voice with Britain in the Atlantic
Alliance and not always remain subservient to the United
States. France did not want to pursue a NATO policy dictated largely by Anglo-American interests; it wanted the alliance to take its interests into account as well.

It was hardly surprising that Russia reacted quickly against
the Common Market and attempted to break up this potential united states of Europe. A strong and united Europe,
economically prosperous and politically stable, would not
only prove to be a powerful barrier to Soviet expansionist
ambitions, but it might well threaten the Soviet *status quo* in
Eastern Europe. The existence of a free Germany had already
had an unsettling effect upon the whole satellite system.

West Berlin, especially, has had a tremendous impact in
this respect. The existence of this city, alongside Communist
East Berlin, had hampered Soviet control of East Germany.
Through West Berlin escaped many young, skilled, and professional men and women of East Germany; it was an escape
hatch that was depopulating East Germany of the very people
it needed to run its society. In West Berlin, the United States,
Britain, and France had, moreover, established agencies to
gather intelligence about Eastern Europe. There was a constant flow of information about the West from West Berlin
into the Russian-controlled satellites; this defeated one of the
major purposes of the iron curtain, which was to stop incoming information that might lead to comparisons of the Communist and free systems. West Berlin, in short, affected the
political stability of all of Eastern Europe. If the existence of
West Berlin and West Germany made the Communist *status
quo* insecure, how much greater the Soviet apprehensions of
a united Europe must have been.

The stability of the Soviet position in Eastern and Central

Europe, as apparently seen by Moscow, depended upon two factors: one, gaining Western recognition of the East German "Democratic" Republic; and two, destroying the freedom of West Berlin. To achieve these objectives, the Soviet Union announced in November, 1958, that at the end of six months it intended to end the four-power occupation and would hand control of East Berlin and the routes leading into West Berlin over to the East Germans. The clear implication was that in the future free access to Berlin would require that the Western powers deal directly and officially with the East German Government. The Russians also repeated their former proposal for the unification of Germany: that East and West Germany should join in a confederation. This, too, was a tactical device to gain the Federal Republic's recognition of East Germany. The Russians obviously wanted to entice the West Germans to start negotiating with the East Germans on the issue of unification; at the same time, it was also clear that the Russians were not in the least interested in any form of unification. Their proposal was, in fact, so constituted that it precluded Western acceptance. A confederation half democratic and half dictatorship was a contradiction in terms and was totally unfeasible. How could a government of such a confederation ever agree on economic policies? Most industry in East Germany was owned by the government; West Germany was a booming private-enterprise state. The G.D.R. had recognized the Oder-Neisse line as Germany's eastern frontier; West Germany did not yet acknowledge the permanent loss of the territories Poland received from Germany at the end of World War II. As if to ensure the rejection of their terms, the Russians also demanded that East Germany, with a population of a little more than 17 million, and West Germany, with a population of more than 53 million, should be equally represented in the confederated government. The Soviet Union naturally did not want the East Germans to be outvoted—with the possible result that East Germany would be voted out of existence—but Khrushchev could hardly have expected the Western powers or the Adenauer government to accept such equality. This lack of Russian interest in German unification was made explicit in 1960, when the Russian Ambassador to West Germany stated that the precondition for German reunification was not German neutrality but the nationalization of West German big industry, the "breaking up of the power of monopoly capital," and the "domination of the working class." None of the Western powers, let alone the Federal Republic, was likely to accept these conditions.

If the Soviet proposals, then, were meant to elicit Western recognition of East Germany, this goal still remained subsidiary to the primary aim of strangling West Berlin. What the Russians were actually calling for when they declared the end of the four-power occupation was an Allied withdrawal from West Berlin, turning it into a "free city." This was, in effect, a demand for the incorporation of West Berlin into East Germany. Once Western troops had left the city, the West Berliners would feel isolated and unprotected, abandoned and completely helpless. They would be surrounded by the Russian Army and the East German Army and police. In these circumstances, the defenseless West Berliners would have to come to terms with the East German regime. On the other hand, if the West would not sign a treaty turning Berlin into a "free city," the Soviet Union would then sign a separate peace treaty with East Germany, thus automatically abrogating the West's right to be in Berlin and making any further Western stay dependent upon the terms that could be negotiated with the now "sovereign" German Democratic Republic. This would mean that the West would remain in Berlin by the consent of East Germany, which could then gradually intensify its pressure and gradually undermine the West's position until it became untenable.

At this point, one way or the other, the Russians would have eliminated a very troublesome thorn in their side. They would then be in a far better position to stabilize the *status quo*. But the destruction of West Berlin would not only have accomplished the Soviet Union's defensive aims; it would simultaneously have attained Russia's long-standing offensive purpose of weakening its opponents, perhaps fatally. If the Russians could drive the Western powers, especially the

United States, out of Berlin, they would also be able, first, to cut off the development of the Common Market before it gathered too much momentum, and second, to shatter the NATO alliance. It was, above all, American power that guaranteed the freedom of the 2 million Germans living in West Berlin. If the United States were to abandon these people under pressure, faith in America's protective power and willingness to live up to its commitments would collapse in Europe. The Germans would be the first to read the lesson: that since America could not guarantee their security, they must approach the Russians independently. Whatever the nature of the terms the Russians would offer them, they would certainly include clauses demanding the abandonment of all Germany's political, economic, or military ties to the West. But without Germany, there could be no Common Market, since Germany's partners were dependent upon it for much of the capital required for their economic development. And if Germany pulled out of the Atlantic Alliance, American troops would have to be withdrawn back to the United States, since it would be politically and strategically impossible to station them in France. Yet, these troops were a symbol of the American commitment to defend Europe; they were psychologically and politically indispensable. No written guarantees could be substituted for this living embodiment of America's stake in Europe. Certainly, the withdrawal of U.S. ground forces at that time would have indicated to the Europeans that America was no longer willing to defend them now that the United States was itself becoming increasingly vulnerable to a Soviet nuclear attack.

This was, in the final analysis, the fundamental issue posed by the Berlin crisis. The Soviet proposals had included the ultimatum that if West Berlin's status had not been "renegotiated" *à la Russe* within six months, the Russians would place the East Germans in control of the railroads and highways leading into West Berlin. If the East Germans then interfered with Western traffic, the West would have to employ force to break any blockade; and Khrushchev stated that any such Western attempts would meet Soviet resistance. The defense of West Berlin therefore posed the definite possibility of total war. But would the United States be willing to take this risk, when it no longer possessed an atomic monopoly? Threatening the Russians with SAC might, at a time of increasing nuclear bipolarity, be ineffective. The Russians, too, were acquiring a capability for massive retaliation. Was Berlin worth the devastation of many American cities and 50 million to 100 million dead and wounded? The Russian challenge was a clever one: It faced the United States with a limited challenge and offered it the choice of surrendering West Berlin or fighting a total war for its preservation. It was America's will that was thus really at stake in Berlin, and a failure of this will would disintegrate the entire American position in the European rimland.

Berlin was thus a major test of postwar American policy. Nor was it a repeat of the 1948 situation. At that time, Stalin had acted upon two assumptions: first, that the far larger Red Army contingents would deter an Allied attempt to break through on the ground; and second, that the United States and Britain could not keep West Berlin alive. The first assumption proved to be correct, but the second was mistaken. When Stalin realized this, he had either to call off the blockade or shoot down Allied planes and risk a war. America's atomic monopoly favored the first solution. By late 1958, the Soviet Union did not have to feel as worried about America's nuclear arsenal; it had a stockpile of its own, and it had just tested the world's first Intercontinental Ballistic Missile (ICBM). American brinkmanship, given this circumstance, would thus be riskier. Yet, if the United States would not accept this risk to prevent Russia from slowly strangling West Berlin to death, the question inevitably arose: What objective was worth the cost of total war? If not Berlin, what was? Berlin was thus a crisis of massive retaliation; for the Soviet action questioned the very feasibility of basic American strategy. Could strategic air power, upon which the Eisenhower Administration depended almost exclusively to preserve the line around the Sino-Soviet periphery, fulfill this task in an age of nuclear plenty, when World War III was merely a pseudonym for suicide? The answer seemed to be that too great a reliance upon SAC was gravely weakening the American ability to preserve this line. Nuclear bombs were just *too* powerful; they were *too* enormously destructive to be used in any situation but the ultimate one. U.S. strategic power was—ironically—*so* great that it tended to paralyze the will to use it; it therefore paralyzed diplomacy as well.

The Berlin crisis, a limited Soviet challenge but one which had enormous stakes for the United States, was the most serious challenge Washington had confronted since 1948–49. The Truman Doctrine, Marshall Plan, Berlin airlift, and NATO had made it very plain to Moscow that Western Europe was an area of vital American interest. Soviet domination over this Western rimland of the Eurasian continent was no more tolerable to the United States than German control. To prevent such hegemony by a great power whose strength, greatly enhanced by its control of Eastern Europe, had consistently been seen as a threat to the United States, and whose antidemocratic political orientation was viewed as a danger to the preservation of an international environment in which democratic values would not only survive but flourish, the United States was prepared to fight. Presumably this knowledge had deterred the Russians in the late 1940's, and it was this fear of war which had led them to redirect their challenges to Third World areas between the so-called free and Communist worlds. But now, ten years after the first Berlin crisis, the Soviets had once more challenged the West in Europe. Indeed, the reopening of the Berlin issue—and especially that for the first time in the post-war era they were publicly demanding that the Western powers abandon territory they controlled and were threatening them with an ultimatum—suggested a new Soviet confidence in the ability of their power to achieve their stated political aim of converting the Western half of Germany's former capital into a "free city." Not only did the West not have a capacity for a limited response to a limited challenge but, worse, the strategic balance appeared to be changing. The Soviets were claiming that they were mass-producing their new ICBM. America's deterrent bomber force, they said, was now vulnerable and its deterrent capacity declining. The Central Intelligence Agency seemed to agree by forecasting a missile gap as the United States entered the 1960's, and many Americans, both in and out of government, became concerned that Khrushchev might be right. Clearly, he was attempting to cash in on what the Soviet leader already asserted was a changing distribution of power which had become favorable to Russia.

6

BERLIN, CUBA, AND THE CRISIS OF MASSIVE RETALIATION

Mutual Deterrence and Suicide

No policy could have been more typically American than massive retaliation. It was a strictly military one, completely divorced from political considerations. The separation of force and diplomacy was, indeed, twofold. First, should it ever become clear that the diplomats had failed to keep the peace, the military would take charge and their aim would be total victory. The enemy was to be punished by completely defeating him. A maximum of violence was required to achieve such a military victory, making nuclear weapons ideal for this task. A combined attack upon the enemy's major population and industrial centers would paralyze the entire country and reduce it to a mass of rubble and radioactive dust. Massive retaliation, in brief, carried the American doctrine of war to its logical culmination. Second, in "peacetime," massive retaliation's function was strictly the deterrence of all-out war. For less than a total challenge, therefore, American diplomacy was unsupported by any usable power. This eliminated any incentive for the Soviet leaders to arrive at any compromise arrangements over the issues that had precipitated the cold war, such as the division of Germany or the incorporation of Eastern Europe into the Soviet empire.

Nor, since the United States had renounced the use of force except in retaliation against a direct attack, could the Soviet Union be deterred from constant probing actions. Indeed the irony of the situation was that throughout this whole period the Russians were constantly probing, seeking to expand their influence by means short of total war—by guerrilla warfare, *coups d'état,* internal Communist parties, anti-Western nationalist movements, "volunteers," and satellite armies. The only thing they had to avoid was an attack upon the United States itself or upon those areas the United States had designated as of vital interest to its security; short of that ultimate provocation, the Soviet Union, the strategically weaker party during the first decade of the cold war, could raise tensions and challenge the United States.

If this was the pattern during the period of America's atomic monopoly and greater strategic power even after Russia had acquired its own atomic bomb, the possibility of challenges in areas vital to the United States—such as Europe—increased as Russia's nuclear stockpile and capacity to hit the United States increased during the late 1950's. As massive retaliation became a two-way street, the Soviet Union's growing ability to impose catastrophic damage upon America meant that the two nuclear states would increasingly stalemate one another's strategic striking power. The "balance of terror," as Churchill called it, would ensure the peace; indeed, in President Eisenhower's words, "there is no alternative to peace." His participation at the 1955 summit conference in Geneva with Soviet Premier Bulganin (Khrushchev was at that time not yet Premier but First Secretary of the Communist Party of the U.S.S.R.) was generally recognized as testimony to this fact. War was no longer a rational instrument of national power; by simply meeting, the leaders of the two most powerful countries of the world were said to have "signed" a tacit nonaggression pact.

Actually, American policy handed the Soviet Union the opportunity to break this stalemate. For the age of atomic plenty has increased America's strategic dilemma. The Eisenhower all-or-nothing strategy has meant that each limited Soviet challenge confronted Washington with the question of whether the defense of the objective under attack was worth the destruction of most of America's cities and their inhabitants. Faced with this prospect, if it responded to the less than total Soviet challenges, the American Government had a strong incentive to do nothing. This meant that Moscow could gradually turn the nuclear balance of power in its favor by imposing a series of piecemeal defeats upon the West. It could erode the *status quo* by nibbling away at it bit by bit, without ever once facing the United States with the one kind of challenge for which it was prepared. According to Henry Kissinger in 1957:

> It can be argued that the fear of all-out war is bound to be mutual, that the Soviet leaders will, therefore, share our reluctance to engage in any adventures which may involve this risk. But because each side may be equally deterred from engaging in all-out war, it makes all the difference which side can extricate itself from its dilemma *only* by initiating such a struggle. If the Soviet bloc can present its challenges in less than all-out form it may gain a crucial advantage. Every move on its part will then pose the appalling dilemma of whether we are willing to commit suicide to prevent encroachments, which do not, each in itself, seem to threaten our existence directly but which may be steps on the road to our ultimate destruction.
>
> To be sure, we shall continue to insist that we reject the notion of "peace at any price." The price of peace, however, cannot be determined in the abstract. The growth of the Soviet nuclear stockpile is certain to widen the line between what is considered "vital" and what is "peripheral" if we must weigh each objective against the destruction of New York or Detroit, of Los Angeles or Chicago.

Was Berlin still a "vital" interest? Or was Berlin now a "peripheral" interest? These were the stark questions which confronted the United States in the late 1950's.

Massive Retaliation and NATO

The question raised by the Soviet challenge was further underlined by the lack of sizable shield forces on the Continent. The original tasks assigned to these troops were twofold: first, to strengthen deterrence by assuring the Russians that an attack upon Europe would break the tripwire and unleash SAC; and second, in case deterrence failed, to implement the "forward strategy" and hold the Red Army at the Elbe while SAC was laying Russia waste. The success of the deterrence of total war, however, dictated yet a third operational assignment for NATO forces: to conduct limited operations and thereby deter less than total challenge. It was preposterous to assume that the United States would continue to risk suicide no matter what the level of Soviet provocation. Would it really be willing to initiate an all-out nuclear war if the Russians seized a small portion of Turkey? Would it really precipitate a total nuclear exchange if the Red Army or satellite East German troops seized all or part of West Berlin or a small enclave of West Germany? Would suicide in these instances be preferable to accepting limited losses? Only a capacity for limited war would allow the United States and its allies to escape this dilemma.

But it was exactly this capacity to respond to limited challenges that was missing in Europe. In a large measure, this was a result of the Eisenhower Administration's determination to "maximize air power and minimize the foot soldier." By January, 1960, NATO had only seventeen or eighteen ready divisions. Apart from the numerical deficiency of NATO ground forces, their equipment with atomic tactical weapons raised the same question as did SAC: Would they be used? Would NATO not grow increasingly reluctant to rely on these forces to respond to Russian moves? When the original decision to equip Allied forces with atomic weapons was taken, it was believed that the Soviet Union would have few, if any, atomic tactical weapons. Thus, the damage caused by the tactical weapons could be absorbed—particularly since East Germany and Poland would have to absorb most of it, and Soviet and satellite troops would have to suffer the atomic blows. The picture changed, however, when the Russians, too, acquired these weapons and thereby ensured that their use would be reciprocal. In these circumstances, the advantages that atomic arms were supposed to confer upon the West began to diminish, if not to disappear.

Nuclear weapons would not protect Europe; they would devastate it. Europe is densely populated; its cities are too close to one another; civil, military, tactical, and strategic targets are all intertwined. A nuclear ground war would be a catastrophe for Europe, probably spelling the end of European civilization. The distinction between limited atomic war and total atomic war was for Europeans meaningless. NATO's capacity to fight a limited tactical atomic war would therefore not allow the West to escape the dilemma of suicide or appeasement. A limited war in Europe was meaningless unless it also limited the devastation. But the concentration on massive retaliation—on NATO's sword—had reduced the apparent necessity of raising sufficient ground forces and strengthening the NATO shield. This, in turn, reinforced the need to stake Western survival on each issue, no matter what the level of provocation, since America was left with no weapon but strategic air power with which to respond to the Soviet challenge in the heart of Europe.

The Berlin Retreat

It was this reliance upon SAC that made it very difficult for the Western powers, especially the United States, to impress the Soviet Union with NATO's unity and resoluteness. On the one hand, the United States was determined to stay in Berlin; on the other hand, having stated that it would defend Berlin by massive retaliation, it simultaneously sought to escape the consequences of its own military strategy. This it could do only by granting concessions. Shortly after the presentation of the Soviet ultimatum, Secretary of State Dulles talked of accepting the East Germans as "Russian agents" at the checkpoints on the routes leading into Berlin. The Secretary also declared that the reunification of Germany could be brought about by means other than free elections. Both statements threatened a complete abandonment of the previous and long-held American positions of nonrecognition of the East German regime and Germany's right of self-determination. The Administration, already pressured by the British, also accepted the standing Russian call for a summit conference. But it insisted on the prior fulfillment of two conditions:

withdrawal of the Soviet six-month ultimatum and a Foreign Ministers' conference to lay the basis for a settlement of the Berlin and the general German issues. The purpose of a "meeting at the top" was, in the Administration's opinion, essentially to ratify decisions already reached at a lower level; Eisenhower definitely rejected a meeting that would settle nothing and end in a fruitless propaganda debate.

The Russians reluctantly accepted the precondition of a Foreign Ministers' conference and at the same time denied that the six-month ultimatum was an ultimatum. But they refused to budge from their position at the Foreign Ministers' marathon held in Geneva in the spring and summer of 1959. It was the West that offered the concessions. In the first place, the United States allowed an East German delegation to sit in on the deliberations and thereby took a step toward *de facto* recognition of the Soviet-installed regime. The Soviet Union had threatened not to negotiate at all if the East Germans were not permitted to attend. Second, the West abandoned its plan for the reunification of Germany at the first sign of Soviet opposition. Third, the Foreign Ministers then took up the problem of an interim settlement for Berlin. In short, after years of stating that it was the Soviet division of Germany that was the cause of European instability, the United States and Britain accepted the Soviet definition of what constituted the principal source of European tension. Furthermore, they offered two concessions: The West would not arm its forces in Berlin with nuclear weapons and would not install missile bases in the city; and the Allies promised to curb their propaganda and intelligence activities in their sector if the Russians would halt similar (and anti-Western) activities in their zone. These proposals were unacceptable to the Soviet Union.

The Russians simply refused to renew their endorsement of Allied rights in Berlin and reasserted that they would end the occupation regime. The Allies thus failed to obtain the Soviet guarantee they sought, but the fact that they had attempted to arrive at an interim arrangement for Berlin at all, and were willing to grant concessions to obtain it, is eloquent testimony to the dilemma in which American strategy had placed them. For, in effect, the Western powers—in this case, America and Britain—were willing to transform the Western position in Berlin merely in return for the withdrawal of the Soviet threat to the city. In an attempt to extricate themselves from the dilemma of suicide or surrender, the two countries were placing themselves in the humiliating position of calling into question their well-established rights in Berlin. No wonder Khrushchev felt that all he had to do was maintain a high level of tension.

His bellicosity and rigidity were thus paying handsome dividends. The more menacing he sounded and the more inflexibly he stood, the greater the number of voices in the West that called for more Western "flexibility" and "new approaches" to the Soviet Union on the whole problem of Germany. Policies which had almost become "untouchable" over the years were suddenly placed in flux and condemned as dangerous. The West was torn apart by precisely this kind of controversy. The British denounced Chancellor Adenauer's "rigidity"; the Germans, in turn, accused the British of "appeasement." Franco-British relations cooled considerably. And both Adenauer and De Gaulle demonstrated increasing suspicions of United States intentions and resolution. America's apparent willingness to discuss Berlin with the Russians seemed to the French and German leaders to show little American conviction or courage to uphold a previous position; to them, Eisenhower was showing far too much flexibility.

As if to prove Khrushchev's theory that his threats of war against the West would have rewarding consequences, and to confirm De Gaulle's and Adenauer's apprehensions, President Eisenhower issued an invitation to Mr. Khrushchev to visit the United States in September, 1959. This invitation represented a major Soviet tactical victory. Such a summit *à deux* would show Khrushchev's equality with the American President and convincingly demonstrate to the world Russia's status with the United States as one of the two great superpowers. And, as Khrushchev knew, it would deepen the divisions within Western ranks by increasing the Allies' apprehension of a separate United States–Soviet agreement at their expense, and conversely, would persuade President Eisenhower that the crisis was caused by the rigidity of certain Allied leaders who were opposed to the "normalization" of relations. It is noticeable, for instance, that after the conference had ended, the President described the Allied position in Berlin with the same word Khrushchev constantly used— "abnormal." This unwittingly strengthened the Soviet leader's diplomatic hand. If the Allied position in Berlin was indeed "abnormal," the Soviet demands then seemed "reasonable," and the Western powers should alter their position to "normalize" the situation. This heedless use of a single word was characteristic of the manner in which Khrushchev was being allowed to set not only the pace of the negotiations, but also the context within which these took place.

The Eisenhower-Khrushchev meeting did result in the Soviet Union's withdrawal of its threat to take unilateral action in Berlin, in return for American willingness to negotiate on the problems of Berlin and Germany at a four-power summit meeting. For American policy-makers, this meant another postponement of the day on which they would have to decide the painful question of whether Berlin was worth the cost of a total war. But if the Administration believed that the crisis had been ended, that from then on it could leisurely negotiate on these issues and, if the Russians did not accept its terms, preserve the *status quo*, it was soon disabused of this notion. Mr. Khrushchev was soon reiterating his threat to sign a separate peace with East Germany.

Shortly before the scheduled Paris summit conference in May, 1960, an event took place that was to shatter the summit conference after only one session and further postpone future negotiations on Berlin. On May Day, 1,300 miles within Soviet territory, the Russians downed an American U-2 "spy plane" loaded with photographic equipment for the gathering of intelligence data. The Eisenhower Administration reacted to this unexpected and unhappy turn of events with considerable diplomatic ineptitude. When Khrushchev initially announced only the shooting down of the U-2, the U.S.

Government responded that the plane had been engaged solely in meteorological observation and speculated that the pilot must have flown off his course. When the Soviet Premier then revealed the real mission of the flight and produced an alleged confession by the pilot, the Administration reversed itself. In a move unprecedented in diplomatic history, it admitted that the U-2 pilot had been taking aerial photographs of the Soviet Union and that it had lied in its previous announcement. Nor did the Administration stop there. It claimed that similar flights had been sent into Russian skies for several years and strongly intimated that such flights would continue. The reason advanced was that Soviet secrecy made it necessary to gather information by this means in order to prevent a surprise attack. But it is one thing to be caught red-handed in spying and to admit it; it is quite another thing to assert that you will continue to do so in the future. In effect, the United States claimed the *right* to fly over Soviet territory (one need only imagine the uproar in the United States if the Russians were to announce calmly that they had the right to fly over American soil and take photographs of military installations).

Such a challenge could hardly have been left unmet. For the Soviet Premier to have bypassed this claim would have been equivalent to acknowledging to the world, to his people, to his domestic enemies, and to his allies that he had surrendered to the United States the right to violate Soviet territory. Khrushchev could not have survived such an admission. The alternative course he took was to strike a belligerent pose in Paris. He launched a blistering personal attack upon President Eisenhower, demanding from him a personal apology for past U-2 flights, a promise that no such flights would be undertaken in the future and punishment of those responsible for the spying operation. Eisenhower's promise that no more reconnaissance missions would be undertaken during his term of office did not satisfy Khrushchev; he apparently considered this to mean merely a temporary suspension. The other conditions demanded by the Soviet Premier were rejected outright by Eisenhower. Khrushchev thereupon suggested that the summit conference be postponed for a period of six to eight months, and he bluntly told Eisenhower that he would not be welcome if he came to the Soviet Union in June to return the Premier's previous visit to the United States. In short, Khrushchev said that he wanted nothing more to do with Eisenhower and that he would wait to negotiate the Berlin problem with the next Administration. A new crisis had been put off for a little while longer.

It was inevitable, therefore, that the Berlin problem would be raised again by the Russians once the new Administration had established itself in power. Khrushchev was still convinced that the global balance was shifting in his favor, and he remained confident that he was strong enough to acquire West Berlin. President Kennedy, fearing that Khrushchev might miscalculate, therefore journeyed to Vienna to emphasize America's determination to defend West Berlin; the United States would stand firm and protect the free half of the city. Khrushchev, however, took these warnings lightly. His response was characteristic: to test the President's resolution by reviving the original threat that the Berlin situation would have to be resolved within six months—that is, before the end of 1961. The fruits of the Vienna summit meeting were thus precisely the opposite of what was intended: the very type of Russian brinkmanship against which Kennedy had sought to caution the Soviet leader.

Kennedy was thus confronted with a crisis. On the one hand, he fully realized the significance of Berlin. While he declared his willingness to negotiate, he also stated that he did not expect the Soviets to confront him with the accomplished fact of a treaty with East Germany. The United States was not willing to discuss merely how the West would withdraw from the beleaguered city, thereby leaving it for the Communists to swallow. The West's right to be in the city stemmed from its victory over Nazi Germany. Western presence and access to the city, and the freedom of West Berlin, therefore were not negotiable. In the President's words: "We cannot negotiate with those who say: 'What's mine is mine, and what's yours is negotiable.'" More specifically, he asked, if the West refused to meet its clear-cut commitments in Berlin, where would it meet them? Yet it was also clear on August 13, 1961, when the Communists built a wall dividing the city, that they had eliminated the escape hatch for East Germans, ended West Berlin's usefulness as a "showplace for Western capitalism," and violated the quadripartite status of Berlin. But the West did not react by resisting the erection of the wall with bulldozers and tanks for fear of military conflict with Communist—especially Soviet—forces. This passivity intensified Khrushchev's conviction that the United States would not fight and that he could, slowly but surely, increase the pressure on NATO and drive the West out of Berlin.

It was this latter conviction, and the consequent American fear that the Russian leader might miscalculate Western resolve and thereby accidentally trigger a war, that accounted largely for the difference between Kennedy's and his predecessor's reactions to the Berlin crisis. Unlike Eisenhower, Kennedy used the tensions over Berlin to further the build-up of American military power; the new President was determined to show Khrushchev that the United States was not bluffing when it declared its intentions to defend West Berlin. Kennedy had actually begun his move to increase the nation's military strength shortly after assuming office. His first consideration had been to reduce SAC's vulnerability during the changeover from bombers to missiles that began in the late 1950's. Bombers located at known sites are highly vulnerable to surprise attack. Thus, even in a situation of mutual deterrence, the possibility that many or most of the enemy's bombers might be surprised and destroyed on the ground remained an incentive to attack. If they could be destroyed, the retaliatory attack by a small remnant force might not be fatal to the attacking nation. In a crisis situation, this possibility could tempt either side to launch a preemptive strike in order to forestall a possible blow by the other side—even if the other side actually had no intention of striking. But solid-fuel missiles, like the air force's Minuteman, can be widely dispersed and protected, or "hardened" underground, instead of being concentrated on a few bases, as bombers are; and the Navy's

Polaris missiles can be moved underwater so that the enemy will at no time know where to strike them.

The importance of the dispersion, the "hardening," and especially the mobility of missiles lies in the fact it deprives a surprise attack of its rationale. When the opponent's retaliatory power consists entirely or primarily of mobile, solid-fuel, long-range missiles, it is impossible to know all the sites at which to hit him in order to destroy his retaliatory capacity. Obliterating the enemy's cities will benefit the aggressor very little if the enemy still retains this capacity. Surprise, therefore, no longer confers any significant advantage to the side that strikes first. Indeed, there is no need any longer to hit preemptively, since enough of the missiles can survive an initial strike and still retaliate fully against the aggressor in a second strike. A first strike in these circumstances—which American policy-makers generally conceded to the Soviets—would be completely irrational.

Yet this change in strategic weapons was a long-range program. Kennedy, as cautious as his predecessor, vacillated between his determination to stay in West Berlin and his equally strong determination to avoid conflict. Thus, like Eisenhower, he was willing to offer concessions and negotiate with the Soviets alone if West Germany and France remained "inflexible." The meager results of these bilateral American-Soviet negotiations were primarily due to Soviet unwillingness to concede the right to any Western presence in Berlin, which, in turn, was in all probability due to Khrushchev's conviction that he need only maintain Soviet pressure finally to evict the Western powers from the Communist-surrounded and divided city. If during this early period of the Kennedy Administration, as during the late years of the Eisenhower era, the Russians were unwilling to risk the final test, they had shown they were not hesitant to push the issue to a point of high tension. If the United States upheld the *status quo,* the manner in which it questioned its own position in Berlin and the concessions it offered in the name of flexibility demonstrated a lack of will and sense of purpose, which augured ill for the future if: (1) the Soviet leaders could keep their challenges below the level of provocation which might arouse an American nuclear response (while the exact level of tension could not be known to them, they did keep well below it) and (2) the Soviets confined their challenges to the periphery of Western power, and especially such isolated outposts as West Berlin. As long as they followed these two fundamental precepts, they could seek to exploit the dilemmas of American strategy.

It was the second rule that they failed to follow when Moscow shifted the challenge to ninety miles from the American mainland—to Cuba—where the United States had no choice but to respond in defense of what Washington conceived to be its vital interests.

Castro and the Missile Crisis

Cuba's revolutionary government had been established on January 1, 1959, after its leaders had overthrown the tyrannical Batista dictatorship. During his struggle against Batista, Castro had identified himself with both democratic government and social and economic justice and had gained widespread popularity among the Cuban people. This public support ensured the victory of his guerrilla army against the larger government forces. The Castro revolution was essentially a social revolution. In the opening months of its rule, the new government moved to remedy the conditions of the people by instituting land reforms and by building low-cost housing, schools, and clinics. But some features of this social revolution were bound to clash with the United States. Castro was highly nationalistic, and therefore anti-American because of past American domination of Cuba. Although the United States had been instrumental in freeing Cuba from Spain, it subsequently passed the Platt Amendment, which granted the Americans the right to intervene at any time in Cuba for the preservation of Cuban independence, for the protection of life, property, and individual liberty, and for the discharge of Cuba's treaty obligations. By 1934, when the amendment was repealed, the United States had intervened militarily

three times; it also had established a naval base at Guantánamo Bay. American capital was even more effective in controlling Cuba. By 1956, the United States controlled 80 per
cent of Cuba's utilities, 90 per cent of its mines and cattle
ranches, nearly all its oil, and 40 per cent of its sugar. It was
thus not surprising that the Cuban revolution should in large
part direct its long-pent-up nationalism and social resentment
against "Yanqui imperialism." America's support of the Batista dictatorship until the moment of its collapse only intensified this anti-American sentiment. "Cuba, si! Yanqui, no!"
became the Castro regime's rallying cry, the ceremonial burning of the American flag its ritual, and the confiscation of
American property its reward.

This anti-American nationalistic feeling—deliberately fostered by Castro to increase the popularity of his regime—led
to an increasing identification of Castro's government with
Communism. Before long, the regime became a dictatorship
with centralized control over all phases of Cuba's life. All
parties were abolished except for one—the Communist Party,
upon whose organizational strength Castro had become increasingly dependent. It was simply a matter of debate as to
whether the Communists dominated the government. The
real point was that the Communists actively supported Castro's revolution, convinced that it was only a transitory stage
to Communism, and that the Castro government linked itself
to the Communist bloc—and then consolidated these political,
military, and economic links. The Soviet Union supplied
Cuba with vast amounts of arms and accompanying military
advisers. Cuban airmen were sent to Czechoslovakia to learn
how to fly Soviet fighters, and a large number of Cuban technicians were trained in Communist countries. Cuba's armed
services soon ranked second only to America's as the largest
in the hemisphere. Diplomatic relations were established with
all Communist countries except East Germany; and economic
agreements were signed with many of the same countries, including East Germany. Cuba's economy became integrated
into that of the Communist bloc; 75 per cent of the island's
trade was with countries behind the iron curtain. In January,

1961, the United States cut off diplomatic relations with Cuba. If Castro had only now attempted to seize the Guantánamo base, there would have been an excuse for open American intervention.

Castro was much too shrewd to do so. Consequently, the United States supported an attempt, in April, 1961, by a small force of Cuban exiles—many of them former Castro associates who had become disillusioned by the Premier's tyranny and his Communist sympathies—to land in Cuba and attempt to overthrow Castro. Plans for this operation had been begun during the Eisenhower Administration, and Kennedy decided to support them when he came into office. The U.S. intelligence community believed that, once the exiles had gained a beachhead in the Bay of Pigs, some units of Castro's army and Cuba's population would welcome the invaders as liberators. But when the American-organized and -financed operation was launched, it turned out to be a dramatic and appalling failure. America had bungled because it launched a major foreign policy move involving American prestige—whether it intervened directly or not—on the glib assumption that a feeble beachhead operation would result in a mass uprising of Cubans against their government. But such an operation was bound to fail without adequate planning and preparation inside Cuba itself, without the binding together of the different anti-Castro factions, and amid conditions in which popular anti-Castro sentiment had not yet ripened. The rumors and press reports, which conveyed the impression of a major invasion, only made the failure appear to be even greater.

If nothing succeeds like success, it can also be said that nothing fails like failure. American prestige, already lowered by Russia's man-in-space achievement, sank to a new low. In Cyrus Sulzberger's succinct sentence, "We looked like fools to our friends, rascals to our enemies, and incompetents to the rest." The Administration had fallen victim to its own half-heartedness. The results of an unsuccessful invasion could have been predicted: an increase in Castro's domestic support, a revival of Latin American fears of "Yankee imperialism," a blunting of Kennedy's initially successful attempts to identify the United States with anticolonialism, and a loss of confidence in America's leadership by its allies.

Finally, Cuba survived as a Communist base from which the Soviet Union could threaten the United States itself and subvert the security of the other nations of the Western Hemisphere. It was in the fall of 1962 that U.S. intelligence suddenly discovered, to its great surprise and consternation, that the Soviets were building launching sites for approximately seventy medium- and intermediate-range ballistic missiles. The very fact that Khrushchev had dared to move his missiles so near the United States, and apparently expected no counteraction beyond ineffective diplomatic protests, was a dangerous sign. The great danger of all-out war is war by miscalculation; to prevent such a miscalculation is therefore an absolute necessity. But American actions had seemingly convinced the Soviet Premier, the apostle of "peaceful coexistence," that the United States would not fight to protect its vital interests. He probably recalled more recent events: the desire of Kennedy to eliminate Castro, but his unwillingness at the moment of truth to send in American forces and, in Berlin, Kennedy's paralysis when the Soviets built the wall. In each instance, Khrushchev had seen the fear of conflict deter the United States. Thus, he apparently came to believe that he could install his missiles in Cuba with impunity; the United States would rather accept this result than risk the use of force.

For Khrushchev, the stakes were high. American failure to respond to his move would have proved to its NATO allies what they feared already—namely, that the United States, having itself become highly vulnerable to attack, could no longer be relied upon for the protection of their vital interests in Europe. Inaction in the face of Soviet missiles installed only 90 miles away from the American coast would have emphasized this consequence of the nuclear stalemate in a most dramatic fashion. And the promised renewal of Soviet pressure on Berlin after the mid-term U.S. Congressional elections, together with the likelihood of an even more cautious American reaction than before, would only have reinforced this impression. This time, the Soviets would probably have issued an ultimatum to get out or else—and the "else" was the fact that the Soviets could for the first time cover a large part of the North American continent with their missiles, which would come flying in over areas where there was no adequate protection against them. The early warning systems against bombers and missiles were in the north, since a Soviet attack had always been expected to come in over the Arctic. American vulnerability to attack had therefore risen. Furthermore, the U.S. position in the Western Hemisphere would have been undermined as well. The sudden and unchallenged appearance of another great power in the area where the United States had long been paramount would have eroded America's authority and status and encouraged the spread of Castroism throughout Latin America. All anti-Castro forces, including the indispensable and all too few genuinely democratic reformers, would have been demoralized and perhaps paralyzed by Washington's inaction.

The political and psychological implications of Khrushchev's limited challenge were thus enormous, for the global distribution of power could well be gravely affected. But Khrushchev had for once overplayed his hand. He had raised the pressure on the United States too quickly and too near the United States itself for Washington to be able to avoid the test. Particularly if previous American actions and inactions had convinced the Soviet leader that he could "get away with it," it was imperative to disabuse him of this notion. Such confidence on Khrushchev's part could only be the result of a conviction that the United States no longer possessed the will to defend its interests. Such a notion was dangerous, for, if it remained uncorrected, it could lead to an even greater challenge, for example in the center of Europe; and if the United States did respond, a violent clash, possibly a nuclear war, would be the result. Characteristically, the Soviets had not committed themselves irrevocably in Cuba. They were willing to gamble for a big payoff, but they were also willing to suffer a serious loss of face in order to avoid a catastrophic clash. American firmness and determination left Moscow little choice. For once, therefore, it was the Soviets who had to decide whether to fire the first shot—to break the American blockade of their missile-carrying ships—and thus risk a possible escalation of the conflict. The Kremlin backed down. The level of tension having been raised, it also was rapidly lowered once American determination and the willingness to use American power became clear. In Secretary of State Rusk's picturesque phrase, "We were eyeball to eyeball, and the other fellow just blinked." Interestingly enough, particularly in view of Kennedy's critics who felt a Soviet humiliation in Cuba would compel the Soviet leader to recoup his lost prestige by forcing the West out of Berlin (with the clear implication that the United States should let him do so or desist in Cuba), Khrushchev called off *both* challenges. America's superior power, as demonstrated in the Caribbean, could also be marshaled in Berlin, and it therefore seemed advisable to terminate the tension over the Western half of the former German capital city as well.

American Strategy and Frontier Defenses

The recurrent crisis over West Berlin from 1958 to 1962, plus the Cuban missile crisis, held several lessons if the United States wished to preserve the frontier line around what was then still considered a cohesive Communist world. First, despite U.S. retaliatory power, the Soviet leadership, when it thought circumstances propitious, did not hesitate to raise international tensions with limited political challenges in order to compel the United States to make unilateral concessions. While Moscow was fully aware of the dangers of nuclear war and the consequent need for the avoidance of acts that would expose the Soviet Union to nuclear conflagration, it had not allowed this recognition to deter it from seeking to exploit the West's fear of nuclear war to transform the *status quo* in its favor. The Soviet leadership has felt confident that it could raise tensions *without* provoking the United States; as long as this tension was not raised too high, it could control the risk of war. To ensure that tensions would not escalate beyond control, the Soviets either left themselves a diplomatic escape hatch or were willing to make timely withdrawals in case they underestimated the American reaction. A Soviet-initiated rise in tension did not, therefore, when met by a determined countermove, spiral this tension further upward; Soviet concern to preserve a ceiling on this tension, lest it precipitate an American nuclear response, tended to lower tension and possibly end the specific crisis. The Cuban missile crisis in 1962 was testimony to the Soviets' confidence that, short of a major provocation, which they were not willing to offer, they could challenge the United States without fearing a nuclear response; their rapid retreat was even stronger testimony to their intense concern to avoid a further upward spiral of tension that might possibly reach the ceiling level.

Second, mutual deterrence was clearly not automatic, needing little attention to maintain it. For technology particularly can upset the stability of the deterrent balance. Simply possessing the bomb was insufficient. The key to a *stable* deterrent balance is an invulnerable retaliatory force; if one's force is vulnerable to attack, it may tempt its possessor to strike preemptively lest his forces be caught on the ground, or lead the adversary to strike first since he fears such a preemptive strike if he does not himself preempt. In the late 1950's and early 1960's, the Soviets were claiming that they were mass-producing missiles that made American bombers vulnerable. If this were true, it meant that the capacity of the United States to deter Russia was declining. This was bound to affect policy-makers in Moscow and Washington, emboldening the former and making the latter more cautious. Russia's willingness to challenge the United States in Europe again after a period of ten years and the manner in which America reacted were symptomatic of this perceived change in the balance by the superpowers. Only in Cuba in 1962, after it had become clear that Khrushchev had been bluffing— that he was not mass-producing ICBMs, that the United States was now ahead because in reaction to Khrushchev's claim Kennedy had started a massive missile build-up on land and sea—did Washington once more regain its confidence and, given the immensity of the stakes, react vigorously. Preserving stable deterrence is thus a continuing, never ending task.

Third, even before the stabilization of the "balance of terror," the United States refused to invoke its great strategic forces to respond to limited challenges; hence the need for limited-war forces. An all-or-nothing option was no option at all. Theoretically, a series of piecemeal defeats could turn the balance of power against America. At some point, the United States would be compelled to take a stand to prevent further deterioration of its position. But the Soviets were not likely to believe in the firmness of this commitment, massive retaliation and the threat of suicide being less and less credible. If, however, America were willing to accept that risk, the Soviet challenge would precipitate a war by miscalculation. Thus by its reliance on massive retaliation the United States could in fact bring about the very war massive retaliation was ostensibly supposed to deter.

Fourth, massive retaliation foreshadowed the gradual weakening of the bonds of America's foremost alliance, NATO. Its European allies had joined NATO to gain the protection of U.S. power, particularly SAC. But in an era in which the United States no longer held a nuclear monopoly, what ally could truly be expected to put its very survival behind the defense of its allies' interests? Baldly stated, what would be the U.S. response to limited Soviet demands in Europe? If America did react all out, Europe would be "saved from Communism" by being reduced to rubble. On the other hand—and this seemed more likely—if America was unwilling to risk its existence for specific issues the Europeans deemed vital, then the alliance was meaningless and the Europeans would have to acquire their own national deterrents. Yet such a diffusion of nuclear arms within the alliance would in turn threaten to disintegrate NATO even further.

Finally, as Berlin and Cuba again demonstrated, the chief function of a military power was to delineate and protect "frontiers." These frontiers had been clearly drawn: along the Elbe and through the middle of Berlin; at the 38th Parallel in Korea and the 17th Parallel in Vietnam; along the coast of China at Quemoy and Matsu; and, more tenuously, at the "northern tier" from Turkey to Pakistan. Any attempt to cross these frontiers, openly by direct attack or covertly by guerrilla warfare, would risk hostilities. Admittedly, the lines drawn outside of Europe were extremely tenuous. METO and SEATO were alliances in areas where nationalist forces opposed the Western-formed and -led alliances. These therefore had little popular support, even in those states which were members. The result was that the Russians could leapfrog the line, as in METO, or that the governments seeking to maintain this line were, despite American help, unable to mobilize the requisite indigenous morale and support, as was to become evident in Vietnam during the 1960's. Indeed, it might well be that the United States would have been better off had it not created what turned out to be poor replicas of NATO. That organization had been formed in an area in which nationalism supported containment against a clearly perceived potential external aggression; the METO and SEATO alliances were organized in non-Western areas where containment was widely perceived as an attempt to preserve Western influence and reactionary regimes. Nevertheless, because the lines drawn created a great danger of conflict, particularly of an American-Soviet clash, this process of delineation had in the 1950's turned the attention of the superpowers increasingly toward the Third World as an area where they believed that the bipolar balance could be transformed in either America's or Russia's favor.

7

THE THIRD WORLD DURING

THE COLD WAR YEARS

The Revolution of Rising Expectations

"Four areas in the world," Guy J. Pauker wrote at the height of the cold war, "are at present or potentially major power centers: the United States, the Soviet Union, Western Europe, and Communist China. In all four, productivity is on the increase, and the political system performs relatively well its integrating and decision-making functions. Despite major differences among them . . . these four areas are likely to be in a position to play major roles in political, economic, and cultural international affairs in the coming decade. In contrast, the Middle East, Southeast Asia, tropical Africa, and Latin America are apt to remain power vacuums during this period, owing to their lack of unity, political instability, economic stagnation, and cultural heterogeneity. It seems highly improbable that ten years from now any of the areas mentioned above will cease to be, respectively, a power center or a power vacuum."

During the 1950's and 1960's such possible vacuums were viewed by Washington as dangerous. The fear was that, as in the eastern Mediterranean and Western Europe immediately after the war, Russian and/or Chinese power would attempt to flow into the void; in fact, Moscow's and Peking's attention had already been attracted. Even after the two Communist powers began to quarrel between themselves, much of their attention and energy was directed toward the Third World. For both nations, despite their fight for leadership of the international Communist movement and differences over strategy and tactics toward Western "imperialism" and the underdeveloped countries, saw these countries' revolt against Western colonialism as part of the disintegration of the international capitalist order and an opportunity for attracting them into partnership with Russia and/or China in the building of a new Communist international order. The challenge of Russian Communism and Chinese Communism in the Third World was, therefore, seen in Washington as stemming not so much from some conspiracy or military takeover as from the totalitarian model for modernization communism offered the underdeveloped countries. The majority of the world's population lived in those countries. If those people in their search for the freedom President Franklin Roosevelt had once called "freedom from want" turned to dictatorial means, it would profoundly affect whether the democratic or the totalitarian way of life would flourish throughout the world. Their choice was therefore critical to American security and, more broadly, an international environment in which open societies and democratic values would be safe. Thus it was vital to help the new countries develop; it was a matter of basic self-interest rather than humanitarian concern for the poor. Said a leading scholar: "Whether most of these countries take a democratic or a Communist or other totalitarian path in their development is likely to determine the course of civilization on our planet."

The task of modernization for the new nations was probably inevitable, for from the beginning colonialism held within itself the seed of its destruction. The nations that emerged from Western imperialism or colonialism after War II were dominated in one of two forms: either as direct rule by the colonial power, or as indirect rule by the native aristocracy in alliance with the colonial state. Still, the essence of colonialism is not the manner in which the ruling nation exercised its power but its political, economic, military, and cultural predominance over a backward territory. By the beginning of the twentieth century, the European states had extended their imperial holdings to two-thirds of the globe. But after 1900, these empires began to collapse. After World War I,

Canada, South Africa, Australia, and New Zealand achieved self-government, and the British Empire began its transformation to a Commonwealth of equal and independent states. But it was World War II that struck the final blow at colonialism. By the end of the war, two decisive factors were at work: The nationalist movements throughout the colonial world were surging forward, and the colonial powers had been immeasurably weakened in strength and prestige. With the exhaustion and collapse of Europe after 1945, one after another of the colonial territories in Asia, the Middle East, and Africa, sought and gained independence, though at times not without a severe struggle.

It is one of the strangest—and certainly one of the most ironic—paradoxes that the distintegration of Western colonialism affords the most eloquent testimony to its success. For the Western powers, including America in the Philippines, justified their imperial domination in terms of bringing the backward peoples of the earth the benefits of Western democracy, medical science, and technology. It was the "white man's burden," or duty, to educate the natives so that one day they could govern themselves. It might well be said that the colonial powers taught their lesson too well. They ruled their colonies autocratically, while simultaneously propagating the virtues of democracy. It was in the name of these ideals that the Western powers first came as colonizers; it was in their name, too, that the nationalist movements challenged their rulers and asked them to practice what they preached. The leaders of these nationalist movements had invariably been educated in Europe or America, or in a Western school in their own country. They fought the European powers in terms of the very principles of democracy and national freedom that they had learned in the West. They saw that these principles were incompatible with imperialism.

Once these countries became independent, they were left with a legacy of extreme poverty, illiteracy, and disease. Rarely in these nations does the annual per capita income attain the $100 level. Because this condition of economic underdevelopment, compared to that of the economically developed nations (indeed, we generally refer to this division as one between the poor and rich nations), is so startling, economic development is the generally recommended remedy. Industrialization modernizes—that is, transforms a backward, traditional, agrarian society into a twentieth-century industrial, urban community. Its effects are several. Industrial strength gives a nation military strength. Any nation-state must obviously be concerned with its defense. But for a new nation particularly, "power" comes ahead of "profit." This power is not primarily important for purposes of attack, although in certain instances it may be; rather, power becomes a symbol of the new nation's sovereignty and independence, and a means of acquiring the status and respect already possessed by the older members of the international society of nations. In addition, industrialization consolidates the rather tenuous bonds holding the infant nation together as a political entity. Industrialization requires a high degree of specialization. The resulting division of labor between the various sectors of the economy located throughout all regions of the country and the need for all these branches of industry to cooperate therefore forges new cohesive links and places the still fragile political union upon the base of an interdependent economic union. Finally, industrialization can create greater welfare for all of the nation's new citizens. This, too, is a fact of great political significance. The people are familiar only with their immediate surrounding area, and they are loyal to this region; national loyalty is unknown. Consequently, the newly formed nation must prove to them that it can offer something they could not otherwise attain. This "something" is an improvement in their standard of living. By achieving this, the nation demonstrates its utility and, in turn, receives from its people the popular support and allegiance it needs to survive and grow.

Yet the question confronting the new countries is whether they can develop themselves economically. The answer will to a large extent depend upon whether their economic progress will be faster than their population growth, or whether their "population explosion" will eat up any increase in national income. The world population by mid-1970 was 3.6 billion. In 1830, it had been one billion; by 1930, it had doubled. Thus, while the first doubling took 100 years, it took only 40 years more to add another 1.5 billion. U.N. experts predict 7 billion by the year 2000. India's birth rate would allow it to build a city the size of New York every year; and China's new population would permit it to add another Canada annually. In 1900, there was one European for every two Asians; in 2000, the ratio will probably be one to four. In the Western Hemisphere, there will, perhaps, be two Latin Americans for each North American. At that rate, the economic level of the underdeveloped nations will at best remain level, at worst decline. These countries may thus come face to face with the Malthusian problem: that is, the constant hunger and grinding poverty which result when the population grows faster than do the means of subsistence. More than 150 years ago, the Reverend Thomas Malthus, who was also an economist, predicted this fate for the Western world—unless the population growth were limited by either "positive checks" such as wars or epidemics, which result in a high death rate, or by "preventive checks," which result in a low birth rate. Yet, despite the huge population increase since 1800, the West has made great economic progress: Agricultural production has provided a plentiful supply of food, and industrial production has raised the standard of living to heights never before attained. The West's recent history would thus refute Malthus's gloomy prediction.

Unfortunately, the conditions that face the underdeveloped nations are quite dissimilar from those experienced by the West. One of the chief differences is that the Western countries had far smaller populations when they began industrializing, and their population increase did not outdistance the economic improvement. But India has set out on its industrial revolution with a population of more than 400 million, which is expected to reach 1 billion people by the year 2000. China already has over 700 million and is expected to reach the same staggering total predicted for India before the close of this century. In Egypt, the population is rising so fast that the completion of the Aswan Dam will only allow the country to remain at its present subsistence level. If the United States had a population density equivalent to that of Egypt, it would have more than 2 billion people instead of 200 million. Under these circumstances, it would hardly be a "developed" nation.

The European nations were also aided by the New World and by their colonial empires, which provided them with outlets to relieve their population pressures. About 60 million Europeans emigrated during the nineteenth and early twentieth centuries. The United States and Canada, rich in resources and fertile land, easily absorbed millions of immigrants and still increased their living standards; Australia, New Zealand, and South Africa experienced similar population and economic expansions, although on a smaller scale. From 1650 to 1950, the European population (excluding Russia) increased by approximately 300 million. But today there are about 400 million people of European descent living outside Europe. If these millions could not have emigrated and if the mother countries had not found many of their colonies profitable sources of cheap raw materials and labor, as well as markets for their products, the West might be living in the same conditions as the underdeveloped nations. The colonies thus served Europe as a frontier similar to that of the American West, which absorbed population that might otherwise have overcrowded the Eastern seaboard and thus added materially to the nation's wealth. But the underdeveloped countries can find no such relatively empty and rich spaces to absorb their surplus populations.

In the West, the Industrial Revolution made possible the use of machinery in agriculture. This permitted a great increase in the food supply; efficient agriculture also meant that food could be produced by a smaller farm population. Excess labor from the land was thereby forced to go to the city, where it was used in the factories; this, in turn, accelerated the industrialization process. Quite apart from modern technology, however, Europe was blessed with sufficient sunshine and rain. Temperate lands are more favorable to food production than the tropical and monsoon areas that make up many of the underdeveloped countries. Europe could thus grow sufficient food for its multiplying population; what it could not produce, it imported from the colonies and the New World in exchange for industrial products. This enabled some European countries to support larger populations than their domestic food resources would otherwise have permitted. By contrast, in the nonindustrialized nations, the majority of the population is still engaged in a primitive agriculture. Moreover, there is generally not sufficient land for any major agricultural expansion; and more intensive farming of land already under cultivation—that is, using better seed, more chemical fertilizers, and insecticides—may yield enough food to keep pace with the population growth. During India's first Five-Year Plan of economic development, about half of the new product was needed to feed new mouths. "If our population continues to increase as rapidly as it is doing," a former President of Pakistan has said, "we will soon have nothing to eat and will all become cannibals."

If this statement is perhaps a little exaggerated, it nevertheless dramatizes the underdeveloped countries' problem of overpopulation. There are simply too many poor people. This might have been all right if the sleeping masses had not awakened—if they had continued to accept their miserable lot as natural and not suddenly become conscious that it was not a fate ordained by God but a man-made one, if they had not made this discovery and therefore demanded to eat more and live better. It is this "revolution of rising expectations" which creates the problem, for it will be impossible to fulfill these expectations unless there is a reduction in birth rates. The population pressure keeps the masses living close to subsistence; and such widespread poverty makes it very difficult, and perhaps completely unfeasible, to accumulate enough capital to stoke industrial growth.

In the West, the birth rate declined after 1850; with industrialization and the growth of cities came the spread of literacy and knowledge of artificial birth-control techniques. Malthus was thus right even for the West, because preventive checks were adopted. But Asia has not yet reached a similar level of economic development, and knowledge of birth-control methods has spread only very slowly. The Indian Government has, for example, instituted a public education campaign in family planning and financed research to discover a cheap and effective means of contraception. It even permits sterilization. And the Japanese Government, because the situation has become so desperate there, too—a population of 90 million with 0.15 acre of arable land per person and a food supply below minimum—has legalized abortion. The United States has encouraged efforts to limit the population explosion by providing birth-control information to governments seeking such information; and in 1967, for the first time, it provided financial aid (over $1 million) to India for the purchase of contraceptives, primarily for use by men.

It is doubtful, however, that the birth rate will significantly decline in most of these countries during the next crucial decade or two. This means that the pace of economic development must surpass the fast-rising populations. Economists seem to agree generally that an annual investment of 12 to 15 per cent of the national income is needed to transform a static agrarian economy into a modern, dynamic, industrialized economy in which capital accumulation begins to sustain itself. But these countries simply do not have that kind of capital. Internal savings in sufficient amounts cannot be squeezed out of peoples living at subsistence level—at least, not without totalitarian controls. An alternative means of obtaining capital is to earn it by trade. The underdeveloped areas are exporters of primary products or raw materials, such as coffee, tea, rubber, and tin. It is precisely this fact that in the past has limited the earning capacity of many of them; for these exports rise or decline with every fluctuation in Western prosperity. A major Western recession lowers the demand and price levels of natural resources; the resulting losses of income may well exceed the Western aid extended during the same period. Furthermore, markets may become glutted with certain items because of overproduction or substitution—that is, a nation may have sought to raise its income by increasing production, but the fact that its competitors had done the same only resulted in lowering world prices, or the Western industrial nations, whose ever increasing demand for raw materials was supposed to furnish the capital for economic development, may no longer have needed them because of the development of synthetics. The lack of stabilized international commodity prices, similar to the parity prices paid to American farmers, plus the inventiveness of modern technology thus hampers the prospects of financing industrialization via trade.

Foreign investment is the third source of capital for economic development. In the past, this burden fell primarily upon private capital, although even during the nineteenth-century days of *laissez-faire* economics, governments loaned much of the money needed for projects and services which, while very necessary for economic development, did not produce immediate returns; these included services like education and such projects as construction of roads, railroads, and harbors. In its days as the world's leading power, Britain exported about 7 per cent of its national income each year. America's economic development would have been neither as rapid nor as extensive without British investments. In order to match those investments today, the United States would need to invest approximately $28 billion per year—more than the underdeveloped countries could absorb annually. Private capital has, in any case, been in short supply for the kind of long-range development that the underdeveloped nations need. Most private American investments outside the United States have been made by a small group of oil companies to build refineries and to discover and pump out oil fields in Latin America and the Middle East.

The reasons for this lack of private Western—and especially American—capital for foreign investment are not hard to find. The American economy has on the whole been booming for most of the post–World War II period. European capital has concentrated on the rebuilding, modernization, and expansion of its own capital plant. American capital has also been greatly attracted, especially since the founding of the

Common Market. Private capital is drawn to investments that will return sizable and relatively speedy profits. But perhaps the basic reason that private funds are so small is that public funds are so small. Businessmen cannot be expected to invest in hospitals, ports, schools, and roads. The returns from such projects are insufficient; and even if there were any profits, it would take too long to reap them. The major burden or responsibility for developing the climate for economic growth therefore falls squarely on Western governments. The first step in promoting more private investment abroad has to be taken with public funds; it is these funds that can raise the economic level of underdeveloped nations to the point where they will begin to attract private capital. Optimists who feel that even this first stage of economic development can or will be undertaken by private funds forget that even in the West the speedy economic growth of the nineteenth century, financed largely by private enterprise, rested upon an economic base developed by the mercantilist state; in brief, it was political authority, the state, that initiated the process that transformed the underdeveloped Western economies into the highly modern, industrialized economies we know today.

Economic development, then, remains the new nations' principal task. But this is *not* essentially an economic undertaking. Fundamentally, modernization, of which economic development is one major aspect, is a political, social, and intellectual task. Moreover, it is a revolutionary process frequently marked by political instability and violence rather than evolutionary peaceful change. One reason for this, in addition to their low level of economic existence, is that most of the nations that have so recently gained their independence lack administrative and political cohesiveness. Generally, the peoples have no single common culture or language; tribes are opposed to one another; different areas are in conflict with one another. There is in these nations no natural loyalty to the state, no tradition of cooperation except, of course, in the one overriding issue of eliminating the colonial ruler. But once that struggle for independence ends, power

tends to fragment. Thus, colonial India disintegrated vio-
lently into Hindu India and Muslim Pakistan following independence, and the latter dissolved further into Pakistan
and Bangladesh—with the help of India, which may itself
fragment further; the Congo (now renamed Zaïre) fell apart
when the Belgians withdrew; Cyprus divided into Turkish
and Greek factions; and Biafra split from Nigeria, only to
lose the subsequent civil war. Even where actual disintegration has not occurred, religious, linguistic, and racial differences and antagonisms tend to tear apart the fabric of these
states with their lack of any history of nationhood. In Bu-
rundi in 1972, for example, Tutsi tribesmen reportedly
slaughtered 120,000 Hutus. Nation-building thus becomes
their first task.

The absence of a strong sense of national consciousness is
reflected in the manner in which many of the leaders of the
new countries build themselves up as symbols of nationhood.
It is not too difficult for them to do this, since their prestige
is usually high as a result of the roles they have played in
leading the nationalist movements for independence. But the
task is an essential one. With Louis XIV, they must say,
"L'état, c'est moi." For they *are* the state; without their
presence as its symbol, the nation would not hold together
as a unit. Furthermore, they also often crush the opposition
party and place their countries under one-party rule.

Such policies may seem undemocratic, but they are to
some degree necessary. Loyalties in the new nations are less
to the state than to ancestors, family, village, or tribe. Wherever the opposition represents these centrifugal forces, an
American-style democracy cannot be permitted to operate,
for it would lead not just to a change in government but to
the disintegration of the state. The alternatives facing the
leaders of these countries are not democracy or dictatorship
but statehood or disintegration. Thus many of the leaders of
the recently emerged nations have emasculated the spirit of
the parliamentary system of government bequeathed to them
by the colonial powers; the conditions for democracy are
simply not yet ripe. Many other nations have not even

bothered to preserve the façade of parliamentary institutions, but have replaced them outright with military governments. In Africa, the world's last continent to be freed from colonialism, three-fourths of the 345 million people lived under one-party governments and military rule ten years after the first nations became independent.

Another reason that modernization must be seen in an essentially political and revolutionary context is that the nationalist revolutions direct their opposition not only against the dominating foreign ruler but also against the domestic ruling class. In colonies ruled directly, such as India, the imperial powers usually abolished the traditional social system, but in territories where they ruled indirectly, they did so via the native aristocracy. As a result, most such countries have been split into two groups when they have gained independence. The first is the ruling minority, composed of the landlords, tribal chiefs, and great merchants, sometimes fronted by an old-regime king. The second group, which constitutes about 80 per cent in most underdeveloped nations, encompasses the peasants, villagers, small artisans, and shopkeepers —those whose efforts have been concentrated largely on the sheer struggle for day-to-day survival. It is this group, which has for centuries borne its hardships silently, that has awakened and is now demanding a better life. For generation after generation, these people—who might truly be called *les misérables*—accepted their condition as if it was God-given rather than man-made. Suddenly, they have become aware that they can change their lot. It is the urban intelligentsia, educated in Western ideas and committed to modernization, that voices these resentments against the old way of life and proclaims the new aspirations most articulately and loudly. Change, change, and more change is the demand of the day.

Without such a social change—that is, the overthrow of the old ruling class—long-range economic development will be inhibited. For instance, American farm experts have been sent to nations where the *ancien régime* still survives. The peasants were to be brought the benefits of American science and technology. But the Americans found, to their great surprise, that the peasants were not interested in acquiring this knowledge, which would help them increase their annual crop. The reason quickly became obvious. If the peasants raised their yield, almost all the increase would go to the landlord, the money-lender, and the tax collector. There was, in short, little incentive for the peasant to work harder or apply new techniques. The limits to what the American specialists could achieve were thus set not by science, technology, or professional knowledge, but by social and political conditions. Assistance programs that should have been successful because they made sense by Western criteria could not produce the expected results when applied in societies that had not yet attained the West's level of social and political development. Economic growth must, therefore, be accompanied by a social transformation; and the change of the social structure is basic to this. The reason this is not a matter of "reform" but of revolution is that the crucial issue relates to power: Who controls the nation—the old ruling class, committed to the preservation of the traditional, religiously oriented, pre-industrial society, or those who seek to secularize, modernize, and industrialize the nation? One thing is certain: Few ruling classes yield their dominant political, social, and economic position without a struggle.

Instability is promoted even where economic development occurs, where national bonds do not disintegrate, and where a modernizing elite is in power. The cause of this is the fact that the slowly rising standard of living does not normally create an increasingly satisfied—and therefore happy and peaceful—population. Quite to the contrary: The masses become more dissatisfied and this raises social tensions. For example, industrialization is accompanied by a major shift of population from the countryside to the growing city because the new factories need manpower; at the same time this permits the small peasants' lots, which cannot be cultivated efficiently, to be gathered into larger lots on which modern machinery can be used to increase the previously all too small food supply. The government needs this produce to feed the growing population and the new urban labor force, and in order to be able to rechannel its precious foreign exchange, too frequently used in the past for the purchase of food, to purchase needed machinery. Most of the increased food supply must therefore be requisitioned. The frequently hungry peasant is not allowed to consume all he has produced; it is unlikely that he surrenders his crop voluntarily.

On the other hand, the large peasant population forced off the land or attracted by the greater opportunities of the city to become the new labor force is also unlikely to witness a significant rise in its standard of living. Capital investment can only be saved from money not paid to the workers; low wages and also the low prices paid to farmers militate against mass consumption and allow the reinvestment of the capital saved into further industrial and agricultural expansion. While there may be some improvement in living conditions, it will probably not suffice to satisfy the "revolution of rising expectations." Dissatisfaction will result from the fact that the population, knowing that it no longer has to live in the poverty and filth of the past, that man can create a better life for himself here on earth through his own efforts, will be frustrated by the continuous gap between achievement and expectation. When this comes on top of a resentment produced by being uprooted from the land, a bewilderment resulting from the anonymity of the city, and anger caused by a miserable existence in the slums, the social discontent and an increasingly sullen, hostile, and more radical mood are bound to rise.

Finally, as should be abundantly clear by now, these causes of instability and turmoil will be enhanced by the intellectual and cultural changes that accompany the transformation of a traditional, static, rural society into a modern, dynamic, urban-industrial state. To put it more starkly: Many of the old customary and religious values that helped man to accept his place in society and conduct himself throughout life simply collapse and the individual becomes disoriented, torn from his age-old moorings for which he has not yet found a substitute. Robbed of the status and function of his ancestors, he is left as an isolated and insecure atom in a rapidly changing environment which he neither made nor comprehends. Secular values, emphasizing material values and progress, replace religious values denying the importance of earthly existence and material possessions. A society in which individual effort is rewarded and a man can rise socially into a higher class replaces a society with a rigid social structure in which birth determined his place. Nationalism replaces local loyalty, and modern means of transportation and communication bring the individual to an awareness of the larger society in which he must now live and work. Impersonal ties to people far away in "his" country replace former face-to-face relations with neighbors, and man must learn new skills and ways of thought. In short, he must forget many of his old ways and cut long-time ties and adjust, readjust, and adjust once more. In the best of circumstances, this is a difficult and agonizing process.

Domestic Instability and International Tensions

It is hardly surprising in these circumstances that the domestic change and turmoil of the underdeveloped nations should have international repercussions that tend to destabilize an international system largely stabilized by the frontiers drawn between the two superpowers and by the nuclear stalemate. For when the internal difficulties of the countries of the Third World spill over into the external arena of international politics, they are likely to attract the Soviet Union and the United States, thus leading to a possible confrontation with its attendant danger of military conflict. The reason these difficulties attract these two superpowers is that they may bring to power a group one country likes and the other dislikes or result in regional expansion and influence that may be perceived as benefiting one and hurting the other. If one of the two nations is unwilling to tolerate what it may, in terms of the global balance of power, consider a local or regional setback, it will intervene; or, if it fears that if it does not intervene its opponent might, the result may be a pre-

ventive intervention. In both cases, it risks counterinterven-
tion.

If a new nation disintegrates into two or more parts, those
who seek to reunify their land or those who seek to establish
their new splinter states may appeal for help to sympathetic
neighboring states who, for reasons of their own, may wish to
see a nation preserve its unity or fragment to support a favorable faction in power. Such appeals are especially likely to be
addressed to Russia or America. One of the more dramatic
examples of the manner in which the survival of the new
states as national entities may involve the superpowers was
given when, in 1960, the Belgian Congo became independent
and Patrice Lumumba, leader of the nationalist party, became the country's new Premier and Joseph Kasavubu its
first President. Almost immediately, the Congo began to disintegrate into disorder. First, the rich mining province of Katanga, upon whose copper and cobalt exports the Congo was
largely dependent as a major source of revenue, split off into
a separate state. In this venture, Katanga's President, Moise
Tshombe, had the support of the powerful Belgian mining
interests, anxious to protect their investments. Then the
army began to revolt because it resented the continued presence of its Belgian officers and wanted them replaced with
native leadership. In a wild spree, the soldiers began to attack white women (including nuns) and children. The Belgian settlers' reaction was to flee. Among their numbers were
the experts the Belgians had expected to leave behind in
order to help the Congolese in their early period of self-
government. All public services now collapsed because the
Congo lacked an educated native elite. The Belgians had
never trained one.

In the midst of this situation, the Belgians flew in paratroopers to protect their nationals. Lumumba, however, saw
this move as a Belgian attempt to restore colonial rule, and
he appealed to the United Nations to send forces to help him
against the Belgians. It was at this point that the cold war
was injected into the Congo. For the United Nations troops,
whose composition did not include any forces from the Great

Powers, did not compel the Belgians to evacuate their paratroopers or agree to Lumumba's demand that they help him
re-establish control over Katanga Province. Secretary General
Dag Hammarskjöld ordered that the international organization's forces were not to be involved in the internal squabbles
of the Congo or employed by the different contending political factions for the purpose of gaining power over their ri-
vals. This, however, had the effect of underwriting the divisions of the Congo, and the country could not survive without
Katanga. Since no leader likes to preside over the disintegration of his nation—particularly when that disintegration is
being encouraged by the former colonial power seeking to
preserve a base of control—Lumumba turned against the
United Nations, bitterly attacked the Secretary General, and
accused Belgium and the Western powers, especially the
United States, of conspiring against him; in these attacks,
Lumumba resorted increasingly to antiwhite racial appeals
and finally asked the Soviet Union for help to prevent the
disintegration of the Congo. He received Russian diplomatic
backing, military supplies and offers of troops or "volunteers"; several neutrals, especially the United Arab Republic, Guinea, and Ghana, also extended their sympathy and
support.

The United States now supported President Kasavubu
(who dismissed Lumumba) and his army commander, Col-
onel Mobutu, who established a caretaker government composed of the Congo's only fifteen university graduates. Mobutu also infuriated the Soviet Union by driving out all
Communist-bloc personnel, who had been aiding Lumumba.
The Russians insisted that Lumumba was still the Congo's
legitimate ruler and demanded his restoration; so did the
neutrals, who supported this demand by threatening to remove their contingents from the U.N. army. This would have
left the Congo in utter chaos. The United States, however,
refused to budge and continued to give its support to Colo-
nel Mobutu, in whom it saw the best means of eliminating
Soviet influence in the Congo and possible Communist penetration into the heart of Africa.

Soviet-American differences now became extremely bitter. The Russians, thwarted in the Congo for the time being, made two demands: the resignation of Dag Hammarskjöld and a veto over the Secretary General's activities. These demands were rejected. But by early 1962, after all efforts to unify the Congo had failed, the international organization reversed its original stand. It finally adopted the policy of forcefully squashing the opposition, the very position Lumumba had originally requested—which, had it been adopted at the outset, might have avoided the subsequent turmoil that led Lumumba to turn for help to the Soviet Union and thereby resulted in U.S. support for the rival faction. In any event, although it was still to be many months before the country was "unified" through the deposition of Tshombe and his Belgian advisers and foreign mercenaries, this task was eventually accomplished, although not without bloodshed. Ironically, this restoration of national order, accomplished with U.N. support, proved to be a posthumous victory for Lumumba who had in the meantime been assassinated. (The CIA reportedly had assassination plans for Lumumba too but was beaten to it.) If the central government had not received American and U.N. support and had been unable to reunite the Congo, it, like Lumumba, would have been compelled to turn toward the Soviet Union. National disunity was clearly dangerous with its superpower interference, attempts to impose "their" factions upon the country, plus the possibility of a military clash. But bipolarity extended superpower competition to all continents.

A more recent example with perhaps more significant implications for American-Soviet relations was the disintegration of Pakistan. A nation divided into West and East with 1,000 miles of India lying between the two parts, Pakistan had been born in a burst of communal hatreds in which hundreds of thousands of Hindus and Muslims slaughtered each other. It confronted the issue of survival in 1971, twenty-four years after its birth, during a period in which India (already hated for its seizure of Kashmir) had tried on several occasions to humiliate Pakistan and destroy it as a possible military threat.

What was to be the breaking point began when Pakistan, ruled for many years by a military regime, held a free election. A majority in East Pakistan voted for autonomy, because under the West Pakistan–dominated government the Eastern half had received less than what it considered a fair share of the national wealth (such as it was) and felt itself to be treated as a colonial appendage. West Pakistan attempted to crush the movement for autonomy with great brutality. The army killed and raped at will, burning village after village; almost 10 million refugees streamed across the border into India to escape this ravaging. The result was the growth of a full-fledged armed independence movement for the establishment of a Bengal Nation, or Bangladesh.

The United States during this period did not utter a single official word of public condemnation against its SEATO partner's brutal behavior (Pakistan, which had joined the alliance to obtain arms against India, had in fact moved away from SEATO toward Communist China as American policy had grown closer to India). Perhaps America's silence and continued shipment of arms to Pakistan were due to Pakistan's help in opening new relations between Washington and Peking; and perhaps this support was reinforced during the sensitive period preceding President Nixon's visit to the Chinese People's Republic by China's strong diplomatic backing for Pakistan. Alone, India supplied arms to the East Pakistan liberation forces and provided sanctuaries for them, thus confronting its traditional enemy, who was greatly angered by India's help for what the Pakistan Government, and China and America, considered rebels. Indeed, Pakistan's President had declared that if the rebels seized control with India's help, this would be considered an Indian attack on Pakistan and constitute a cause for war. India turned for support to the Soviet Union and received it in the form of a twenty-year friendship treaty intended to deter a Pakistani attack. This move away from India's historic policy of non-alignment was also presumably intended to deter open American support for Pakistan and provide India with the confidence to move against Pakistan. While denying that the new treaty represented a departure from nonalignment, India did have a good short-term reason for wanting to go to war quite aside from the longer-range aim of once and for all eliminating Pakistan as a rival on the Indian subcontinent. This more immediate objective was to end the burden of the millions of refugees, a cost sufficiently great to slow down India's rate of economic growth. In a real sense, a war was cheaper than continuing to support the refugees. Thus, under circumstances in which both sides claimed the other shot first, war erupted. Pakistan lost its Eastern half; Bangladesh attained statehood. India's policy of dismemberment succeeded, Russia reaped the rewards of India's victory, and its influence on the subcontinent reached new heights, while the United States—and to some extent China—lost prestige with the world's biggest democracy by siding with its weaker, military-ruled rival, whose soldiers' brutality had undermined the legitimacy of its cause in the eyes of almost all the world's nations.

Even if a new nation with tenuous bonds does not disintegrate, the political leaders may well invoke the only emotion the people ever shared in order to hold the nation together. This emotion is, of course, the nationalism born of the hatred of the former colonial power and directed against both that country and, more broadly, "Western imperialism." The granting of independence does not necessarily mean that colonialism is no longer an issue; rather, to preserve national unity the fight must continue. The same technique may be invoked by a country with the even more common condition of a stagnant economy in which the "revolution of rising expectations" turns into a "revolution of rising frustration." The political leadership will then be tempted to preserve its power by externalizing domestic dissatisfaction; foreign scapegoats will be needed to relieve internal stresses and strains. It is easier for leaders to play a prominent and highly visible international role before their countrymen than to undertake the hard and difficult work of modernizing their nations. The people can take pride in their leader's—and hence, their nation's—new status and identity in an international society which, under colonialism, had been denied importance and dignity as a nation and a people. Nkrumah of Ghana, Sukarno of Indonesia, Ben Bella of Algeria, until their deposal by military regimes, and Nasser of Egypt were among the most prominent and skillful practitioners of the art of channeling domestic grievances into international adventures. The most dramatic example of the dangers this can hold for the peace of the world was given by Nasser, who, as in 1956, provoked a war with Israel in 1967 when he confronted increasing economic hardship at home and a militant anti-Israeli Arab nationalism in Syria, a notoriously politically unstable and stagnating country. Nasser, increasingly compelled after 1958 to turn his attention and energies inward to "Arab socialism" in his fight for Arab leadership, had after more than a decade of rule still not managed to launch Egypt on a path of self-sustaining economic growth. Egypt was desperately short of funds to finance its development, buy food, support its 200,000-man army, and provide enough jobs for its unemployed and underemployed population. The national debt in 1966 was estimated at $2 billion; more than $100 million was overdue to Western states; foreign credit was very tight, and the balance of trade was declining. The second Five-Year Plan, already extended to seven years, was shelved. An estimated 30–50 per cent of the productive capacity of the government-owned industry was idle because of a lack of money to buy parts. The growth rate, which in the early 1960's was 6–7 per cent, had fallen to an annual 2–4 per cent, hardly sufficient to keep up with the population growth. The birth-control program had failed to have any significant impact; the birth rate added 800,000 people annually to a population of over 30 million. The pace of inflation was approximately 15 per cent a year. Nasser's program of nationalization and expropriation had brought domestic investment to a near halt and discouraged foreign investment. And his virulent anti-American attitude, which in 1964 had led to the burning of a U.S. library and a speech telling the United States to choke on its foreign aid, led to reduction and, finally, a cut-off of the American surplus food shipments his people desperately needed. So he had to buy his food elsewhere—at

least when the Russians did not give it to him—and use up
funds that might have been invested in the economic development of Egypt. The heavy expenditures on military equipment, probably amounting to one-third of Egypt's annual
budget, also diverted funds from development.

Arab socialism, having lost its glamour and thereby weakened Nasser's claim to Arab leadership, left him only the
arena of foreign policy in which to recoup his prestige and
hold on the Arab masses. But here, too, his stature had declined. He had reached the height of his self-proclaimed
leadership of Arab nationalism at the time of the seizure of
the Suez Canal a decade earlier. Nationalism had also affected Nasser's neighbors. Iraq refused to subordinate itself
to his direction, and Syria quit its short-lived union with
Egypt in 1961. Nasser then resumed his verbal attacks on the
traditional monarchies of Jordan and Saudi Arabia; Egyptian
forces also helped the revolutionary forces who had overthrown the Yemenite monarchy supported by Saudi Arabia.
He was clearly seeking to extend his influence southward
into the sheikdoms and sultanates of South Arabia, a British
protectorate scheduled to become independent in early 1968.
This would give him control over the Red Sea entrance to
the Suez Canal. But the Egyptian Army was unsuccessful in
destroying the royalist supporters. By 1967, the pressure of
inter-Arab rivalries was thus added to the pressure of economic failure for Nasser to reassert his leadership of Arab
nationalism.

First, he had to act if he was to be successful in establishing
his influence in the former British protectorate of Aden upon
its independence. Second, the Jordanians, in response to Nasser's hostility, taunted Nasser with hiding behind the U.N.
forces stationed between the Israeli and Egyptian forces at
the close of the Suez War. Third, the Syrians, trying to dis-
place Nasser as the leader of Pan-Arabism, openly and repeatedly called for Israel's destruction and stepped up their
terrorist raids into Israel. After a retaliatory Israeli raid, the
Syrians even claimed in May, 1967, that the Israelis were as-
sembling their forces for an invasion of Syria. This rumor,

reportedly also brought to Nasser's attention by the Soviet Union, which was seeking to exploit the Arab-Israeli-Western quarrel for its own purposes, was found to be untrue by U.N. observers. But Nasser, the great hero of the Arab peoples, either felt compelled to act or saw in the invasion rumor his opportunity to restore his leadership of Arab nationalism. Since Arab nationalism competed in terms of who was the most anti-Israeli—Israel being alleged the extension of Western "imperialism" into the Arab-world—there was bound to be trouble. This was particularly true because, after eleven years of receiving Soviet training and arms, Nasser seemed very confident that his forces could beat Israel, which this time would be fighting by itself, without the aid of France and Britain.

The Egyptian leader therefore made several moves. He moved reinforcements into the Sinai Desert. Next, he demanded and obtained the withdrawal of the U.N. peace-keeping forces; Egyptian and Israeli forces thus confronted each other for the first time since 1956. In addition, he proclaimed the blockade of the Gulf of Aqaba, through which Israel received its oil and other goods. Israel had long declared this to be a vital lifeline, since Nasser barred its shipping from the Suez Canal, and he knew Israel had stated that it would consider a blockade intolerable and an act of war. In short, Nasser was deliberately provoking a military conflict. Finally, he signed a pact of alliance with Jordan. This meant that Arab armies were surrounding Israel: Syria in the north, Jordan with its highly regarded army directed to cut Israel in two at its narrow waist, and Egypt in the south. All these moves were accompanied by increasingly shrill calls for a holy "war of liberation" and the extermination of all of Israel's inhabitants—in brief, genocide.

In these circumstances, war was inevitable, unless Israel was willing to accept a major political defeat, an unlikely prospect. Whether peace could be preserved, primarily by Nasser's "unblockading" the Gulf of Aqaba, depended now on the United States and the Soviet Union. Washington was, however, caught in a dilemma. On the one hand, it had recognized Israel's right to send its ships through the gulf after compelling it to withdraw in the wake of its 1956 victory. But it also recognized that if Nasser did not relent, a forceful test might be necessary; seeking support from other maritime powers, it found the major nations were reluctant to use force. On the other hand, it was deeply involved in Vietnam and therefore reluctant to become engaged in a second conflict with Egypt. Furthermore, a key question for American policy-makers was whether such a test would precipitate a clash with the Soviet Union, which had with great fanfare sent warships into the eastern Mediterranean, fully supported the Arabs in their aims, continuously denounced Israel as an aggressive tool of American imperialism, and perhaps even spurred Nasser on with the false story of an imminent Israeli invasion of Syria.

For Moscow, the Arab-Israeli conflict had, as earlier, not merely regional but global implications. If Western influence could be expelled from the Middle East and if Russia could establish itself as the dominant power over this oil-rich region, Europe might possibly be weakened and perhaps even neutralized. The Soviet political support and naval show of force undoubtedly contributed to Nasser's intransigence. Certainly it helped restore his reputation in the Arab world, and, had the blockade been successful, the Soviet Union would have earned the Arabs' everlasting gratitude, since it would have been chiefly responsible for Egypt's political victory, having demonstrated its ability to inhibit the American Navy and having eroded American commitments to Israel. Thus Moscow was unwilling to restrain Damascus or Cairo.

Since Washington was unable to arrange a diplomatic solution, the Israelis, tired of waiting for one, attacked. Routing the air forces of their Arab opponents in a brilliantly coordinated set of air strikes in the first hours of hostilities, they defeated the Egyptian Army in short shrift and reached the Suez Canal in three days—two days ahead of their 1956 record! They then routed the Jordanian Army and captured half of Jerusalem and the western bank of the River Jordan. Finally, they turned on the Syrian Army and eliminated the bases from which Syria launched the terrorist raids and shelled Israeli settlements. Nasser's dreams of an Arab empire were shattered, despite his efforts to salvage his reputation by blaming his defeat on alleged American and British air intervention on behalf of Israel. The Soviet Union reaped an ambiguous legacy. On the one hand, the Arabs were bitter because they felt that Moscow had deserted its friends when the situation became critical. On the other hand, the humiliating and complete defeat of the Arab armies left Egypt and Syria more dependent on the Soviet Union for political support, economic help, and further military aid and training, since they had by their own propaganda alienated themselves from the West. Arab nationalism and intra-Arab quarrels had once again intensified the Arab-Israeli conflict and precipitated war; and the bipolar competition for influence in the Middle East had once more turned the area's problems into the "Balkans of the twentieth century," an inflammable area of political instability, regional rivalry and Great Power conflict likely to explode at any moment and spread the resulting war far beyond the immediate area. Domestic Arab problems only aggravated the tendency of leaders to engage in adventurism, export internal dissatisfaction and grievances, strike tough and inflexible poses, and expose the world to the dangers of a superpower clash.

Even more broadly, Washington defined the greatest danger for American security as stemming from the new states' functional—not ideological—attraction to Communism. Confronting an amalgam of political, social, and cultural changes, not just an economic transition, experiencing revolutionary transformations, not just evolutionary progress, the non-Western nations have no guarantee that they will successfully climb what Robert Heilbroner has termed the Great Ascent; even the attempt may well call for some sort of left-wing authoritarian rule. In this context, the Soviet Union represented itself as a model of development. The Soviets could point to the Soviet experience and say: "In 1917, Russia was also underdeveloped but now, within the space of one generation, it has become militarily one of the two superpowers, the second largest industrial country in the world. You, too, can be industrialized quickly and live a better life." To people who already suffered from chronic hunger and poverty, it presumably would not matter greatly that the Soviet Union achieved industrialization by means of totalitarian governments that brutally squeezed the necessary sacrifices out of the people; the loss of liberty would not mean much to people who had never known it anyway, who have lived for centuries under authoritarian governments, whether domestic or foreign. Soviet totalitarianism would provide the organization and efficiency to squeeze the sacrifices from the masses, the discipline to hold the nation together, to speed up the pace of the cultural revolution while controlling the social tensions produced by the early stages of development, and, where necessary, to ruthlessly depose the traditional ruling class blocking the path to modernization. In short, just as capitalism was the chief means of modernization in the nineteenth century, Washington feared that Soviet Communism would be able to present itself as a successful model for modernization for the new nations seeking to enter the twentieth century. (After the Sino-Soviet schism, China too promoted itself as a model for modernization, one superior to European Russia.)

It was in terms of this competition of models that the United States and other Western states first offered foreign aid and technical assistance. It was also the reason Khrushchev visited many of the new states, especially in Asia, and offered material help wherever he went. And, as we already know, it was primarily to try and demonstrate that Russia's economy was not so bountiful that Secretary Dulles had withdrawn the Aswan Dam offer. The Third World nations were to see firsthand that Russia was bluffing when it extended aid and that Communism was not a successful economic-political system and model for them.

Global Inequity and Social Politics

In the rationales for sympathy and material and political

support for the countries of the Third World, it is clear that besides simple humanitarian sentiments for peoples living in such abject poverty, squalor, disease, and ignorance, security considerations were uppermost. Perhaps the basic reason for such concern sprang from a logic frequently articulated by government spokesmen, academicians, and journalists but also often implicit in policy: namely, that a world divided into rich and poor nations was an explosive world, for it set the majority of the poor against the privileged minority. Such a gap was no more acceptable internationally than it had been within each of the Western nations 100 years ago. The two situations were believed to be so similar that the "lessons" of the previous experience were applied to the international division of wealth. As the Industrial Revolution gathered momentum in each of the European countries and America, it created a privileged minority which owned most of the wealth. The distribution of income was, to say the least, unequal. Laborers, including many children and women, worked fourteen to sixteen hours per day, six or seven days a week, earned little beyond what was considered a living or subsistence wage (and sometimes less), and lived in overcrowded slums. The rich got richer, and the poor got poorer. This trend was so obvious that Disraeli talked of England not as one nation but as two. But the prevailing *laissez-faire* philosophy argued that nothing could be done to alleviate this situation. Government intervention, whether to end the grosser forms of exploitation such as child labor or to redistribute the income to help the poor lead a decent and dignified life, was rejected as contrary to the "iron laws of economics." Any outside interference with the workings of the market would stifle the private incentive and initiative that stoked the competitive capitalistic system. These "laws," which condemned a large section of the population to a hopeless and miserable existence, received even further support from Darwin's theory of evolution, with its emphasis on the "struggle for survival" and the "survival of the fittest." This philosophy, adapted by Herbert Spencer and called Social Darwinism, argued very simply that the rich were wealthy because their success in the competitive struggle had demonstrated that they were the most fit; conversely, the poor were destitute because they were unfit. It never occurred to Social Darwinists to ask themselves whether everybody had had an equal start or opportunity in this struggle. Perhaps this question was not asked because the Darwinian answer seemed so eminently right that it would be pointless, even silly, to doubt it—particularly since it apparently had God's approval. For it was He who must have endowed the rich with their superior talents and withheld these abilities from the poor. It was upon the men of wealth that human progress rested. Poverty, malnutrition, disease were admittedly evils, but they could be corrected and abolished only by the long-term evolution of the human species, which would ensure that only the superior qualities of man would survive. Social legislation to support the unfit—that is, political interference with God's purpose, the laws of nature and economics—would at worst burden society and ensure its stagnation, and at best slow down the evolution toward the healthy and wealthy paradise of supermen.

These philosophical justifications for leaving the poor very poor, if not to die, were ultimately rejected in all Western societies. The long working hours, the unsanitary and unsafe working conditions, the teeming slums were a blot on the West's conscience. They were also politically shortsighted and economically foolish. Politically, the division of people into "haves" and "have-nots" could only end in revolution, with the bourgeoisie being overthrown by the working classes, or proletariat; or, if it surrendered its democratic beliefs and values, the bourgeoisie could perhaps retain its power by establishing an authoritarian government and crushing any proletarian protests and uprisings. Neither of these alternatives was a very happy one for the ruling middle classes. Nor did this policy of squeezing the workers for maximum profit make sense economically, since the less money people have, the fewer things they can buy. Thus, social justice made sense —morally, politically, and economically.

In every Western society, government in the late nineteenth century began to intervene increasingly in the economy. While all governments—national, state, and municipal —were involved, it was national governments upon which the main responsibilities devolved. Their growing awareness of social problems and ills eventually led to the regulation of business; the passage of minimum-wage and maximum-hours legislation and the abolition of child labor and "sweatshop" working conditions; the organization of trade unions, thus enabling workers to bargain collectively with their employers for better wages and terms of employment; measures to counteract the sometimes violent swings of the business cycles; the implementation of the progressive income tax; and the initiation, during depressions, of unemployment insurance, public-works programs, and other "pump-priming" projects to increase the purchasing power of the people, thereby stimulating renewed demand and production. These measures, especially in the United States, widened and raised the base of wealth, giving rise to the twentieth-century mass market. They also led to a discovery so simple and yet so hard to understand that Europe, particularly Continental Europe, is just learning it: namely, that a worker is also a consumer. If he is paid a good wage, he will also buy the goods he produces. This is profitable all around: The worker is economically satisfied and therefore gains a vested interest, politically, in the social and economic order; capitalists earn handsome profits by selling volume at reasonable prices, and they retain their social status and political control.

It was this same problem of an inequitable distribution of income that was seen as once again plaguing the world. Only this time the problem did not exist within nations, but *between* nations. The rich countries were becoming wealthier, the poor ones more poverty-stricken. The iron laws of economics seem to hold the same fate in store for them that they once did for the Western working classes. Had the Marxist prophecy that the exploited proletariat would overthrow the bourgeoisie been defeated domestically only to reappear internationally and defeat the West on the global plane? Would the poverty-stricken nations of the world, the international proletariat, rise up in revolution against the privileged and wealthy Western countries, the international bourgeoisie? If the avoidance of this end was one basic reason for concern about the gap between rich and poor countries, another was more positive: the kind of world which the United States wished to help create. The two world wars of this century had been fought not only to forestall the creation of a power in Europe so strong that it could physically threaten the United States but to preserve a world in which democratic values would not only survive but prosper. Similarly, many during the 1950's and 1960's reasoned, modernization and Western help for this task would help bring about a world in which Western values would be more secure.

Although the nature of the problem seemed clear to many a policy-maker, it never attracted anywhere near the extent of public support that the more easily understood military preparations did. Such support, had it been realized, could perhaps have been translated into a more sustained effort to start the underdeveloped economies on a steady rise to the point where they could have become self-sustaining. What was probably required, as Barbara Ward had long suggested, was a progressive international income tax by which all the advanced Western nations would contribute 1 to 2 per cent of their annual national income for this development process. While the World Bank's Pearson Commission in 1969 endorsed the 1 per cent figure, no Western country was giving sums amounting to that percentage by that time. Despite the rapid economic growth of the industrial states during the 1960's, their foreign aid spending had not kept pace, indeed, had declined. This was particularly true for American aid, which as a percentage of the gross national product (GNP) had slipped from 0.83 per cent in 1961 to 0.69 per cent in 1965. At the time of the Marshall Plan to Europe, the figure had been 2.75 per cent of the GNP; by the middle 1960's, this figure had declined to less than 1 per cent. In short, at a time when the American GNP had risen by hundreds of millions of dollars, the national effort was puny compared to its increasing capacity to pay. A U.N. report issued in 1972 showed that this was occurring at a time when the gap between the rich and poor nations was continuing to widen. During the 1960's, while the per capita output, industrial and agricultural, of the developed countries rose 43 per cent, that of the underdeveloped nations increased 27 per cent. What these figures mean can be simply illustrated: A country with a $2,000 per capita output will add $200 to its production with a 10 per cent increase; for a country with a $200 output per year, an additional $200 represents a doubling of its output. Given an annual population rise of 2.3 per cent. What these figures meant can be simply illustrated: Latin America (compared to 1.3 per cent in North America, 1.1 per cent in Russia, and 0.8 per cent for the rest of Europe), the rate of production in the have-not states is barely staying ahead of the growing population.

Indeed, the term "economic aid" is itself something of a misnomer. After 1950 and the eruption of the Korean War, most economic aid was, in fact, military aid. Moreover, since Western Europe's recovery, most of this aid was channeled to Turkey, Pakistan, South Vietnam, South Korea, and Nationalist China. The sum that was left was used for economic assistance. But there was another snag. A good part of the remaining sum was devoted to what is called "defense support"; this provided money to sustain the economies of allies like South Korea or South Vietnam, which, in the absence of this support, could not maintain their standing armies. Only the final sum remaining after all these deductions was employed for the fundamental task of capital development, and of even this amount, a large sum was used for technical assistance. This involves such necessary programs as sending agronomists to the developing states to teach farmers how to get their hens to lay more eggs or how to use better irrigation techniques to enhance their crop yields. Although a vital aspect of economic development, this did not meet the problem of capital accumulation. According to the Pearson Commission, American nonmilitary aid had fallen to a low of 0.38 per cent of the GNP by the last year of the 1960's. More extensive economic aid programs, more liberal trade terms which would include higher and stable commodity prices, and tariff concessions on imports to the developed countries are thus a continuing need (the Common Market countries are much more generous in giving trade preferences to the new nations).

Apart from the issue of public support for foreign aid, the existing aid programs suffered from a number of other liabilities. All too often, American dollars have been offered with the explicit or implicit assumption that the recipients should associate themselves with U.S. cold-war policies; that even if they do not formally ally themselves with the United States, they should often thank it for its generosity, praise it for the morality of its anti-Communist stand, and certainly refrain from criticizing it. The United States has been reluctant to give dollars to nations that would not join its side. After all, could any nation really be neutral in a struggle between right and wrong? Was not democracy good and Communism evil? If countries wanted U.S. money, surely the least they could do was to fight with America "the battle of the righteous." Why, indeed, should the United States help those who were afraid or unwilling "to stand up and be counted"? And what was really wrong with attempting to win friends and allies with economic aid? The answer, perhaps, was "Nothing"; but it simply did not work. An economic aid program could not achieve its purposes unless its aim were fully shared by the recipient; it had to coincide with his aspirations. And the basic aspiration of most of the underdeveloped countries has been to concentrate their attention and energy on internal matters, to raise their standard of living and strengthen their independence, and to minimize their involvement in the cold war. Most therefore preferred to remain nonaligned in the struggle between the West and the Communists, avoiding all "entangling alliances." Any attempts to use economic aid as a means of forcing them into an American alliance system could only fail.

In preferring a generally nonaligned position, the underdeveloped nations were following America's own earlier experience. After it had gained its independence, it, too, abstained from all entangling alliances and preoccupied itself with internal developments; as an underdeveloped country itself, it was very much aware that its newly realized independence meant very little until it had gained economic and political strength. Moreover, having just thrown off the shackles of colonialism, the Americans had no desire to be once more tied to the European powers. For they knew that if they joined any alliance system, the European powers would again have a large voice in their affairs, simply because they were the far weaker party. The United States would become involved in their quarrels and wars; and this would mean that it would have to maintain a sizable military establishment, which, in turn, would divert much-needed capital from its economic growth. It was for these reasons that Washington, in his Farewell Address, advised the country to isolate itself from Europe's conflicts until it was strong enough to "choose peace or war, as our interest, guided by justice, shall counsel." It was for the same reasons that John Quincy Adams, when he was Secretary of State to President Monroe, advised against accepting the British bid for joint action against the Holy Alliance if it attempted to reimpose Spain's control over its former Latin American colonies. The United States, Adams said, refused to become a cockboat in the wake of the British man-of-war. Adams knew that he could safely reject the British bid, since Britain's own interests would make it necessary for it to oppose the Holy Alliance—economically, because it had trade interests in South America, and politically, because a Holy Alliance powerful enough to extend its power across the Atlantic was a coalition strong enough to dominate the European Continent and threaten Britain's security. Adams therefore unilaterally declared the Monroe Doctrine with every confidence that the British Navy would enforce it.

The underdeveloped countries of the world, with one or two important exceptions, have felt much as the United States did in that earlier period and for similar reasons. This policy of nonentanglement was dictated, in addition, by their lack of national cohesion. The divisive forces in the new nations are far stronger than they ever were in the early United States. Yet even that young republic had to be careful, for, quite apart from the strength of state and regional loyalties, the nation soon became bitterly divided between the Jeffersonian supporters of the French Revolution, who emphasized its democratic character, and their Federalist opponents, who stressed the Revolution's terror, bloodshed, and attack upon religion and property. Later, with the arrival of massive waves of immigrants in the nineteenth century, involvement in Europe's quarrels posed a more serious danger to the bonds of unity. Allegiances to the "old country" would have badly divided the country, as they tended to do even as late as the World War I period. The new citizens first had to be "nationalized," or "Americanized"; their sense of identification as Americans in fact depended upon alienation from— and opposition to—the Old World. Still, the United States, for all its internal schisms, was born as largely a middle-class society with capitalistic and democratic values. The new nations, as we have already seen, are less fortunate, because they suffer from intense class, religious, linguistic, ethnic, and racial differences of a kind and intensity that the American republic rarely experienced. Not surprisingly, therefore, these new nations generally flaunt their anticolonialism more vigorously than the United States ever did. Any demand on the Americans' part that these nations "stand up and be counted" by aligning themselves with their former masters in the West in return for aid funds is likely merely to force them into a coalition with the Russians.

The American position was also severely handicapped by the continued discrimination which prevented blacks from realizing their full measure of civil rights and equal opportunities in American society. To a world in which the vast majority of the population is nonwhite, the persisting segregationist practices and exploitation of blacks in the South and the North were flagrant violations of the democratic principles of freedom and human dignity so often proclaimed by the United States. The peoples of the underdeveloped areas not only claimed equal status as nations but also sought equality as human beings; when they heard about segregation in America, they could only be reminded of the old days when the white man had treated them as inferiors simply because of the color of their skins. This situation began to change during the Kennedy and Johnson Administrations, as blacks listened to Martin Luther King articulate their aspirations for a life of more dignity and full participation in American life, as the ghettos exploded, and as the government itself began to act by removing certain discriminatory practices against blacks, as well as providing greater opportunities in such areas as jobs and housing. However, racial problems continued to haunt the United States on the foreign front. In Rhodesia and South Africa, minority white-controlled governments determined to stay in power used abhorrent methods such as apartheid and the strictist police surveillance. The United States, despite its often expressed disapproval of these policies, did not follow through in its actions. Rhodesian chrome was still imported despite a U.N. embargo, and in South Africa American companies, although often providing their black workers with better working conditions and pay than local companies, continued to invest heavily. America, the world's first state to insist that all men were created equal, seemed all too often to say to the world that there was a qualifying phrase "except blacks."

One further attitude hampering U.S. relations with the developing states has been the American lack of sympathy for class struggle and social politics as somewhat alien to the United States. America has managed to avoid the kind of domestic conflicts over basic values that the countries of Europe experienced and that now plague many of the underdeveloped nations. Americans are, indeed, so overwhelmingly committed to middle-class values that divergences, real or apparent, are likely to be condemned as "un-American." "Americanism" is an absolute. Deviations are "sinful" and must be rooted out so that the "American way of life" will remain pure and unadulterated. The principal challenges to these values have until recently come not from within the system but from outside the U.S. borders, and the United

States has reacted to foreign threats—German, Japanese, Communist—in two ways: internally, by hunt for "subversives" that inevitably has infringed upon civil liberties and endangered the security of traditional freedoms; and externally (that is, up to the present Communist threat), by the total destruction of the hostile regime so that American principles could continue to live untainted. Thus, domestically, the Communist threat in the early 1950's led to McCarthyism, a search for heresy in which the goal of eliminating alleged un-American attitudes and behavior justified any means, including disregard for "due process of law," which is the basic guarantee of all civil liberties. At times, this hunt went to frightening lengths, as when the U.S. Information Agency actually burned "suspect" books—and, even worse, when the careers and lives of people were jeopardized and sometimes ruined. At other times, it became so ridiculous that it would have been funny if the implications had not been so frightening—as when a member of an Indiana school board suggested that *Robin Hood* be banned since it was obviously a "pro-Communist" book in which the hero took from the rich to give to the poor. In foreign policy, the reaction to the Communist threat to the American way of life was to support almost any "anti-Communist" regime. Thus, the United States associated itself with traditional regimes whose days were numbered because they had alienated mass support: Bao Dai in Indochina and King Faisal in Iraq were two such examples. The fact that these countries' governments were pro-American and anti-Communist qualified them in American eyes as "democratic," or at least potentially so; and by the same token, the United States opposed internal movements to overthrow them and condemned these as Communist or pro-Communist. This attitude was typical of American absolutism and inability to understand the deeper social struggles of Asia and the Middle East. In the attempt to contain Communism—that is, to preserve the global *status quo*—the United States became committed to the domestic, social, and political *status quo* in these countries. Thus America, in seeking stability, is paradoxically trying to preserve freedom by supporting ramshackle autocracies that are unrepresentative of their peoples' aspirations. But this internal contradiction within the U.S. alliance system must eventually resolve itself. American support for traditional regimes only bottles up the social and political resentment and ferment even more, thereby adding to the explosive forces that must someday burst forth and further upset the global balance of power.

Latin America is a good example of the manner in which U.S. foreign policy, even when realizing the need for development aid, becomes a prisoner of its own domestic experience. Much has been said in this country about Cuba as a base for subversion of other Latin nations. If such subversion were successful, this would constitute a great threat to the United States. But this possibility has to be seen within its proper context. Cuba may well be a Soviet foothold in the Western Hemisphere, but it is by identifying themselves with nationalist hopes and against social injustice that the Soviets could extend their penetration into America's own backyard—and thereby undermine the Monroe Doctrine. Possibilities of success for such penetration were enhanced by a number of factors: resentment against a history of past American interventions in the Caribbean and Central America; vast-scale private American capital investments and economic control of many Latin American economies; frequent American support for the privileged few who, usually closely linked to American capital, seek to preserve their position by ignoring social grievances and establishing right-wing military dictatorships; and finally, and above all, the sheer misery, grinding poverty, mass illiteracy, and constant hunger of the vast majority of the people, who, although they live in the countryside, are landless.

Latin America, in short, shares the two aspirations that are sweeping through all the underdeveloped areas: the urge for a better life for the mass of people who, dispossessed and exploited, are filled with deep and bitter social resentment; and the desire of countries to determine their own national destiny and become free of colonial rule—in this instance,

America's. The United States has exercised its colonial domination by indirect means, usually an alliance with the native aristocracy or wealthy and privileged governing class. The absence of direct political and military rule may have granted Americans the self-righteous belief that they were free of Europe's taint of colonialism, but it has not disguised this fact for Latin America. The Monroe Doctrine turned the southern part of the hemisphere into a U.S. sphere of influence; America did not have to resort to direct rule. Invested American capital spoke louder than guns; and political orders were unnecessary when a nation was a "banana republic" or an economic satellite. The economies of Latin American nations remained backward, undiversified, and agrarian; they therefore continued to depend for a livelihood on the export of one or two raw materials to the United States, their largest market. In good years, they earned money; in bad years, the normal measure of unemployment, poverty, and hunger increased. Their very lives depended on the fluctuations of the business cycle, as well as, of course, their obedience to American political wishes.

In these conditions, the success of Castroism depended on two factors. First, it would depend upon the Latin American governments themselves: whether they would undertake large-scale social and economic reforms or cling to their privileges; whether these privileged few were wise enough to understand the need for internal changes or whether they would prefer to commit suicide after fearfully clinging to their fading power for a few more years. Public pressure for change was rising. The only question was whether this change would be revolutionary or evolutionary. If the ruling classes remained as hostile to reform and as irresponsible toward public welfare as in the past, Castro would be able to export his revolution. For wherever there is social injustice, Castro—or Communists speaking through a Castro—will find receptive audiences. The destruction of the *ancien régime* will in these circumstances appear as the sole way of gaining a job, a piece of land, or enough food. Revolution and a "radical solution" will seem the only hope for a better life. But, even where governments will undertake social reforms, the danger of revolution will remain if the gap between the people's aspirations and their present miserable standards is not closed with sufficient speed. It was on this inability to remedy quickly the lot of the bulk of Latin America's population that Castro had placed his hopes for the future.

Second, the success of Castroism would depend on the effectiveness of an American policy directed toward alleviating the conditions that fostered popular resentment in Latin America. Whether America would be able to lead this revolution, however, was another matter. For it was a task that would require American support of non-Communist left-wing movements and acquiescence in the expropriation of American property —both rather difficult in view of the false but popular identification of democratic "socialism" with revolutionary Communism, and because of the powerful influence in government of American industry and capital, which stood to lose their investments and cheap raw materials. Moreover, the United States would have to inject into the Latin American economies billions of dollars of primarily public capital in order to help them achieve a self-sustaining rate of economic growth, to develop conditions in which private capital would be attracted to projects other than raw materials such as oil or iron ore, and to aid in the transformation of backward societies into modern, urbanized, industrial nations. Latin America's projected 50 per cent increase of population during the next twenty-five years—approximately 90 million people— only underlined the urgency of this developmental task. In the absence of an adequate effort, the already far too low standard of living would deteriorate even more. This could only ensure the success of future radical revolutions and the complete alienation of Latin America from the United States. Effective economic aid, in short, would require a towering effort, even greater than that made in postwar Europe. For the task in Europe was to reconstruct a continent shattered by war; but the resources, the skills, and the industries were already there. These were all absent from the Latin American nations. Europe was also a modern society; the Latin American nations were largely agrarian, and their traditional ways had to be uprooted and their entire societies transformed.

It was to meet the challenge of the Latin American "revolution of rising expectations" that President Kennedy, soon after assuming office, called for an Alliance for Progress between the United States and the nations of the south. He pledged $20 billion of primarily public capital over the next decade to Latin America and, even more significantly, placed great emphasis upon the need for social politics. In the absence of the necessary reforms, he realized, the possibilities of economic and political development were slight. The Alliance, in short, was a post-Castro attempt to abort any future Castros.

Would the ruling oligarchies, however, surrender their power, status, and prestige, or commit themselves to fundamental reforms? In the words of a veteran observer of the Latin American scene, Herbert L. Matthews:

> In the whole of Latin America, the rich are getting richer and the poor poorer. This is the worst, the most difficult and the most dangerous feature of the area. The Alliance for Progress was created primarily to tackle this essentially social problem, but social imbalances (as the United States is discovering in the case of segregation) are devilishly hard to correct.
>
> The most serious feature of this problem centers around agriculture and land reform. The frantic urge to industrialize that seized Latin America after the Second World War was, in part, satisfied at the expense of the agrarian sector. Yet virtually all the countries are from half to three-quarters agricultural. Latin exports are overwhelmingly agricultural and mineral.
>
> The abnormal and dangerous urbanization, caused by the flight of impoverished peasants from the rural areas to the urban centers, has led to some of the largest cities in the world and some of the worst slums. Countries with plenty of land were, and are, importing food at high cost.
>
> Most landowners are resisting the reforms that their governments and the Alliance for Progress desire. . . . Much will depend on whether the ruling classes see the need to make drastic structural reforms. Much, also, will depend on the state of the world and the world markets for raw materials, not to mention

the ability of the United States to invest and to aid. The rise of dynamic revolutionary leaders is always possible—not another Fidel Castro, who is *sui generis,* but Latin America has always been a region where personalism plays a great role.

There are revolutions and revolutions. The fascist-military type in Latin America comes from the right; the socialistic-communistic from the left; and in between is the sort of peaceful, voluntary, gradual but genuine type of revolution which the Alliance for Progress is trying to promote.

Latin America is such a dynamic area of the world that it is bound to have revolutions. The only unknown factor is: what kind?*

The most likely type would seem to be that of the radical right or left if, as seems to be the case, the oligarchy continues to be concerned less with Castroism than with the loss of its privileges. Furthermore, the oligarchy knows from past experience that the United States will continue to extend aid irrespective of demanded reforms: first to protect private corporate investments, and second, out of fear of any revolution which, rightly or wrongly, is labeled as Communist or Castro-supported.

The paralysis imposed on the Alliance by Castro was abundantly illustrated at the time of the Dominican intervention. The background for this event was the overthrow in 1961 of the cruel thirty-one-year-old Dominican dictatorship of Rafael Trujillo. Following a brief intervening period of political turmoil, Juan Bosch, a man of genuinely democratic convictions, had been elected to the office of President. Seven months later, Bosch was overthrown by a military *coup d'état* whose leaders announced that they would re-establish a "rightist state." In April, 1965, the pro-Bosch forces revolted against this right-wing military government. But the leadership of this revolution swung increasingly, according to Washington, in a Communist direction. Communists were thought to be active in the anti-junta movement, and Washington feared they would gain control of the pro-Bosch forces and that the result would be a second Cuba in the hemi-

* The *New York Times,* March 15, 1965.

sphere. The rebels claimed that while some Communists might support their movement, their revolution was led by non-Communists who only sought a return to constitutional government. President Johnson, however, ordered American intervention before the evidence was clear that the revolution was in fact Communist-controlled—even though this action would once more raise the old specter of American intervention, so common in the days before Franklin Roosevelt's "Good Neighbor" policy. But in 1965 the problem was that the U.S. fear of a Communist capture of the Bosch movement would lead Washington to intervene on behalf of a right-wing military junta. In short, the United States would be siding with the very forces who supported the *status quo* and opposed the Alliance for Progress. At the same time, by opposing the non-Communist element in the revolt, which enjoyed widespread popular support in the Dominican Republic, Washington might drive many Latin Americans into a militantly anti-American direction. If the United States were willing to risk intervening and alienating the people whose support was needed for the Alliance for Progress, it might at least have waited to see if the "Castro-Communists," as Washington called them, would capture the pro-Bosch movement. If it were in America's interest to avoid the establishment of a second Cuba, a firmer case for intervention would then have been laid; it might even have diminished the criticism and consequences of such an action.

What the Dominican intervention did in fact demonstrate was that the Alliance for Progress continued to be haunted by the Cuban leader. Castro was responsible both for the Alliance and for its failures. Without him, there would have been no large-scale effort to develop Latin America. But also the U.S. fear that any Latin revolution would be a Communist revolution requiring preventive action would not have sprung up without Castro. American policy, in Latin America as in other areas of the world, thus continued into the middle 1960's to be motivated by a bipolar image of the world. Nowhere was this to be more evident than in South Vietnam and the American interpretation of the nature of that war and the reasons for the American intervention. Also, no experience could more searingly and searchingly have compelled the country to reassess its foreign policy and note that bipolarity was itself in the process of change.

Was U.S. Third World Policy Imperialistic?

Especially since the American involvement in the Vietnam war, some radical writers, often referred to as the New Left, have said that American actions as in Cuba and the Dominican Republic were hardly accidental; nor was the failure to provide meaningful economic aid for the modernization of the new nations a mere oversight. Indeed, this line of argument maintains, while these nations may have been new in the sense of formal political independence, they were in reality economically controlled by the dominant economy in the "global capitalist system," the U.S. economy; the so-called new and independent nations thus in fact remained colonies. "Neo-colonialism" was the term popularly used to refer to their alleged status. Whereas in European eighteenth- and nineteenth-century colonialism the European state had usually invaded a piece of territory and established direct rule of the newly acquired colony, American imperialism in the contemporary age of nationalism controlled its colonial appendages through less visible but equally binding economic chains: corporate investments, economic aid, and the needs of the Third World countries for advanced technology and for markets in which to sell their raw materials. And, of course, the U.S.-supported reactionary political and social elites who survived only with American backing which, when necessary, was supplemented with American training and arming of local police and military forces, CIA bribes, subsidies for private armies, and all sorts of "dirty tricks," including assassinations and *coups d'état*.

Why all this bother about the poor countries of the world? Because they are, according to this radical critique, extremely profitable. They are sources of cheap raw materials to stoke

Western industry; they constitute potentially sizable markets for Western goods; and they provide places for the investment of private capital at large returns. Capitalist economies like that of the United States, the leading Western capitalist state, constantly need profits; without them, unemployment would increase, standards of living decline, and the struggle between capitalists and those who worked for them resume. This struggle is muted when some of the enormous profits reaped by the capitalists trickled down to the workers in the form of higher wages and living standards, thereby drawing their revolutionary fangs and winning their support for capitalism. In short, even with the best of intentions, America as the guardian of Western capitalism could not surrender its "neocolonial control" over the less developed states. It was structurally necessary; if capitalism was to be preserved and social revolution avoided, the Third World countries had to be maintained as dependencies and raw material suppliers. Hence the American pursuit of counterrevolutionary and interventionist policies.

In fact, the economically imperialist interpretation of postwar American foreign policy is testimony to the significance of faith and attitudes over facts. Little evidence supports such a purely economic interpretation. The vast bulk of American private investments has been made in the American economy; and of the approximately 5–6 per cent of American investment that was made abroad, most, even at the height of the Vietnam war in 1968, went to Western Europe, Canada, and Japan. In short, investment in non-Western economies was hardly significant for the welfare of the American economy. In trade, the pattern was identical. The United States trades primarily with the other industrial countries. They have something to sell to each other. Again, the Third World states are not essential to the well-being of the American economy. It is primarily in the area of natural resources that the dependency argument carries a degree of plausibility, for clearly America, like other Western industries, needs raw materials. But even here the case is far from persuasive. Substitutes, alternative raw materials, the domestic availability of a vast ar-

ray of raw materials in fact make the country far less dependent upon the Third World than the imperialist interpretation
would suggest. (Admittedly, the cost of materials from domestic sources will be higher than from the less-developed
countries, although not necessarily higher than the prices
these countries hope to demand or, in the case of oil, are already receiving.) The United States, in fact, possesses most of
the raw materials it needs, including energy resources, especially coal.

What is equally clear is that the imperialist interpretation
which suggests that capitalist countries either exercise control
of Third World economies in order to make a profit, or have
no control which leads to a collapse of capitalist economies,
could not be more wrong. The Western states that, since
1945, have achieved the highest rates of economic growth are
countries like Japan, West Germany, and those of Scandina-
via, states that obviously had no colonies and that exercised
no "control" over non-Western countries. They bought what
they needed. Imperialist control was completely unnecessary
for these states with "capitalist" economies; indeed, such control was inversely related to their prosperity. It was former
colonial states like Great Britain and the last colonial state of
all, Portugal, whose economies fared the worst of all Western
economies. Thus, domination of the underdeveloped countries for the purpose of having access to their raw materials is
not required. Indeed, and no doubt disillusioning to the New
Left critics who would like the Third World countries to
withhold their resources to bring down American capitalism,
these nations, radical or not, sell their resources to all Western countries—if the price is right.

But to return to the main point: The picture of the United
States controlling Arab oil countries or even Latin American
states is ludicrous. As became clear in 1973 with the Oil Producing Exporting Countries' (OPEC) fourfold increase of oil
prices, and should have been clear even before that historic
date, the Third World, country after country, has been ex-
propriating American investments and property. Nationalization has been the trend in this age of nationalism, and there is

little that can be done about it except to acquiesce and officially protest—but not too heavily—and seek some compensation for the expropriated industry. But the United States does not send marines in or overthrow governments to save a corporation's sugar fields or banana crops or to lower oil prices. Economic and other pressures, as well as covert operations and overt interventions, have been resorted to only where the government in Washington perceived the stakes to be far broader than simple expropriation—that is, where the stakes were not simply those of corporate property, indeed where the stakes were perceived to be far broader than merely economic ones. In Guatemala in 1954, in Cuba in 1961, in the Dominican Republic in 1965 (and later, as we shall see, in Chile in the early 1970's), the American government intervened—even if, as in Cuba, unsuccessfully—because it viewed the governments in these countries and their international orientation in the context of cold war bipolarity. All these countries seemed to be slipping into or aligning themselves with the Soviet camp. This appearance, which led to the U.S. interventions, may have been in error, but, it needs to be noted, it is not one that stems from an *a priori* anti-left or anti-Socialist animus; the United States has allied itself and cooperated with Democratic Socialist or Labor party governments in many countries, especially in Europe, as well as with non-democratic Communist regimes in countries such as Yugoslavia and China.

American policy in the Middle East is probably the strongest refutation of the imperialist interpretation. If the corporate capitalists did indeed control Washington, it is impossible to understand why the United States has since 1948 so strongly supported Israel, alienated most Arab states, jeopardized access to the oil needed so badly by Europe and increasingly by America, and risked the nationalization of Western oil companies (almost everywhere now controlled, even if not yet totally owned, by OPEC). In fact, what this policy shows is that economic considerations, if present and important, are not at all necessarily predominant in the making of the nation's foreign policy. If only the United States did control Saudi Arabia, Iran, Kuwait, and Venezuela! (In fact, if the imperialist theory *were* correct, the Western industrial states would be in the process of becoming the colonial appendages of OPEC.) American motivations in foreign policy must be sought elsewhere than in the economic realm, primarily in security considerations and fear of Russian power and the identification after 1946–47 of the expansion of Russian power with the expansion of Communism. In a bipolar era of two relatively cohesive alliances, NATO and the Sino-Soviet alliance, this identification was easy to understand, even if it was not always correct.

8

THE AMERICAN EMPIRE

Peace-Keeping in the "Provinces"

The world that emerged from World War II and dominated most of the twenty years from 1945 to 1965 was bipolar. The United States and the Soviet Union, plus their allies, confronted one another directly and globally. In a series of crises, they drew the "frontiers" between their worlds and extended their competition to the Third World. This bipolar world was very dangerous, because the distribution of power in the state system between two poles is extremely sensitive. Both are constantly alert to the slightest shifts in power lest they upset the equilibrium and give one adversary a superiority of power. Each side perceives a gain of power and security for one as a loss of power and security for the other. Each views the opponent's moves, even if alleged to be defensive, as deliberate and offensive; and moves in areas of secondary importance are ranked as significant and countered because they are seen as symbolically vital. Drawing "frontiers" around spheres of interest deemed essential to each state's security, and then guarding this territorial *status quo* against encroachment, subversion, or defection becomes the heart of bipolar competition.

It was through this competitive process that the United States became what some critics called a "world policeman." Others referred to its role as "imperial." Quite distinct from the term "imperialist" with its attribution of economic motivation, they referred to the extensive role a Great Power plays when, stronger than its allies, the responsibility of preserving the balance of power in the system falls largely on it. "In this sense," Raymond Aron has said, "a bipolar system inevitably requires an imperial diplomacy on the part of each of [the] two superpowers designed to limit its rival's expansion." Through a process of challenge and response America had become involved in all continents of the world and, motivated by political, rather than economical goals, acquired an "empire" primarily around the Sino-Soviet periphery. Thus initially in the Eastern Mediterranean and Western Europe, then in Asia and Middle East and, to varying degrees, in Africa and Latin America, Washington reacted to what it saw as Soviet and/or Chinese attempts to exploit power vacuums, intraregional conflicts, and differences between Western countries and the Third World with what Kennan described as "long-term, patient, firm, and vigilant containment." As a result, the United States, the formerly isolationist nation which felt that no quarrels anywhere affected its security, became the world power that became involved everywhere.

The second characteristic of the American empire was the continuous peace-keeping operation to protect its "frontiers." Strategic deterrence was the principal means of preventing a major incursion anywhere, such as in Western Europe, or a strike against the empire's center, the continental United States. Limited challenges were met by a variety of means: nuclear blackmail by a mixture of military and diplomatic means, and actual frontier crossings by "frontier wars."

As a third distinguishing feature of this empire, these limited challenges normally have taken place at the farthest point from the center. This is, of course, where frontiers meet and where the opponent finds it easiest to cause trouble and the defender is likely to show the least resolution. The frontier is far away and may not seem clearly related to the security interests of the center; it is also nearer to the opponent, and its defense therefore may involve a big fight— indeed, such peripheral involvement may seem like an overextension of the center's power, which, it will be claimed, is not only dangerous but also expensive and unnecessary. Yet these frontiers have been guarded by the Roman Legions of our time—the American armed forces. The foreign policy of the imperial power is fundamentally one of filling holes in the dike. When the occasions have arisen in the ex-colonial areas of the world, the two superpowers have agreed to allow U.N. forces, staffed primarily by nonaligned members, to keep the peace in order to avoid a clash between themselves.

As a fourth and key characteristic of the empire, its preservation has been perceived by the center as depending upon its will. The belief is that deterrence, both total and limited, requires that the opponent believe that the center will honor its commitments. It follows that if commitments to maintain a particular frontier are no longer credible—no matter how distant or unimportant this frontier may seem to some—the hostile "empire" may come to believe that other frontiers too may be crossed with impunity. It may be true that one frontier is less vital than another, but how is the opponent to know which one? Yielding a less important part of the empire may tempt the opponent to test the center's will in an area the latter considers more significant, since he cannot know whether the center, having shown a lack of will to defend one part of the empire, may consider another frontier more significant and show a greater determination to defend it. The failure to honor a commitment in one area may then be seen by the adversary as an indication that another commitment elsewhere may also not be honored. Thus, a commitment, whether eagerly sought or reluctantly accepted, becomes a matter from which it is presumably virtually impossible to withdraw without disastrous consequences.

This is because, fifth, the empire is recognized as such in the "provinces." The latter know that their defense depends upon the center, and they are therefore constantly alert to signs of a weakening will. The provinces on the periphery, precisely because they are keenly aware of their geographic location and know that the defense of their security may at times seem either hazardous or unimportant to the imperial power, will live in a continuous state of apprehension lest they be left undefended; if they are, they may well consider approaching the opponent and bargaining for the best terms possible. As President Kennedy said with regard to Soviet policy on Berlin: It was designed to neutralize West Germany as a first step toward the neutralization of Western Europe.

If the United States did not meet its commitments in the divided city, it would mean the destruction of NATO and a resulting dangerous situation for the whole world. All of Europe was at stake in West Berlin. Yet, the fact that the provinces constantly look to the center for protection does not mean that they regard all imperial frontiers as of equal significance. On the contrary: Those in their particular area take priority. Fearful that the center's power may become committed and perhaps weakened elsewhere, they oppose (as Europe has repeatedly done when America became involved in Asia) the defense of other regional frontiers.

The final characteristic of the imperial power has been that it commands and trains its foreign legions. NATO, always commanded by an American, has a highly centralized command and integrated forces; only one of the provinces, France, has pulled its forces out while remaining nonetheless dependent upon the United States for its basic defense. When several of the provinces show concern for their self-protection by building nuclear forces for purported use in those situations they deem vital even if the center should regard them of secondary interest not "worth" a total war, the imperial power either seeks to gain control of these forces (Britain's) or opposes their development (France). The provinces are not to decide when the empire will defend its interests and risk military conflict; these are for the imperial center to decide. The United States also trained soldiers from non-Western states, some in America, some by sending military missions to their countries. Indeed, after Vietnam, since America is unlikely to fight another protracted conflict with its own ground forces, this burden is likely to be shifted to native troops if areas important to American security are attacked—presuming a future President is even willing to become involved after the nation's searing experience in Vietnam.

Vietnam as a "Frontier War"

The United States became involved in the war in Southeast Asia because, first of all, it was a frontier war. The issue, as Eugene Rostow of the State Department has written,

> . . . is to maintain the policy which former Ambassador George Kennan, 18 years ago, first labeled "Containment." Kennan's idea—that of mutual respect for the frontiers of the Communist and free worlds—is a necessary if not a sufficient condition of Peaceful Coexistence. It implies that we halt aggression at the boundaries of the Cold War as we did in Greece, Korea and Berlin, in the natural hope that the passage of time will reduce the danger of general war. It has been a demanding and wearisome policy. But it has kept the Cold War within tolerable limits and has helped to preserve nuclear peace.
>
> In Indochina the North Vietnamese government has broken the first and most basic rule of Peaceful Coexistence: That the frontiers of the two systems not be altered unilaterally, or by military action. To cite a clear parallel, it has been deemed self-evident in Washington and in Moscow that it would be unthinkably dangerous for either East Germany or West Germany to attack the other, either openly or through infiltration. Yet what North Vietnam, with Chinese backing, is attempting in Indochina—to conquer a country the United States has agreed to protect—is the precise analogue of such a hypothetical German conflict, or of the Korean war of 1950–53, or of the Soviet Union's early postwar probes against Greece, Turkey and Iran.

Second, it was a war fought at a great distance from the center, in a place where the frontier was very accessible to the enemy. South Vietnam was a badly divided society: refugees (approximately 1 million, about half of them Catholic) against indigenous South Vietnamese; Buddhists against Catholics; lowlanders against *montagnards*; and peasants against urban inhabitants. Loyalties were, as in most new nations, primarily local. Hostility to a central government was deeply ingrained since, as in most underdeveloped countries, the government historically has been that of the colonial power, as represented by the tax collector and recruiting sergeant. Transportation and communication were primitive and industrial development nonexistent. In addition, this was a new state that had emerged from the 1954 Geneva conference concluding the First Indochina War between France and the Vietminh forces, with no established political institutions and a precarious economy. Not surprisingly, the Vietminh expected South Vietnam to collapse: The Geneva agreement called for a general election to be held in 1956, and it was assumed by Hanoi that a majority of the 12 million South Vietnamese would vote for the man who had led the nationalist struggle against the French, Ho Chi Minh (who obviously could have delivered most of the North's 15 million votes). Thus the country would be reunited under Communist control.

It was for this reason that neither the United States nor the new Diem government in the South favored the election; the former wanted the 17th parallel to be accepted as the new frontier, and Diem, a fervent Catholic and anti-Communist, was not about to eliminate himself. Their opposition was decisive, irrespective of the issue as to whether the unsigned Geneva declaration about the election was politically binding. Thus Hanoi's chances for a peaceful takeover of the South ended, and so did its stance of reasonableness and restraint. At the time of the Geneva settlement, approximately 5,000–6,000 local hard-core guerrillas, presumably the Vietminh's political and military elite, went underground and became anonymous peasants. About 90,000 others went north. Within a few months, the guerrillas who had stayed in the South began to murder village chiefs. The Second Indochina War had started; the immediate guerrilla objective was to isolate the central government from the majority of its population and substitute Vietcong control over the peasantry by killing the government's local representatives.

This war, in short, started in quite a different manner from the Korean War. Korea had begun with a clear-cut, aggressive attack which aroused the American public and united the principal Western allies against the common threat. It had also been a conventional war in which regular Communist forces had been checked by regular South Korean, American, and U.N. troops. By contrast, Dienbienphu had been a decisive moment in contemporary history, for, apart from defeating France and throwing off French colonial shackles, the battle demonstrated that *guerrilla warfare* could defeat the larger, stronger, conventionally equipped army of even a major power. It also showed that nuclear weapons would be useless in countering the tactics of such a war. An internal uprising by guerrillas, directed and organized by the North, was therefore a shrewder manner of "crossing" the 17th parallel. It would lend the resulting struggle the aura of a civil war, which, if taken at face value by the United States and the West, would paralyze any united response and cause domestic doubt about the morality and wisdom of fighting in such a conflict—at least long enough for the guerrillas to win. Diem's increasingly autocratic rule and his failure to enlist the support of his population, especially the peasantry, through political, social, and economic reforms prepared the ground for a successful guerrilla campaign and lent support to the view of the conflict as a civil war.

Yet the war was seen in Washington as a test of the center's will, which was so necessary to maintain all frontiers. The Asian balance depended upon the United States until the non-Communist states of the area became economically developed and possessed sufficient capabilities of their own. Commitments—and the administrations of Presidents Eisenhower, Kennedy, and Johnson all considered the United States to be committed to the defense of South Vietnam—were interdependent. The United States could not choose to defend West Berlin and Quemoy but not Matsu and South Korea (an American protégé which did not even have a formal treaty of defense with the United States). Washington, as the imperial nucleus, could no more forgo the defense of the frontier in South Vietnam than in Greece and Turkey, in Western Europe and Berlin, or in Korea and Cuba. One did not need to subscribe to President Eisenhower's domino theory that if one country fell it would, in its turn, knock down the next one and so on down the line, to know that the political and psychological impact of an American pullout would be severe. In the words of a man who was not a hawk and is extremely knowledgeable in Asian politics, Edwin Reischauer, former U.S. Ambassador to Japan:

> While there is extreme disapproval of our Vietnam policies in much of the world, this is not true in several of the countries closest to Vietnam. There is, in fact, strong approval in Thailand, Laos, the Philippines, Taiwan and South Korea; and in several other Southeast and South Asian lands, there is a considerable degree of quiet support, masked either by discreet silence or by an official stance of mild condemnation. Many of these countries are themselves unstable and either fear the sort of internal subversion that has torn South Vietnam apart or are apprehensive about the intentions of their great Chinese Communist neighbor and suspicious of the loyalties of the sometimes sizable populations within their borders. They would feel much less secure if the United States, after having committed itself to the fight, were forced to admit defeat at the hands of Communist insurgents. In fact, *such an outcome of the Vietnam war would send a massive psychological tremor through all these countries, further threatening their stability and perhaps sharply shifting their present international orientation.* [Italics added.]
>
> Conversely, all those who hope for Communist takeovers in the less developed countries of the world, whether in Asia or elsewhere, would receive a shot in the arm. America's defeat in Vietnam would seem to be proof positive of the Maoist doctrine that what the Communists call "wars of national liberation" are irresistible. It would be far better proof than Ho Chi Minh's victory over the French in North Vietnam, or the Communist triumph in China, or the sweep of communism in the wake of the Soviet Army in North Korea and East Europe, because in none of these cases was the military power of the United States directly involved. . . . The possibility that Communist insurgency will develop or succeed in other Asian lands depends, primarily, on internal conditions in each country, but a clear-cut defeat of the United States in the Vietnam war would certainly be one external factor that could have a seriously adverse influence on this situation.

In short, a North Vietnamese victory and American withdrawal would be widely recognized in the "provinces" as a failure of will by the imperial power. China's and Vietnam's neighbors would very probably detach themselves from the United States and seek friendlier relations with China, as Cambodia did when, as a result of Laos's neutralization in 1962, Communist power approached Cambodia. For they would be recognizing the inability or unwillingness of the United States to maintain an Asian balance, and therefore the worthlessness of American commitments.

The Misconduct of Counterguerrilla Conflict

During the Kennedy and Johnson administrations, justifications for an increasing military commitment to South Vietnam were made in terms of America's global responsibilities for maintaining the general peace and stability of the international system. Despite this, the wisdom of the policy was debatable. During his years as President, Kennedy sent 16,500 military advisers; Johnson, beginning in the spring of 1965, augmented this number to more than 500,000. Particularly significant during the years of piecemeal commitments was that at no point did policy-makers in Washington ever sit down, take time, and ask themselves some fundamental questions about Vietnam: Was it vital to American security interests and, if so, how vital? Could the situation in South Vietnam be saved militarily, given the nature of the Saigon government and its seeming lack of popular support? If American forces should be sent, in what numbers? And how could they be effectively used in an unorthodox type of war? What cost, if any, was South Vietnam "worth"? As incremental commitments were made whenever conditions in South Vietnam appeared ominous, these questions continued to be avoided. During the Kennedy period, military advisers managed to prevent total collapse, but by 1965 his successor —who had spent his time since Kennedy's assassination passing a major domestic reform program and getting re-elected —could no longer operate on this basis and avoid the central question of what the United States ought to do. South Vietnam was about to be cut in two, and the Vietcong would then be in a position to mop up first one part, then the other. In the face of this reality, Johnson sent in 200,000 troops that year, extending U.S. involvement and turning an incremental policy into a long-term commitment. After years and years of neglect and procrastination and with the situation growing worse daily, Washington had neither the time nor the inclination to make a carefully calculated basic decision; when the crucial decision was made, it was made by a new President—whose primary interest, experience, and skill were domestic—on the advice of the Kennedy staff and Cabinet he had inherited. Long-range policy had thus become the prisoner of a number of prior short-range decisions that had been made to tackle immediately critical problems.

The key to the successful deployment of American arms— the political structure of South Vietnam—was virtually ignored. For years, the United States had supported Ngo Dinh Diem, whose increasingly authoritarian rule and aloofness from his people had alienated most of them. By the time the military overthrew Diem, with Kennedy's knowledge and tacit blessing, the Vietcong already controlled much of South Vietnam; the social, political, and economic reforms needed to win the war had for too long been disregarded. The very fact the United States acquiesced in the coup against Diem should have alerted future administrations; that Kennedy had himself said Diem had "gotten out of touch with the people" testified to the political bankruptcy in Saigon, as well as to the questionable wisdom of having begun the military commitments in the first place. Diem's successor governments proved no more able to rally popular support for a vigorous prosecution of the war against the Vietcong. Saigon's succession of corrupt, reactionary, and repressive regimes apparently never reawakened thoughts in the minds of U.S. policy-makers of Chiang Kai-shek and his Nationalist government in postwar China. The Truman Administration at the time had decided China could not be saved, except perhaps—and it was only *perhaps*—at an enormous military and economic cost, which it felt the American public would not be willing to pay and which would, in addition, have diverted the nation's resources and efforts from its area of primary interest in Europe where these could be productively used to enhance American security. In Secretary Acheson's words at the time: "Nothing that this country did or could have done within the *reasonable* limits of its capabilities" could have changed the result in the conflict between Mao and Chiang [italics added]. In short, containment could not be affected through a sieve. By attempting it in South Vietnam, Truman's successor Democratic administrations were in fact risking major domestic discontent. They were also risking a public questioning of the fundamental assumptions of American postwar foreign policy; if these administrations could not win (and quickly at that) the limited war in which they were involving the nation, they were likely to make it impossible for any future administration to engage in such wars; even more, they were likely to endanger the "imperial policy" itself by undermining its assumptions.

And the possibility of achieving a quick victory over the Vietcong was remote, for a guerrilla war is anything but the traditional type of Western warfare. Its aim is to capture the power of the government from within, and to do so by eroding the morale of the army and by undermining popular confidence in the government. To achieve this objective, it is necessary neither to inflict complete defeat on the government's forces nor to compel them to surrender unconditionally. Indeed, until the final stage of the war, guerrillas do not even meet these forces openly, and then they do so only to apply the *coup de grâce*. Guerrilla forces fight a guerrilla war because they are compelled to; in the initial phases, they are the weaker side militarily. Guerrilla war is therefore a protracted conflict in which the guerrillas resort to hit-and-run tactics—here, there, everywhere—and engage only those smaller and weaker government forces they can defeat. In order to cope with such tactics, year in and year out, the government troops must be dispersed to guard every town, every hamlet, and every bridge against possible attack. Unable to come to real grips with the enemy and impose a heavy defeat upon him as in a conventional and set battle, suffering defeat after defeat, however small, the army is subject to great loss of morale and its mood becomes defensive.

Although such tactics gradually weaken the military strength of the army, the guerrillas' main effort remains directed at the civilian population. As they are the weaker side, the guerrillas' principal aim becomes one of wresting the allegiance of the population from the government. Without popular support, the government will simply collapse. The guerrillas proceed to do this in two ways. First, by their increasing control of the countryside, where the vast majority of the population live, and by their defeats of government forces, they demonstrate to the peasants that the government cannot protect them. The execution of the village headmen, who are generally government representatives, and of any persons who may have helped the government forces proves this most vividly. Second, and even more important, the guerrillas exploit any existing popular grievances. Communist guerrillas do not pose as Communists, and they do not receive popular support because they are Communists. The populace will support them because it believes the guerrillas will oust the government with which it is dissatisfied and that a new government will meet its aspirations. Mao Tse-tung has said that guerrillas need the people as fish need water; without popular support, the guerrillas would not receive recruits, food, shelter, and, above all, information on the government forces' disposition. Thus, in contrast to conventional warfare, in which each army seeks the destruction of the other's military forces, in guerrilla warfare the guerrillas seek to win the support of the people. A government that has the allegiance of its population does not provide fertile soil for guerrillas; the outbreak of guerrilla warfare is therefore one indication that a government is unpopular. The guerrillas gain the support of the peasantry because they successfully represent themselves as the liberators from colonialism or foreign rule, native despotic governments, economic deprivation, or social injustice.

Counterguerrilla war is therefore not a purely military war, but a political war as well. While the defeat of guerrillas in the field must be vigorously pursued, the principal task is to tackle the political, social, and economic conditions that bred the support for the guerrillas. Fundamentally, counterguerrilla warfare is therefore an extremely difficult and sophisticated form of war to wage—far more so than the traditional clash of armies—because the war cannot be won without thoroughgoing reforms. Yet these have to be carried out in the midst of battle. Such a war is also likely to take years; five to ten years is not at all out of the ordinary. And finally, it takes approximately fifteen counterguerrilla fighters to one guerrilla—in short, a sizable army, and one trained not in conventional fighting but in counterguerrilla tactics. What all this means is that the United States will find such wars extremely difficult to fight. America likes its wars "strictly military." A war that is concerned primarily with social and political reforms—and thus opens itself up to all the usual domestic criticisms of "socialistic," "pro-Communist," and "do-gooder" reforms—runs completely counter to the American approach. Its length would also cause great frustration, because the United States likes to get its "boys home by Christmas"; not a lengthy, drawn-out affair, but a quick and happy ending à la Hollywood is the American way of fighting. If this new kind of warfare did not yield swift and successful results, the American temptation would be either to pull out or to seek a short-cut to victory by purely military action.

American policy-makers, however, misplaced their confidence in the nation's military prowess and its ability to change the guerrillas' "rules of the game." In 1965, the illusion of American omnipotence had not yet died. Had not the United States successfully confronted the Soviet Union in Cuba and compelled it to back down? Could there really be much doubt that its well-trained generals in command of armies equipped with the newest and latest weapons from America's industry and under the leadership of that most efficient Pentagon manager, Secretary of Defense McNamara, could beat a few thousand "peasants in black pajamas"? Could America not, with its sizable forces and its superior mobility and firepower, find the enemy's troops and destroy them, compelling that enemy to desist from taking over South Vietnam? Characteristically, then, the principal emphasis was strictly military.

In a war that required forces to secure villages and to stay there in order to root out the Vietcong cells and possibly give Saigon the opportunity to prove to the villagers that "their" government did care for them, the military carried out massive search-and-destroy operations. The guerrillas, even when defeated (as they usually were when they were found), returned after the helicopters had left and continued to control the countryside. Since such large-scale operations could hardly be launched without preparation at the base camp and were usually preceded by airstrikes and artillery bombardments of the area in which the troops would land, the Vietcong generally disappeared and the whole operation ended in frustration.

The American military clearly did not understand the political nature of counterguerrilla war. They had been trained for conventional battle and their strategy was to bring maximum fire power to bear, even when, for example, by destroying a village from which a few shots had apparently been fired, they alienated the villagers without whose support the war could not be won. The government, too, tended to become increasingly enamored of the military approach—probably because the political nature of the war remained so elusive and difficult to grasp. The military "kill" thus became the prime aim, because that seemed tangible and attainable. The war was also extended by air to the North. The purpose in the beginning was clearly not primarily military. Guerrillas can live off the land and capture many of their weapons from their enemies; and, in any case, the sustained American attacks on Chinese supply lines in North Korea during the Korean War had shown that air power alone was unable to stop the flow of supplies to the fighting zone. The aim of the attacks was political—to persuade North Vietnam to call a halt to the war. The gradual extension of these attacks was intended to stress the fact that the United

States meant to protect South Vietnam and would not withdraw; that the price Hanoi might have to pay for victory would be disproportionally costly, and therefore that it had better desist. But the bombing did not weaken Hanoi's will to prosecute the war, cut the supplies sufficiently to hamper the fighting in the South, or greatly reduce troop infiltration. This, in turn, led to increased military and political calls for *more* air strikes and against new targets. It was not that air power could not by itself win the war; rather, it could win the war only if it were used with maximum efficiency. Air power, in short, came to be seen by some as an immaculate way of fighting the enemy, of efficiently inflicting great destruction on him, throttling his supply lines, breaking his morale, and finally compelling him to seek an end to the conflict.

This objective, however, remained unattainable. Even the more stable Thieu-Ky military regime, which sought to legitimate itself in the election of 1967, failed to implement a program of social and economic reform; it was particularly remiss in not carrying out a necessary redistribution of land from the usually absentee landlord to the peasant. Without such reforms, the ground could not be cut out from under the Vietcong. Militarily, every increase of American forces was met by increased infiltration of both guerrillas and conventional troops from the North to the South. Nevertheless, optimistic battle reports and forecasts of victory were frequent. It was the 1968 Tet (or Vietnamese New Year) offensive that was to be the Johnson Administration's Dienbienphu. Tet showed once and for all—and Americans could see it nightly on their television sets—that, despite the repeated optimistic predictions of the past, the enemy had again been badly underestimated. He had launched a major countrywide offensive and penetrated Saigon, Hué, and every other provincial capital; a Vietcong squad had even penetrated the American Embassy compound, thereby scoring a significant symbolic victory. Above all, the Vietcong had clearly demonstrated that neither an American Army of a half-million men nor Saigon and its vastly larger army could give the people living in the urban areas security—and the Communists already controlled much of the countryside.

American power and its effectiveness in unorthodox warfare were revealed as greatly exaggerated. Tactically, American forces had seized and retained the offensive, claiming the destruction of large numbers of enemy soldiers, but strategically the Vietcong had maintained the upper hand. The Americans were still very much on the defensive and, by using about 80 per cent of their forces to find and destroy North Vietnamese troops in the relatively unpopulated central highlands and frontier regions, were unable to secure *and* protect the 90 per cent of the population living in the Mekong Delta and coastal plains. The pursuit of victory through attrition clearly could not be transformed into military and, especially, political advantages. Indeed, in question was not just America's protective capacity but also its wisdom. Having left the cities unprotected, except for elements of the South Vietnamese Army (Tet revealed Saigon's impotence dramatically), allied forces then had to fight their way back into the hearts of the various cities and towns the Vietcong had infiltrated. If, after almost three years of American help, South Vietnam was still that insecure and the enemy that strong, the wisdom of continuing the war, let alone sending further American reinforcements, was bound to be intensely debated.

This was particularly so because many Americans increasingly perceived the war to be morally ambiguous, if not downright immoral. There had never been a clear-cut crossing of the 17th parallel dividing North and South Vietnam; this made the accusation against Hanoi as an aggressor less believable. The undemocratic nature of Saigon's government and its apparent lack of popularity gave credence to the view of the war as a rebellion or civil war against Saigon's repression. (Interestingly, in 1950, the South Korean Government had a similar autocratic reputation, but the attack across the 38th parallel focused attention on North Korean ambitions and justified the American intervention. No one in the United States raised questions about defending a "corrupt dictatorship.") The massive and often indiscriminate use of American fire power leading to widespread destruction of civilian life and property, the creation of thousands of refugees, and, presumably, the hostility of the very people upon whose support military success depended had already pricked the conscience of many Americans concerned with their nation's historic image as a compassionate and humane country. The tanks rumbling into cities after Tet, the dive-bombing of apartment houses, the civilian suffering and personal tragedies left many a television viewer asking himself whether there was any point in destroying a country in order to defend it.

Within the United States, Tet coalesced the opposition that had been growing throughout 1967 as the war had continued, seemingly without end, and President Johnson's initial support eroded on both right and left—the former demanding an end to the war through escalation and the latter through de-escalation, if not outright withdrawal. (Sometimes, in fact, the same people held both views.) The articulate opposition to the conflict by a number of liberal and moderate Republican and Democratic senators, especially the chairman of the Senate Foreign Relations Committee, J. William Fulbright, made the opposition of other politicians, some university professors, many students, and a number of editorial writers and television commentators respectable instead of "un-American." Indeed, after Tet, Fulbright and his committee became an alternative source of interpretation and policy recommendations to the President.

At the same time, two senators from the President's own party, Eugene McCarthy and Robert Kennedy, were contesting Johnson's renomination as the Democratic standard-bearer. Running as "peace candidates," they provided a rallying point for the ever larger numbers of Americans disenchanted with the war. Then, in March, 1968, at the end of the speech that laid the basis for the Paris peace talks, the President announced that he would not run for a second term. In the words of the astute political commentator Tom Wicker of the *New York Times,* Lyndon Johnson's tragedy was that he "came into office seeking a great society in Amer-

ica and found instead an ugly little war that consumed him."
The changing American mood was evident in the 1968 election campaign. Vice-President Humphrey, nominated in Chicago after bloody clashes between police and antiwar students
(many of them McCarthy supporters) and bitter disagreement among the delegates over the Vietnam platform, was
mercilessly heckled during most of the campaign. As a member of the Administration, he found it difficult to disavow
the war; when he did take his own "risk for peace," it was
very late in the campaign. In these circumstances of Democratic disunity, former Vice-President Nixon, a long-time
hawk, found it inexpedient to charge the Democrats with
a "no-win" policy; instead, he softened his views on the war,
and indeed, in his speeches the menace abroad suddenly ran
a poor second to the "moral decay" at home. Generally, candidates from both parties fell over themselves in their eager-
ness to abandon both anti-Communist slogans and the war,
offering instead hopes for an "honorable" peace in Vietnam
and for "law and order" at home. Halting Communist aggression was abandoned as an issue; stopping further costly
foreign adventures—"No more Vietnams"—became the issue.

"Imperialism" Re-examined

Vietnam raised two major questions for the future of
American foreign policy. One was whether the United States
could in the future pursue a strategy of limited war. The direct result of Vietnam, this question remains even if the necessity of an alternative to suicide-or-surrender in the face of
a limited external challenge is acknowledged in the abstract.
The other, and more fundamental, question was whether the
United States would continue to implement an "imperial
policy." Vietnam was widely perceived as the product of
U.S. global policemanship; the assumptions underlying that
role were therefore subjected to rigorous examination, with
the result that a more limited role was prescribed.

Vietnam, even more than Korea, seriously strained the domestic consensus required for the conduct of "frontier wars." One lesson it has taught is that, apparently, in a democratic country committed to the territorial *status quo*, public support for military action requires the presence of widely understood imperatives. The most important of these is the existence of a "clear and present" danger to American security. But a limited war fought across an ocean seems far away, the danger to the country is less apparent, and public concern and fear are much smaller. Only a total threat, like World War II, or limited challenge close to American shores, like that in Cuba, pose so overwhelming a menace that public opinion unifies in support of whatever political and military actions are required, that criticism is largely muted and that, above all, domestic considerations remain subordinated to foreign policy commitments.

The second imperative is identifying the opponent. As a nation of predominantly European immigrants, the United States is "nearer" to Europe than to other continents. Germany, especially Nazi Germany, could therefore arouse American opinion. Distant non-European antagonists whom Americans hardly know, and with whom they cannot easily identify in terms of a common culture and past history, fail to elicit the same intense hatred or fear. In Korea, by marching across the 38th parallel, the North Koreans left no doubt that they were the aggressors. In Vietnam, by calling for an uprising in the South and infiltrating troops and supplies across the 17th parallel, North Vietnam avoided such a clear-cut identity; by exploiting the seeds of revolt in South Vietnam, Hanoi was able to give the struggle in the South the appearance of a civil war.

The third imperative is that limited wars avoid massive involvement and costs, particularly the danger of a nuclear war. But, in reality, limited wars have become less limited. Korea escalated as the United States advanced into the North and precipitated Chinese intervention. Subsequently, strong pressure was exercised upon President Truman to attack China, regardless of the risk this entailed of a very much enlarged war, possibly even a world war if the Soviets came to China's aid. Johnson escalated the air attacks on the North, which it was hoped would quickly bring Hanoi to its knees. Open interventions by the North Vietnamese regular army and by the Chinese were constant possibilities; they were among the reasons Johnson did not expand the war into Cambodia and Laos to cut off the enemy's supply lines, or march northward across the 17th parallel. Nor could some sort of Soviet counteraction—perhaps in Europe—be entirely discounted as the United States became more deeply involved in Vietnam.

Finally, limited wars must be won quickly while domestic opinion, which "rallies around the flag" initially, is still largely disposed to support the President. Yet a counterguerrilla war is, by its very nature, drawn out. To uproot in every hamlet the guerrilla's cell structure, which gives him his control of the countryside, to destroy his forces, and to carry out a reform program—such policies make counterguerrilla war a lengthy affair even for a nation more adept than the United States at "social politics." The result was that for many years Hanoi showed itself uninterested in a negotiated settlement. Basically betting that the fragmented, war-weary South Vietnamese society would collapse, it also hoped that domestic pressure in the United States would compel the abandonment of Saigon. The split of the Democratic Party and Johnson's withdrawal from the Presidency were incentives for Hanoi to wait things out and erode American support for the war. But the fact that Korea had destroyed Truman and Vietnam had consumed Johnson raised the question not only of whether the American public would ever tolerate another frontier war, but also of whether it would continue to support the imperial policy that had twice in twenty years resulted in limited wars and that had continuously since 1945 threatened to involve the nation in various conflicts and quarrels around the globe.

Ironically, it was the "realists," the former supporters of containment, who turned into its critics. American power, they asserted, was very great, but the United States was not omnipotent and therefore could not pursue global commitments: It simply did not have the wealth to take care of all possible foreign policy obligations and at the same time handle its pressing domestic needs. Policy-makers therefore had to carefully rank the external priorities—usually Europe and Latin America are considered of primary importance—and concentrate on these. By being selective in commitments, the nation could bring the ends of policy and the means of its implementation into balance. Vietnam was thus seen as a tragic product of an indiscriminate anti-Communism which led the nation to overextend itself. It also was seen as a chastening experience which would result in the reduction of American commitments, a concentration on urgent domestic problems, and a generally more sober and restrained international behavior.

After Vietnam, these broad prescriptions were probably useful reminders to policy-makers but they were less useful as guides in the day-to-day conduct of foreign affairs. For it was reasonably clear that American policy-makers, during World War II and in the immediate postwar years, had been aware of the nation's limited power, of its need to be selective in making commitments according to some criteria of priorities and to apply power discriminately. Indeed, during the war they had planned no overseas obligations whatsoever. The whole point of Franklin Roosevelt's policy toward Russia was to overcome Stalin's suspicions of the West and win his friendship for, and commitment to, postwar cooperation. The expectation was that the United States, the Soviet Union, Great Britain, and China would, in a new era of goodwill, jointly keep the peace. America's partners would preserve it in Eurasia; the United States would limit its responsibilities to its own hemisphere. It was the disintegration of these hopes, as Soviet hostility became apparent, England and Continental Europe collapsed, and Nationalist China lost the mainland, that left America as the only countervailing power to Russia. Even then, American responses were limited to those countries and areas where the Soviets challenged the territorial *status quo* left by World War II.

Aware of the need to be selective, the Truman Administration decided that priority should be given to Europe, the cradle of the American heritage, the area where an imbalance of power had twice in this century sucked the United States into total wars and where great potential power existed because the skills, resources, and industry were already present. Europe needed time and dollars to help it revive after the exhausting experience of two great wars in thirty years, and the United States could supply both. This focus on Europe was the chief reason the United States did not intervene in any major way in the Chinese civil war. While the United States furnished the Nationalists with some economic and military assistance, limits to its intervention were dictated by the resolve not to become militarily engaged. Similarly, in husbanding the nation's resources and trying to keep a balance between America's commitments and "limited power," troops were withdrawn from South Korea. Continental Asia was strictly of secondary interest. There was little that could have been done to save Chiang Kai-shek's regime, because its erosion was due to internal reasons, but the Republic of Korea was a protégé whose government America had helped establish and then provided with various kinds of aid. Thus, when it was attacked, the United States felt obliged to come to its aid.

The extensive American involvement was not thus due to a desire to be a global power, or to an unawareness of the maxim that a nation should order its foreign policy priorities; it was due, rather, to the bipolar distribution of power in the external environment, which left the Americans little choice. Even the 17th parallel and the beginning of the American political involvement in South Vietnam stemmed from this bipolar period. Not surprisingly, it was this simple division of power which also tended to give rise to the militarization of containment. Although during the first few years the policy of containment was in existence its implementation was mainly economic, the attack upon South Korea and the resulting fear that the Soviets might try something similar in Europe led to vast American and Western rearmament. After Korea, the concept of deterrence as a drawing of frontier lines and a threat of major retaliation if these were crossed was extended from Europe to the Middle and Far East. Because the rise of nationalism in these areas was frequently accompanied by anti-Western overtones, the alliances formed to support such lines proved relatively useless, caused a great deal of regional turmoil, and threatened to involve the United States in highly unorthodox wars.

While the wisdom of drawing such lines outside of Europe was questionable, the gap between the desires of American policy-makers to limit the nation's commitments and the extent of its involvement due to the nature of the external environment was very evident. The gap was a reminder of the difference between wish and reality and that nations, like individuals, often must do what they do not want to do. This hard truth is nowhere more clearly observable than in the underlying meaning of the sensible proposition that a nation should not squander its resources but choose obligations it can undertake wisely. The implicit conclusion is that it should honor only those obligations, all others, presumably not as vitally related to our security interests, being expendable.

Yet can this rule be applied without regard for the specific circumstances of a particular event or challenge? Can one not equally well say that a great power like the United States is committed—period? Korea provides the example. Because the Truman Administration did not wish to become involved in Asia and instead concentrated on Europe, the American forces sent into South Korea for the purpose of disarming the Japanese were withdrawn and the American defense perimeter in the Pacific was publicly defined in terms of the island chain, including Japan, off the Asian coast. The Soviets and North Koreans apparently drew the logical conclusion that the United States had written off the Republic of Korea. Consequently, in June, 1950, the North Korean Army marched southward across the 38th parallel, and America was suddenly and unexpectedly engaged in its first frontier war.

Why did it fight if South Korea was not a vital interest? Was it only because Korea was a protégé? The answer was that while the southern half of the peninsula was not in itself significant—and certainly the Americans were not legally obligated—the political and psychological consequences of inaction would affect the global balance. In Asia, re-establishment of a balance after Chiang Kai-shek's defeat depended upon creating an American-Japanese alliance; a demonstration of fear or indifference to the fate of a friend would hardly win Japan to an alliance. A nation that permitted Communist power to establish itself 100 miles across the water from Japan was hardly to be relied on. Similarly, the United States had just committed itself through NATO to the protection of Europe; if Korea were allowed to fall, the newly acquired European allies, who still recalled America's post-World War I withdrawal and isolationism and who still were apprehensive about a recurrence, might disregard NATO and try to bargain for the Kremlin's best terms. In short, it was believed that the impact of not defending South Korea in a bipolar world would result in the neutralization of Japan and Europe. Suddenly, American security was recognized as very much involved in this area of secondary interest. Thus a noncommitment, deliberately excluded from the defense perimeter because it did not seem vital, overnight became a primary commitment; yet a prior commitment pledging American help in case of attack, supported symbolically by a few thousand troops, might have deterred the Communist invasion and spared the Americans a costly war.

One need but compare the situation in Europe, including the divided city of Berlin, where such a defense commitment has kept the peace for more than twenty years, even though a spark between the confronting American and Soviet forces might well have erupted into a major fire extremely difficult to extinguish. The lesson is that, regardless of its preference not to be committed in some areas or countries, America might still on occasion need to become involved. Despite a nation's best intentions, commitments are not always determined by *a priori* selection but by contingencies and events over which even a Great Power has little or no control. The United States became involved in the two world wars during this century even though no commitments to France and Britain existed: It had no choice but to become involved in order to preserve the balance.

One question remained: Had the Americans not been so passionately anti-Communist after 1945, would they have undertaken so many commitments, even becoming involved in some instances of noncommitments. Was not their globalism the offspring of their penchant for crusading against opponents who they felt had provoked them? The presumption of anti-Communism as a principal motive of postwar American foreign policy assumed that the cold war was somehow not the typical power struggle inherent in an anarchic state system that left each state to be its own protector and therefore compelled it to concern itself with its power status relative to other potentially hostile states. The record of U.S. foreign policy since 1945 was, in fact, less that of a crusader than that of a practitioner of the ancient art of power politics. The purpose of containment, the American synonym for a balance-of-power policy, was precisely that—to contain Russia and, after 1949, Communist China—by establishing a central strategic American-Soviet balance supplemented by regional balances where required. The aim of American policy was not the launching of holy anti-Communist crusades to overthrow the government in Moscow or Peking. Passionate anti-Soviet and anti-Chinese speeches and talk of "liberation" were not translated into policies. In other words, American policy had been "limitationist," and the power behind it had on the whole been used with restraint, as shown for example in Berlin, Korea, Hungary, Cuba, and Czechoslovakia. But anti-Communist rhetoric had tended to create a widespread public impression of a policy lacking moderation and proportion, and pursuing instead an ambitious and often wasteful adventuristic world role. Nonetheless, despite extravagant declarations of intentions, the objective of containment was what George Kennan had called the mellowing of Soviet power; presumably this logic also applied to China. If they could be prevented from expanding, both Communist countries would, in time, become derevolutionized, no longer acting as messianic powers with a secular mission to convert men to the true faith. "For no mystical movement," Kennan had said, "can face frustration indefinitely without eventually adjusting itself in one way or another to the logic of that state of affairs." This was the fundamental assumption upon which, correctly or not, American foreign policy had been based.

As a nation which had put isolationism behind it, and as a state which, once it had become actively engaged in international politics, quickly learned to play power politics as had others before it, the United States was never so blinded by an allegedly indiscriminate anti-Communism that it could not adopt the age-old technique of divide and rule. Thus, within a year of Truman's militant anti-Communist speech, known afterward as the Truman Doctrine, the United States, offering help to Communist Yugoslavia after Tito's break with Stalin, demonstrated that American policy was anti-Soviet. Even in its relationship with Communist China, the United States negotiated formally or informally with Peking whenever Washington felt its interests were involved (as in ending the Korean War). If full-fledged diplomatic relations between these two powers did not exist, the responsibility was not Washington's alone. It had been moving toward official recognition when the Korean War occurred; strident anti-Americanism, similar to the anti-Russianism that has left a deep schism between the two Communist giants, also blocked better Sino-American relations for more than twenty years.

Anti-Communism has, in fact, been less a motive explaining American foreign policy than a tool used by American leaders for mobilizing public support. As suggested earlier, the United States is essentially an inwardly oriented society. Nor is this accidental, for, quite apart from the historic tasks of westward expansion and modernization, a political system in which the people vote and the governors must therefore be responsive to mass preferences is a system that concentrates upon domestic affairs and welfare issues rather than on a burdensome, costly, and distracting foreign policy. To arouse the public to support external ventures, the struggle for power and security endemic in the state system must be disguised to appear as a struggle for the realization of the highest values. From the beginning of its existence, the United States has felt itself to be a post-European society— a New World standing as a shining example of democracy, freedom, and social justice for the Old World. Anti-Communism fitted beautifully into this traditional dichotomy. America could thus practice *Realpolitik* as long as it could be disguised as *Idealpolitik,* which fitted its national style of conducting foreign policy; power politics needed ideological justification in a nation that had always felt that the use of power internationally was evil. Domestically, power was legitimated by the democratic purposes for which it was used; so, externally, its employment had to be justified in terms of making the world safe for democracy.

If anti-Communism served well as an instrument of internal mobilization, its "feedback" upon the foreign policy it was intended to serve was, because of the competitive nature of American party politics, frequently harmful. Once an administration had aroused the public, the opposition party could always seek to exploit foreign policy issues by accusing those in power of "appeasement" and being "soft on Communism." This in turn made it difficult to recognize a Communist regime, build bridges to Eastern Europe, and negotiate arms control agreements with Moscow; but, with the exception of recognizing China, it did not block these efforts. Some other consequences were more harmful, particularly during Democratic administrations, when leaders recalled it was their party that, in the aftermath of Nationalist China's collapse, had suffered bitter attacks of "sell-out" and "treason" and lost a Presidential election. The desire to avoid accusations of being soft on Communism had affected Truman's decision to advance northward across the 38th parallel before the 1950 mid-term elections; it had made it impossible to negotiate any settlement of the war that would leave Korea divided; made it impossible for Kennedy, who had campaigned on a tough anti-Castro platform, to reject the Eisenhower-initiated invasion plan about which the new President had serious qualms; led the Kennedy and Johnson administrations to make their piecemeal commitments in Vietnam, lest the Democrats be charged with the "loss of Indochina" as well as China; influenced Johnson to bomb the North; persuaded him to land troops in the Dominican Republic to prevent "another Cuba" from being established. These examples illustrate the high price paid for the need to moralize power politics in a competitive political system.

Nevertheless the balance of power sought by the United States after 1945 was not an end in itself. It was the means to the end of preserving the security of a democratic America; in turn, successive administrations felt that this required the maintenance of an international environment congenial to the survival of democratic societies. The fundamental orientation of American foreign policy was, therefore, to support the democracies, old and new, in Western Europe and Japan through alliances—and one state, Israel, which had no formal alliance with the United States (although, for all practical purposes, it might as well have). Admittedly, the United States also acquired a set of dictatorial allies and friends, usually of right-wing coloration, which appeared to weaken Washington's democratic rationale and lay its foreign policy open to the charge of hypocrisy. One reason for this has been, as we just saw in the case of South Korea, that the security of Japan required the defense of the authoritarian regime in the southern half of the peninsula. Similarly in Europe, the desire for air and naval bases to strengthen NATO, composed of the principal remaining democracies in the world, led to the inclusion of Portugal as an ally and Spain as an associated power. It might be preferable to have democratic allies, but in a world most of whose states are not democratic it is not always possible. Security and democracy are therefore bound to appear on occasion as conflicting values; which is to be given priority is the difficult and often agonizing choice. If in the name of security a democracy somewhat indiscriminately picks up a large number of dictatorial allies to enhance its power, acquire strategic position, or play off one country against another, it may indeed sully its purposes; on the other hand, if in the name of democracy it refuses to align itself with any undemocratic regimes in order to keep its hands clean, it may remain pure but weaken itself against its principal adversary. Thus, in the real world, a democracy must at times sup with a dictatorship, be it of the Right or Left, although when it does so it should remember to eat with a long spoon. The question is not whether a democracy should ever ally itself with an undemocratic government or come to its rescue if it sees that its *own* security is involved—as, for instance, Great Britain did when it went to the rescue of an undemocratic Poland attacked by Nazi Germany in 1939 or the United States when it sought to bolster undemocratic Turkey and Greece against perceived Communist expansionist pressures from Russia in 1947—but how often, for what purposes, how long, for what ends, and at what level of commitment such as association should be forged. On these issues, honest men can and do differ vigorously. In the absence of war, how can it be proven that America's relations with Portugal and Spain, for example, contributed to the prevention of hostilities and therefore the protection of Western Europe; perhaps war would not have occurred without them and we need not have stained our cause. Perhaps the United States could have achieved its diplomatic objective of restraining Russia even without aligning itself with Tito's Yugoslavian dictatorship after 1948 (or, after 1972, with Mao's totalitarian regime in China to exploit the Sino-Soviet schism). Interestingly enough, although not a single Communist state has ever evolved into a Western-style democracy or been overthrown by force from within in favor of a parliamentary form of government, some of America's authoritarian allies, as those on the Hispanic peninsula and Greece, were overthrown, collapsed, or began to evolve in a more democratic direction—which, in itself, suggests an essential difference between Communist totalitarian and right-wing authoritarian regimes in terms of the degree and permanence of governmental control and subjugation of population, despite similarities such as arbitrary government or the loss of civil and political rights in both types of regimes.

In any event, the principal thrust of American policy since

World War II, as before the war, has remained the preservation of a balance of power that would safeguard democratic values in the United States and other basically Western countries. Indeed, this has been a consistent policy since World War I, whether the threat came from the expansionism of the Right (Germany twice) or the expansionism of the Left (the Soviet Union once). American policy-makers in the twentieth century have opposed both types of regimes, for they threatened not just our security but, more broadly, the international environment in which democratic values could prosper. And this remains the crux of American opposition to Soviet Russia: that Russia's great power is a threat to Western values and Western-style open societies. Indeed, Communism, as reflected in the organization of all Communist societies (including Yugoslavia), remains the antithesis of societies that believe in individual freedoms, whether of speech or religion, free-party competition and genuine political choice, and a distinction between state and society. The basic purpose of American foreign policy, after all, is the protection of a democratic social order in a hostile world and it is America's counterbalancing power which has protected its own democracy; without that power, Soviet power and the Soviet Union's social values and order would have prevailed. As Henry Kissinger as Secretary of State succinctly expressed it, "If we do not lead, no other nation that stands for what we believe in can take our place."

A New Mood

Whatever the validity of the criticisms of America's cold war policies and the value of advice about ordering of priorities, what was clear was that they reflected a mood of weariness, disillusionment, and retraction from global commitments and involvements. One feature of this mood was the attempt to curb Presidential power in foreign policy, especially the power as Commander-in-Chief to commit American forces to battle. Under the Constitution, the President is chiefly responsible for the conduct of foreign policy; it is not surprising that those opposed to these policies focus their attention on him. Just as conservatives during the 1950's wished to limit Presidential authority because the President was, in their minds, not anti-Communist enough and might, therefore, upon the advice of the "pro-Communists" in the State Department, sell the country down the river (as the State Department had already "sold" Eastern Europe and Nationalist China), so liberals started in the late 1960's to seek to restrain his authority because in their opinion, he, the military-industrial complex and the C.I.A. supporting him were too anti-Communist, intent on involving the country in too many places, in too many costly adventures abroad. Conservative or liberal, the remedy for the "Imperial Presidency's" alleged abuse of its authority and its virtually solo determination of foreign policy was identical: to reassert the control of Congress in the formulation of external policy and to restore the Constitutional balance that had purportedly been upset. Thus, the President would presumably be restrained so that he would no longer be, for conservatives, able to "appease" America's enemies or, for liberals, able to act in an interventionist and warlike manner.

A second symptom of the new mood was that greater attention should be paid to the nation's domestic problems. These became very clear as the affluent society began to reveal its seamier and more violent sides in the 1960's, such as urban slums, air and water pollution, and the dissatisfaction of the poor, who were composed primarily of the discriminated-against sections of society—Blacks, Puerto Ricans, Indians, Chicanos, and Orientals. It was on such problems that critics of the war wanted to spend money to improve the quality of American life for all citizens and prevent the fabric of their society from being torn apart. Instead of crusading for democracy abroad, they argued, the United States should start crusading to make *America* safe for democracy. Liberal critics of the war in Vietnam quoted Edmund Burke to the effect that "example is the school of mankind, and they will learn at no other." The example should be one of a free society enjoying its freedom fully; yet these blessings could not be fully realized in a nation whose excessive preoccupation with foreign affairs drained its power and resources, both human and material. A "strong" foreign policy was unlikely to bring with it any lasting greatness, prestige, and security; rather, the constant expenditure of energy in foreign adventures would ruin the domestic base. The cold war preoccupation was corrupting the very nature of American society. Institutional imbalance was eroding constitutional processes, particularly when powerful and energetic Presidents in the name of national security not only committed the nation to war but also appeared to sanction the assassination of such foreign leaders as Castro (with Mafia help), lied to the American people and Congress about what they were doing or why they were doing it, acted secretly (even bombing Cambodia secretly for years), and in various ways violated the constitutional rights of some American citizens. And the large-scale devotion of the country's financial and intellectual resources to its external commitments meant a corresponding neglect of domestic issues. Foreign policy, in short, was tainting the American promise and vision; the priority of foreign policy, therefore, had to be ended. This had always been the heart of the old isolationism: America could only take care of her own needs and remain pure in a morally wicked world if she stayed out of or minimized her political involvement in it. The domestic consequence of playing an extensive role internationally was to endanger the very democracy such a role was intended to protect.

Perhaps the most revealing symptom of America's reaction to Vietnam was the reassertion of the deep-seated attitude toward the exercise of power internationally as immoral and corrupting. Once power politics could no longer be moralized in the context of the democracy-dictatorship dichotomy, the sense of guilt awakened by its employment returned. Vietnam seemed to prove again that in the exercise of power the nation had forsaken its moral traditions and violated its own democratic and liberal professions. Not surprisingly, sensitive men deeply committed to humane values—and daily watching the exercise of power in the form of violence in history's first televised war—repented their former support of containment-through-power as if in giving that support they had been unknowing sinners. Thus Senator Fulbright, who had been a leading advocate of postwar foreign policy while it could be disguised as a moral conflict, now attacked America's global role as evidence of an "arrogance of power." He did not merely assert that the United States had overextended itself and that its commitments needed to be cut down to its capacities. Nor did he say that Vietnam had been an unwise commitment although the basic policy of containment had been a correct one. He stated something far more fundamental: that all Great Powers seem to have a need to demonstrate that they are bigger, better, and stronger than other nations, and that it was this "arrogance of power," from which the United States now suffered, which was the real cause of international conflict and war. In brief, it was the exercise of power *per se* that, regardless of a nation's intentions, made it arrogant. Power itself is a corrupting factor; even if justified in moral terms, its use is immoral except in clear unambiguous cases of self-defense. No title for a book could have been more characteristically American. Power is evil and its exercise is tantamount to the abuse of power; abstention from power politics, providing an example to the world of a truly just and democratic society, is a more moral policy. America should be loved for its principles and for practicing what it professes, rather than feared for its might. Democracy and "power politics" were simply incompatible.

If Vietnam and the consequent mood had not led to a reappraisal of America's foreign policy role and objectives, the result of the bipolar distribution of power and the intensive concern with security, the changes in the international system would have required such a reassessment. Vietnam perhaps speeded up this process of reappraisal, but it was in fact already going on at the time of the military intervention. Two changes were particularly significant and were to have a profound impact upon American-Soviet relations: the erosion of NATO's once cohesive bands and the disintegration of the alliance between Russia and China as the former "Sino-Soviet bloc" or "Communist world," including Eastern Europe, became increasingly polycentric.

9

THE PASSING OF BIPOLARITY

The Erosion of NATO

Having committed their wealth and manpower to the defense of Europe, Americans may deem the states of Europe, particularly the Continental states, ungrateful that during the 1960's they should increasingly have questioned America's authority to speak for the alliance. But the NATO partners had good reason for doing so. First, the European nations had recovered their economic health and sense of confidence; and their continuing economic integration still held out the possibility that someday Europe would emerge as another superpower. To be sure, this union might not turn out to be the federation envisaged by the functional advocates; for the establishment of a European supranational authority cannot, as expected, be an automatic result of the spillover process. The spillover would work "automatically" only if all the member states agreed to form a federal union. During the 1960's, however, General de Gaulle opposed a union in which the Six would lose their individual identities. He therefore sought a "Europe of Fatherlands" in which power would remain in Paris, Bonn, Rome, the Hague, Brussels, and Luxembourg; the Six were, however, to coordinate their political policies through regular meetings of the chief executives, foreign ministers, defense ministers, and other ministers. But if Europe's future as a confederation or federation remained undetermined—and a confederation may, as in the case of the American Confederation, be only a stepping stone toward federation—its future as a closer union seemed less in doubt, despite differences among the Six. For Europe was no longer the weak, divided, and demoralized continent of 1945.

When NATO was formed, Europe had been almost power-less. The imbalance of power within the alliance resulting from Europe's virtually exclusive reliance upon the United States for its defense had placed Washington in a primary and Europe in a subordinate status. Washington's voice had been, and remained for some time, the voice of the alliance. It was Washington that had determined over-all Western foreign and defense policies. While Washington had taken into account its allies' objections and had on occasion adjusted its policies to their wishes, its voice had nevertheless remained the determining one. If France objected to West German rearmament, Paris could delay but not prevent it. If France and Britain acted to defend what they deemed their vital interests, as at Suez, and the United States disagreed and opposed them, they had to withdraw in humiliation. The final decisions were made in Washington in terms of what the United States defined as the West's vital interests. But once Europe had recovered, and even surpassed, its prewar economic vitality, it demanded recognition as America's partner plus a greater share in the determination of NATO's political policies and strategic decisions.

This desire for equality with Washington—and with London, as head of the British Commonwealth—had, of course, been one of the original motives behind the French proposals for European integration. Not surprisingly, therefore, once a more equitable distribution of power had been restored within NATO, the French insisted that the political relationship between the United States and its allies had to be changed, too; and they claimed to speak for Continental Europe. The subsequent Franco-American differences may well be ascribed to De Gaulle; but Gaullism, in the sense of what might perhaps be called a nascent European identity, was paradoxically both the product of America's postwar policy of rebuilding Europe and proof of its success. Just as once the youthful American republic strengthened its unity by rejecting Europe, so the embryonic Europe of the Six consolidated its bonds by opposition to its "outside" ally, America; this opposition was consistent with the changing distribution of power within the Atlantic Community. It would have been unnatural for the Six not to rebel against their subordinate, or "satellite," status in an alliance controlled by Washington with its junior partner in London.

Besides equality, however, the Europeans also sought a greater voice in alliance policy formulation because of fear. As the United States became more vulnerable, they have had to ask themselves whether they could continue to rely—ten or twenty years ahead—upon American protection against the Soviet Union. Without sufficiently large and credible national nuclear forces of their own, they would continue to be completely dependent upon American power for the most important aspect of their existence, their national security. But what would happen if the Soviets ever made demands considered vital by the Europeans but not by Washington, either because this was its true assessment of the demands or because it did not consider the demands worth the price of all-out war? Could the small British or French strategic force be relied upon to deter the Soviet behemoth?

Paradoxically, Europe had also grown less fearful of a Soviet threat and therefore felt less dependent upon the United States. This was partly due to the growing friction between Russia and China, which, it was expected, would increasingly turn Soviet energies toward Russia's Asian neighbor. It was also due to the belief (also widely held in the United States) that industrialization was transforming the Soviet Union from a power concerned with achieving a Communist world victory to a nation concerned with consolidating the security of its postwar territorial gains and focusing more attention on economic growth for the satisfaction of the Soviet citizen who had so long been deprived by the leaders' concentration on heavy industry and arms. Fundamental domestic changes would dissipate Soviet Russia's ideological commitments to world revolution and allow it to adopt a live-and-let-live attitude for a genuine peaceful coexistence with states of other political and economic persuasions. *Soviet* Russia would be "derevolutionized," and, while *Russia* would remain a superpower, its interests would presumably be more limited than global.

Finally, the loosening Western alliance reflected to some

degree the different geographic position of the partners and to the diverse historical roles played by the United States and Europe in the postwar period. Both factors contributed to, and underlined, all of the other differences within the Atlantic Community. From 1945 onward, each of the major European countries, including Great Britain, had relinquished or been divested of its colonies until, by 1960—with but a few relatively minor exceptions—their extra-European role had come to an end. By contrast, during this same period the United States had become a global power. Hence, at a time when its allies were essentially looking inward, seeking a new role, modernizing themselves, and groping toward a larger political organization and identity, the United States found itself having to become concerned with those areas of the world previously under the controlling hand of Europe. Undoubtedly, the European powers resented their reduced role. Tensions were inevitable. Perhaps more important, the nations of Europe were deeply concerned over any major diversion of American resources and attention away from Europe and to such underdeveloped areas as Korea and Vietnam. They were equally concerned over the possibility that the United States, in its new global role, might involve them in an all-out war resulting from a head-on confrontation (as had seemed possible in Cuba) or from the escalation of an ongoing limited conflict (such as the Vietnam war). Conversely, U.S. resentment over their lack of sympathy and support for its extra-European ventures merely deepened the already existing American disappointment over the failure of the Europeans to take on a far greater share of their own defense.

The resulting European "revolt" against American hegemony largely revolved around the issue of nuclear weapons, since these have played a triple role within NATO: as the symbol of Great-Power status, as a means of influencing Washington's policy (by contributing to American strategy, which has relied so heavily on nuclear weaponry), and as a means of defense. But it was in the nuclear field that the United States was not willing to surrender its primacy and the accompanying political dominance that the virtually exclusive possession of nuclear weapons gave it. Partly, Washington had become too used to wielding the determining voice in the alliance, and consequently, when its protective capacity was questioned, it tended to react with hurt pride, as if the issue at stake were a matter of American honor. Partly, too, Washington feared the diffusion of nuclear weapons, which would seem to increase the opportunities for accidents and miscalculations that might trigger nuclear war. In brief such a diffusion would tear the alliance apart. For almost two decades the United States had possessed the power to determine an issue on which Europeans might have to die; but now that France, for example, could decide for which issues Americans might die, the United States balked. What this meant was that the issue of more than "one finger on the trigger" tended to rupture the American-European partnership. The bonds of internal cohesion of the "entangling alliance," and therefore the external security the alliance provided for its members, were thus coming apart under the pressure of this ominous question: How does an alliance preserve its unity in the nuclear age when each major crisis poses the risk that actions by one member may precipitate a nuclear holocaust for an issue that the other members may not consider worth so high a price? Washington, particularly during the Kennedy years, was therefore insistent on maintaining its nuclear monopoly and the political supremacy of the alliance.

One of the principal ways it sought to do so was by supporting Britain's bid to join the new Europe. British membership, it was hoped, would mean that one of the leaders of the resurgent Europe would be a close friend who would act as the spokesman for the American point of view. This would result in a more harmonious American-European relationship. Britain had already achieved its national deterrent and, unlike France, whose atomic development was vigorously opposed by the United States, had received extensive U.S. help. Britain's reasons for developing a deterrent were exactly the same as those stated by France in its quest for nuclear arms—namely, to gain prestige, security, and particularly a voice in Washington. Indeed, it was the "special relationship" between nuclear Washington and nuclear London that had been the incentive for France to follow Britain's lead.

But continental Europe no longer recognized Britain's leadership. Even throughout the 1950's—before De Gaulle—it had been somewhat suspicious of the intentions of America's junior partner. Since the end of World War II, Britain had stayed out of all European integration schemes for two main reasons: first, because it considered its close ties with the Commonwealth and, more generally, its global interests to be incompatible with integration into Europe; and second, to preserve its special position as America's closest ally. The only European organizations Britain had joined were those that committed America to Europe. On the other hand, Britain was so dependent for its livelihood on trade that it could not afford to be shut out of the Common Market. To reap its advantages, Britain had therefore proposed that the Common Market be included in a large free-trade area including Sweden, Norway, Denmark, Switzerland, Austria, and Portugal. Members would abolish the tariff barriers among themselves, but they would establish no common tariffs against third parties. The British purpose was clear: to eliminate tariffs on industrial goods but not on agricultural commodities, which it received from the Commonwealth countries under preferential tariff arrangements. Thus, London wished to exploit the economic benefits of the Common Market for which it was in a strong competitive position. At the same time, it also wanted to maintain the advantages it derived from its Commonwealth association. Needless to say, the Common Market countries did not take too kindly to this attitude, especially the fact that London seemed little concerned with the Inner Six's primary purpose of forming a closer political union.

Britain's position therefore continued to deteriorate. The Commonwealth, traditionally an outlet for British goods and in this respect Britain's own common market, was buying fewer and fewer British industrial and consumer goods, either manufacturing these themselves or receiving them more cheaply from the United States or Common Market countries. But by the early 1960's, after the searing experience of Suez in which London had been forced to desist from its course of action by pressures from America, presumably its close colleague, Britain had begun to realize the advantages of a European political union. Increasingly, in the scale of world powers, London's voice would be heard less and less in comparison with those of Washington, Moscow, Brussels (the new Europe's capital), and Peking; nations would pay principal attention to these centers of power, not to a comparatively feeble London. Britain therefore sought entry into Europe. But De Gaulle and Adenauer were suspicious of Britain's bid. What they feared was that if Britain maintained its special relationship with the United States, Continental Europe would remain in its subordinate status in what they felt was an Anglo-American—dominated alliance.

The crucial task for Britain was therefore to prove its loyalty to the Europe it had shunned at the time of ECSC, EDC, and EEC. Instead of shattering EEC, as it had tried to do, it had to demonstrate that this time it was wholeheartedly committed to the political aspirations of European union. This is exactly what it failed to do in a year and a half of negotiations. Entry into Europe meant accepting the Six's common external tariff, which would, in effect, have ended the preferential tariff relationship Britain enjoyed with the Commonwealth countries—and this tariff was the economic link that had become the Commonwealth's principal bond. Yet, month in and month out, Britain sought special arrangements, arousing, as before, the suspicion that all it wanted from the Six was the Common Market's economic benefits. Confronted by a choice between the Commonwealth and Europe, Britain hesitated, implying all too strongly a choice for the Commonwealth.

London's stand on the nuclear issue reinforced this anti-European impression. Since it was economically weak, Britain's only real bargaining point with the Six was, in fact, its nuclear force. If Europe was in the long run to have an economic and political identity, it also needed a nuclear one. As a potential great power, this was fitting; for bargaining, this was essential; for defense, in case of American nonprotection, this was vital. For France, still developing her nuclear deterrent, Britain's help in this area, plus the contribution of its bombers, would have been very important. By breaking its special nuclear relationship with Washington and offering its nuclear knowledge and deterrent to the new Europe, Britain would have demonstrated that it was sincere in its application and that it wished to help build this greater Europe politically, economically, and militarily. But, in late 1962 at Nassau, Britain made its choice between Brussels and Washington in forty-eight hours and chose the latter. To maintain its "independent" national nuclear force, Britain became absolutely dependent upon the United States, which promised to supply Britain with the Polaris missile, for which Britain would build its own submarines and warheads. London's decision ended the negotiations and Britain's bid for entry into the Common Market. Just as it had chosen the Commonwealth as between the Commonwealth and Europe, it had now made its choice between the United States and Europe. The logical conclusion of Britain's continuing "special relationship" was De Gaulle's veto of Britain's entry in January, 1963.

Thus, by the middle 1960's, the members of NATO had arrived at a turning point of their relationship. On the one hand, it was quite clear that the United States retained its predominant position in the alliance. It possessed overwhelming nuclear superiority and this was reinforced, starting in the 1960s, by American business, which with its immense amounts of capital and technical and marketing skills wished to profit from the Common Market by establishing industries behind its tariff barrier. America, because of its world power and the huge sums of money spent on research and development, had a lead in computers, electronics, space, and rocketry. Although the subsequent American-owned industries in Europe were not to account for more than 5 per cent of the total business activity in any one country, they were concentrated in a few highly technological sectors that not only shaped the contemporary economy—such as chemicals and oil—but also tended to reshape the environment of the future: U.S. companies thus manufactured 75 per cent of all computers in Europe, 33 per cent of all cars, 35 per cent of Britain's tires, 40 per cent of France's farm machinery, 70 per cent of its sewing machines, 75 per cent of its electrical and statistical machines, and 90 per cent of its synthetic rubber. There were, of course, many reasons for Europe's technological lag—e.g., national markets and industries had been too small in the past, not enough money had been spent on research and development, even by private enterprise, managerial training and skills had been inadequate, as were the general and higher educational system. Moreover, beyond this technological gap was a psychological, political, economic, and social gap.

On the other hand, the Europeans were in revolt against America's political primacy. Even Britain, which reapplied for Common Market membership in 1967, only to be turned down again by De Gaulle, became more "European." And although a majority of British public opinion remained opposed to going into Europe, Britain's Government, led by Conservative Prime Minister Heath, who had conducted the Common Market negotiations from 1961 to 1963, finally took the island nation into the Europe whose divisions it had historically exploited in order to assure her own security. Together with Ireland and Denmark (Norway voted to stay out), Britain's 1973 entry substituted the Europe of Nine for the Europe of Six. Whether this enlarged Europe would once more give impetus to the movement for a monetary and eventually a political union remained to be seen; so did the answer to the question whether this would lead to greater friendship and closer relations with the United States once more or to more intense political competition and major economic and financial rivalry. A confederation cannot balance American power in NATO or economic strength in Europe. Only a Europe with economic vitality and a government politically able to establish a European foreign policy and the military strength to support it can in the long run define and support its interests and once more play a major role in the world.

As the 1960's ended, Europe had, however, shown no sign

that it even wished to play such a role again. Its growing economic and financial strength, like Japan's, had not yet been translated into political and military terms that looked much beyond Europe. Political unification, even cooperation on forming a joint European foreign policy, still seemed far off. French-British nuclear cooperation for the establishment of a possible European deterrent had not started; and the role of West Germany in such a venture—a Germany that if left out would feel discriminated against and resentful, but if involved might scare many of its partners away and arouse intense Soviet opposition—had scarcely been given any thought. The European countries remained preoccupied with their individual affairs: Britain with its entry and the attendant problems, France with its "independence," and West Germany with improving its associations with the Eastern countries it had attacked not so many years before.

One thing, then, had become clear. The alliance was in a state of disarray in an era of *détente,* when the perception of an external military treat had faded and commonly held security interests were no longer subordinated to individual national interests, especially of an economic nature.

The Sino-Soviet Conflict

The disputes between Russia and China, paralleling those among the Atlantic alliance, stemmed from the tendency of China, first, to assert its equality with the Soviet Union, and second, to take independent actions in foreign policy. Peking's first major opportunity for the former came during the East European crisis in late 1956. The Hungarian revolt had overthrown the Communist regime, and only intervention by the Red Army had kept Hungary within the Communist bloc; and Poland had also struck for a measure of independence from Russia under the leadership of a man whom Khrushchev had personally attempted to keep out of power. For a while, it looked as though Russian power in Eastern Europe might collapse. At this point, the Chinese came to Russia's rescue. They did so by issuing a statement approving of Russia's suppression of the Hungarian "counterrevolution" and by sending Chou En-lai to Europe to reconcile Moscow and Warsaw. In Stalin's time, such Chinese intervention in Europe would have been inconceivable; now the Chinese were actually helping Russia stabilize its position in its own satellite sphere. They achieved this by stressing the unity of the Communist bloc under the leadership of the Soviet Union and at the same time supporting the aspirations of the East European states for greater control over their domestic affairs. This position was not as incompatible as it might seem. The Chinese argued that the Communist states must stand together against the capitalists, and since Russia was the strongest Communist nation, it was the obvious leader. But Russia's primacy did not mean that the other Communist states (including China) could not take "different roads to socialism."

The idea that this assertion of China's independence might lead to a break with Russia gained support as China began to take a different stand on international issues with increasing frequency. For instance, during the Middle Eastern crisis in the summer of 1958, the Chinese sounded far more belligerent than the Russians. In late 1959 and 1960, the Chinese took further actions apparently in opposition to Soviet wishes. First, they crushed a revolt against their rule in Tibet; perhaps remembering Hungary, the Russians did not criticize this Chinese act. But they openly criticized China's dispute with India. The quarrel with India, which involved minor military skirmishes, was over the precise location of the Sino-Indian frontier in the Himalayan mountains. This was a clear test of strength, and the Chinese were apparently determined to press their point of view in an attempt to inflict serious damage on the prestige of their main Asian rival for power. China's actions were a shock to Asia. Up to then, the Asians had interpreted the Chinese Communist revolution largely in terms of their own experience. Chiang Kai-shek had been tied to the landlord class; his overthrow was therefore a blow for social progress. The Nationalist leader had also been allied to the West; his defeat was therefore an advance toward national independence. Now the Chinese were showing themselves to be aggressive. This hurt the Communist cause in Asia, and no one realized it more keenly than Premier Khrushchev. He made no attempt to hide his annoyance. Few things could have mattered less to him than a few square miles this way or that on the Indian-Chinese frontier. Compared with the need to make a favorable impression on the underdeveloped countries, this matter was picayune; for the issue at stake was a triumph of Communism throughout the formerly colonial world and a shift away from the West in the global balance of power.

The Chinese did not really disagree. They merely believed that the Communist victory must be won in a different way. It was on this central issue of the proper strategy with which to win the global victory that Russia and China differed with increasing vehemence; and their "debate" focused on the two interrelated issues of war and peace, and policy toward the leaders—the so-called national bourgeoisie—of the underdeveloped countries. The Soviet position was that in a nuclear war the Soviet Union would not only destroy its enemies, but be destroyed itself; therefore, unnecessary risks were to be avoided—or so the Soviets argued after Cuba—and the two nuclear superpowers even had to cooperate on some arms-control agreement to avoid nuclear accidents and miscalculations. Consequently, the main line of the Soviet attack upon the West's position shifted to Asia, the Middle East, Africa, and Latin America; great energy has been devoted to the encouragement of the revolutions raging throughout the underdeveloped areas.

The aim has been obvious: the establishment of friendly political relations with the nationalist regimes, whose emotional dispositions are generally anti-Western. The Soviet Union has tended to encourage their nonalignment (often a pro-Soviet nonalignment in fact, as Nasser's Egypt) in the cold war. This was clearly a tactical device. If Russia opposed their wish to remain disassociated from the cold war—even if some of them wished to exploit the bipolar superpower antagonism to advance their interests—the new nations might become alienated. An attitude of "if you're not with us, then you must be against us," an attitude Stalin and Secretary Dulles had both frequently expressed, might drive these states back into the capitalist camp. If their neutrality were supported, however, their separation from the West would be reinforced and world capitalism would be further weakened.

The Chinese Communists had a somewhat different point of view. They seemed far more willing to risk war. It was often said that this attitude was probably shaped by China's gigantic population. It could afford to lose 400 to 500 million people, in which case it would still have a population of 200 million or more. No other country in the world could survive such mammoth losses. "On the debris of a dead imperialism," Peking had itself pronounced, "the victorious people would create very swiftly a civilization thousands of times higher than the capitalist system and a truly beautiful future for themselves." Nor did China yet possess a large industrial establishment, as does Russia, whose destruction its leaders would be unwilling to risk in a total war.

Simultaneously, the Chinese had grown increasingly skeptical of aiding the new nationalist governments not under Communist control. Though often anti-Western, these govenrments were also bourgeois—and thus by nature anti-Communist. Economic aid and technical assistance therefore only built up nations whose true colors would sooner or later come to the fore. Consequently, the Chinese preferred to encourage local Communist parties to seize power. In any case, they held that the Soviet Union should channel its aid exclusively or primarily to Communist countries, especially to China.

These Sino-Soviet disagreements over tactics, however, exaggerated the differences between the two Communist powers. Even if nuclear weapons had not existed, the Soviets would not necessarily have been eager to attack the West. Neither Lenin nor Stalin thought of the world revolution in exclusively, or even primarily, military terms. Khrushchev's policy of "peaceful coexistence" was hardly novel. The Communists have been coexisting peacefully with the non-Communist world since 1917. Communists think of victory over capitalism in long-run historical terms; and history, according to them, is determined by economic forces. Hence the struggle will be conducted in primarily social and economic terms, not military ones. This does not mean that the role of military power is unimportant. But its principal use is political—to harass, pressure, frighten, gain limited objectives, not to precipitate an all-out war that would risk the security of the bastion of the world revolution. This was as true in the pre-nuclear period as it is in the nuclear one. And it was equally true for the Chinese as well.

Peking might well talk of several hundred million Chinese surviving a nuclear attack, but it was also very well aware that such a war would endanger Communist control of the country. The Chinese might talk of constructing a superior post-nuclear civilization, but they had also been anxious to avoid any major clash with the United States. In Korea, they warned the United States several times not to advance to their frontier and they finally intervened only for the same defensive and security reasons that had led to America's intervention after the invasion of South Korea. In the Formosa Straits, they had not invaded even the offshore islands when the United States openly supported the Nationalist troops on these islands. The whole Chinese approach was, in fact that of protracted guerrilla warfare—in China itself, in North and South Vietnam, as well as in Laos—rather than direct military attack. In the final analysis, for all the Chinese leaders' militant talk, they had acted with great caution. And for all his talk of peaceful coexistence, it was Khrushchev who had threatened to attack London and Paris during Suez, who had precipitated the Berlin crisis, who had broken the test-ban moratorium, and who had sought to install missiles in Cuba.

The real difference between the Russians and the Chinese had not been that one favored peace and the other desired war. Rather, the key issue that divided them had been how much pressure should be exerted against the United States, how far Washington could be pushed before it would react. Moscow's view has been that the United States could not be pushed as far as Peking has asserted. Clearly, this was the vital question, and not only between the two Communist powers;

in each crisis, this question split policy-makers within each country as well. For the answer determines both the opportunities that could be exploited and the consequences that might have to be suffered. If not much pressure was applied because of the high risks, then the gains would be small, if any; this is why the Chinese charge the Russians with betraying the cause through a cowardice that led them to "kowtow" to the United States. If a great deal of pressure were exerted, the "profit" might also be far higher, but so were the risks; this was why the Russians accused the Chinese of a recklessness that could end in suicide by provoking the United States. Wisdom in these circumstances counseled caution.

The issue of strategy toward the West and the underdeveloped nations was, furthermore, closely related to the issue of leadership of the Communist bloc. The Soviets had long dominated the Communist world. As the capital of the first Communist-controlled nation, Moscow had since the early 1920's controlled the international Communist movement; and it had been Moscow that had formulated the movement's policies. After World War II, it established control over the states of Eastern Europe, which were unable at that time to pursue an independent policy. Only Yugoslavia had not been controlled by Moscow, and when it did oppose Stalin's efforts to control it, Tito was read out of Stalin's empire. Communist China's birth—another state controlled by the indigenous Party—had thus presented a real problem for the Soviets. Potentially far more powerful than Yugoslavia, China was determined to be Russia's equal, not its subordinate, in the Communist bloc. Peking had therefore sought to share Moscow's authority to formulate bloc policies. But Khrushchev would have none of this. Moscow, like Washington, had too long defined the policies for its followers and thus become a poor alliance-manager. Instead of sharing authority with Peking, Khrushchev acted as Stalin had—and ironically, he did so first on the issue of de-Stalinization! He had decided to de-Stalinize at home and within the bloc; China was expected to adopt the same policy. It was not that the Chinese had been particularly fond of Stalin, for they had not. Nor was it that the Chinese did not recognize the need for de-Stalinization, particularly some relaxation of the Soviet grip on the satellites and permission for each to travel its own "road to socialism"; they did recognize this need. What offended the Chinese, and therefore initiated the Sino-Soviet dispute, was that Khrushchev pronounced policy for the entire Communist bloc without even bothering to consult them.

It was this conflict over authority, then, that was a key issue of the Sino-Soviet conflict. If to this extent it was comparable to the Franco-American conflict, it has also proved to be totally different in one respect: Unlike the French and Americans, the Chinese and Russians conducted their struggle in ideological terms. And because of this, the struggle held more ominous implications for the Communist bloc. Paradoxically, the very ideology that bound them together also tended to divide them. On the one hand, Moscow and Peking interpreted the world through the same ideological framework; Communism provided both of them with a *Weltanschauung*. Both held the same view of man, society, and history. They both saw world conflict in terms of class struggle and the final triumph of Communism, and they both defined capitalism as their common enemy. On the other hand, precisely because of the intimate relationship between ideology and action—ideology providing the framework through which events in the world are analyzed and defining the general purposes of the movement—ideology became a divisive factor. Moscow had long been the Communist Rome, and the ruler in Moscow therefore became the Communist Pope when he assumed power. If an ideology claimed to represent the truth, there could only be one correct interpretation of that truth. Thus there could be only one center for the interpretation and application of the doctrine. No ideological-theological movement can tolerate two Romes and two Popes. A schism—and a fight for the leadership of the movement—had therefore to develop, since one of the Romes and one of the Popes must *per se* be heretical. Hence Moscow denounced Mao for having deserted Marxism-Leninism and, by fragmenting what had been a united Communist front against the United States, for having aided the devil's cause, imperialism. Denouncing the actions of the Soviet Communist Party as "Khrushchevism without Khrushchev," the Chinese charged that it had been seized from within by "revisionists" who were in fact capitalists, cooperating with Washington in order to contain China! Peking called for the overthrow of the Soviet leaders.

Since Mao attributed the caution of the Soviets toward the United States as well as their hostility toward China to the *embourgeoisement* of the Soviet leadership, he launched his Cultural Revolution after 1965 in order to purify his nation and keep it loyal to the true Marxist-Leninist faith. All persons, no matter what their positions and functions, were to be rooted out if they were suspected of "taking the road back to capitalism." Purges—especially by mobs of youths called Red Guards—were conducted in the army, government, industry, agriculture, even the Party itself. The President of China and the General Secretary of the Party were among those deposed as the conflict between Mao and his followers on the one hand and his opponents on the other raged on for several months. Central authority seemed to have broken down. In these circumstances, the army increasingly came to the fore, restoring national unity and central control. During the internal conflict, Mao—who had certainly condoned, if not instigated, the Indonesian Communist Party's attempted *coup d'état* in 1965, which ended in the decimation of the Party and the assumption of power by the Indonesian Army—managed to offend Burma, alienate the Japanese and North Korean Communist parties, set off riots against the British in Hong Kong, renew the border skirmish with India, and intensify his campaign against the two powers he saw in collusion against China, "revisionist" Russia and "imperialist" America.

The Sino-Soviet schism was by the late 1960's dramatically clear. The epithets hurled between Peking and Moscow reached a ferocity unknown since the early days of the American-Soviet cold war. Improvement in the relations between the two large Communist powers would at best have to wait until Mao's death. For Mao and his followers, the struggle against Russia tended to be primary. The infidel had to be eliminated first before resuming the conflict against the evils of imperialism; internal betrayal within the Communist movement had to be rooted out lest those who had strayed from the true faith corrupt and weaken the movement beyond repair for the ultimate struggle. Thus avoiding conflict with the United States became important. During Vietnam, for example, China continuously counseled Hanoi that revolutions had to be self-sufficient and repeatedly stated that only an American attack on China itself would precipitate Peking's intervention. In brief, North Vietnam should not and could not count on active Chinese help to help defeat American forces in South Vietnam. Mao's policy was therefore militantly anti-American rhetorically, but restrained in its behavior. Yet even after Mao's death a complete Sino-Soviet reconciliation seems unlikely for, quite apart from any ideological issue, these two powers remain divided by the same issues that divided NATO: differences of power, of geographic position; different evaluations of international problems; and the obvious conflict between a power with global interests and an ally whose interests were essentially regional. Russia and China also had a long history of conflict which antedated their becoming Communist states and still affected the intensity of their antagonism. Peking was bitter about Russian retention of lands seized by the Tsars when China had been a weak state exploited by all the major Western powers, especially by Russia. But Moscow considered these lands Russian, regardless of how they were acquired. The two large Communist states also had a number of clashes along their 4,500-mile border, the longest in the world. Both had heavily reinforced their troop strengths; the Soviet Army, larger than the one in Eastern Europe, reportedly possessed large quantities of tactical nuclear weapons. And the bitter feelings of these two countries toward one another, especially of the Chinese toward the Russians, intermittently erupted into public print. Thus the Russians called Mao China's Hitler and compared today's Chinese with the Mongol hordes who overran Russia a millennium ago; and the Chinese talked about the "Soviet revisionist clique" as a "dictatorship of the German fascist type" and quoted Marx as saying already in the middle of the last century that Russia's aim had been, and always would be, world hegemony.

The Soviets even had to bargain with the East European people's democracies because, as a result of the Sino-Soviet conflict, these increasingly nationalistic states gained a degree of independence from Moscow in return for their support of Moscow against Peking; indeed, it is doubtful that most can any longer be called satellites. Their conflict with the Soviet Union, moreover, has taken on a dynamic of its own. Romania is the most defiant of the people's democracies; in 1968, Czechoslovakia was also moving rapidly toward greater independence when Soviet fears that Prague's reforms would jeopardize the survival of Communism in a country bordering on West Germany (Romania, which does not share a frontier with the Federal Republic, is also, internally, a quite orthodox Communist regime) led to the Red Army's intervention. Yet, even while this intervention reminded the East European nations of the limits of Soviet tolerance, none of them is as completely subservient as it was during Stalin's reign. Indeed, they looked westward to varying degrees, especially in the economic-technological realm, which could help their economic growth. Concomittantly, they needed a relaxation of international tensions or *détente;* a return of the cold war would reduce their links to the West and bring back greater Russian control and intervention in their affairs. On the whole, therefore, they approved of the changing nature of American-Soviet relations "from confrontation to negotiations," which had been going on throughout the last half of the 1960's and which was to become dramatically visible with the advent of the Nixon Administration.

A Backward Glance

Twenty years after World War I, a new world war had already started. Twenty-four years after that war, in 1969, the two superpowers, while they remained in conflict, were keenly aware of their stake in preserving the peace. Even before the Nixon Administration, the "hot line" between the

White House and the Kremlin for use in case of crises and emergencies, the limited test ban, the agreement to outlaw nuclear weapons in space, the antinuclear proliferation treaty, and the outlawing of biological weapons had been among the fruits of this awareness. But there was additional evidence. The changeover from "soft" to "hard" strategic weapons not only had enhanced American and Russian national security during the 1960's, but, by removing the dangers of pre-emptive and preventive strikes, had stabilized the bipolar strategic equation, and this was likely to continue for as long as the relative strength of the United States and the Soviet Union was maintained within the permissible range needed to preserve the stalemate. The Soviet-American arms control negotiations of the early 1970's aimed at the freezing of offensive and defensive weapons were particularly significant in this respect and symbolic of the new "adversary partnership" between the two nations (see below).

These "arms-control" measures—safer weapons systems and strategies—are supplemented by other actions. The United States restrains Chiang Kai-shek from attacking mainland China; it does not intervene on behalf of the Hungarian rebels in Russia's East European security belt; it compels its two closest allies, Britain and France, to desist from their attack upon Egypt because it is in America's interest to keep Nasser from being overthrown, an act that might have compelled the Soviets to intervene and would have tainted the Western anticolonial stance; it negotiates with Moscow bilaterally on Berlin when its allies oppose such negotiations for fear of an agreement at their expense. In its turn, the Soviet Union tacitly cooperates with the United States in the United Nations in the establishment of a peace-keeping force to be stationed between Egyptian and Israeli forces in 1956, and does not intervene when Israel defeats the Arabs in 1967; similarly, despite harsh verbal attacks on the United States and on the U.N. Secetary-General, the Soviet Union acquiesces in the dispatch of U.N. forces to the Congo a few years later; it does not support Chinese Communist attempts to capture Formosa; it signs the limited testban treaty despite Chinese Communist opposition (just as the United States signed despite French objections); it supports India when China attacks it and constantly denounces Chinese militancy; it does not intervene militarily when the United States bombs and shells fraternal North Vietnam; and while it has increased its supplies of arms and ammunition to Hanoi, it has not denounced the United States with great ferocity, but negotiates with it on such key items as the nonproliferation treaty and SALT.

In retrospect, then, could it not be said that this period, despite all the crises, was remarkably stable and "peaceful" in the sense that conflicts in the international system were resolved and adjusted without triggering a world war? And was it, in fact, not the simple and direct confrontation of the two great nuclear powers that accounted for these conditions? When one nation pushed, the other had to push back; and this occurred no matter how distant the arena from Moscow or Washington. The two superpowers, precisely because their attention was riveted on each other, were constantly on guard against any disturbances of the balance between them. The recurrent confrontations in the postwar period, as Kenneth Waltz has pointed out, were in this context an essentially healthy sign, since they meant that attempts at expansion were being met with counteraction. "Rather a large crisis now than a small war later is the axiom that should precede the statement, often made, that to fight small wars in the present may be the means of avoiding large wars later." Furthermore, the general caution and responsibility in handling crises was reinforced by each power's knowledge that if it miscalculated, it might be risking suicide; whereas in an earlier age, a nation in its power calculations could easily overestimate its own strength and underestimate that of its opponent, nuclear arms have compelled policy-makers not to commit such errors, and this has had a restraining effect. A *Pax Atomici* it was, but it was precisely this *pax* that constituted the principal restraint upon the superpowers and transformed their relationship to one of a more "limited adversary" nature, which stressed not only their continued competition for influence in the world but their cooperation if that world were to survive and each of the powers' interests were to be relatively satisfied.

10

FROM COLD WAR TO *DÉTENTE*

From Idealpolitik *to* Realpolitik

Vietnam had left the nation disillusioned with anti-Communism as a rationale for American global involvement. The war having been justified in its name, the reaction was that the price was too high. Before Vietnam, the nation could be mobilized to stop Communist aggression; after Vietnam, the concern became avoiding engagement in further adventures overseas. Even more basically, anti-Communism had been weakened by the increasing pluralism of the formerly cohesive Sino-Soviet bloc. In the bipolar world, it had been relatively easy to moralize about power politics precisely because the bipolarity had been one of power *and* values. Globalism, which had made sense as long as any Communist expansion meant an addition to Soviet strength, could thus be explained in terms very understandable to Americans, that is, democracy versus dictatorship. But it was one thing to "fight Communism" as long as there was only one Communism to fight; once Communism became a many-splintered thing, which Communism were they to "fight"? Were all Communist states, because they were Communist, their enemies? Or did they now have to distinguish among them, determining which was hostile, which friendly, which neutral—in short, which posed a threat to American interests? More specifically, in these new circumstances, what changes in the distribution of power could America safely allow, and where, if anywhere, and against whom did it still have to draw "frontiers"? Quite apart from the fact the answers to these questions were more difficult to arrive at than during the simple days of bipolarity because each situation would now confront policy-makers with alternative policies, thereby arousing great debates and possibly intense controversy, anti-Communism would no longer be very useful as a means of eliciting popular support, since the United States might well be supporting one Communist state against another.

One crucial question this posed for the future conduct of American foreign policy, therefore, was whether, in the absence of anti-Communism, the United States would "dirty" its hands by playing straight and unadorned power politics. While *Realpolitik* was synonymous with *Idealpolitik,* it had been easy to be a leader and organize various coalitions whose basic task was to push back when pushed. The state system's requirement to keep the balance could, in other words, be performed by the United States as long as it could disguise from itself what it was doing and pretend it was engaged in a noble task. *But could a nation that historically has condemned power politics adapt its outlook and style to a world in which justifying foreign policy in terms of ideological crusades was outmoded; could it "play the game by no other name" in an increasingly multipolar world?*

The Nixon Administration thought so and, somewhat surprisingly, attempted to conduct its foreign policy accordingly. Surprisingly because the President, as Congressman, Senator, and Vice-President, had been an exponent of virulent anti-Communism, the "illusion of American omnipotence" and an inflexible moralism which tended to reject having anything to do with Communists lest one be tainted with "un-American" virus. But as President he and his National Security Assistant Henry Kissinger, a German-born Jewish immigrant and Harvard professor, who later also became Secretary of State, both rejected the traditional American justification for participating in foreign affairs. International politics was not a fight between the good side and the bad side. All states had the right to exist and possessed legitimate interests, a right as true for Communist as for non-Communist states. A nation, therefore, did not launch crusades against an adversary on the assumption that differences of interests represented a conflict of virtue and evil. The better part of wisdom was to learn to live with other states, defend one's interest if encroached upon, but also attempt to resolve differences and build on shared interests. Nor would such differences be easily or quickly resolvable, for when states held conflicting views of their interests these views were usually deeply held and not easily relinquished. Summit meetings were important as part of a negotiating process, but one summit did not all problems solve, and to raise false hopes that it would was to produce the cynicism and disillusionment that would endanger diplomacy itself. Good personal relations among leaders might smoothe this process, but they were not a substitute for hard bargaining; accords basically reflect the ratio of power between the nations the leaders represent.

And what about dealing with a Communist dictatorship whose values and practices were abhorrent to us? The most the United States could expect was to influence the international behavior in a responsible direction; American power was too limited to transform another nation's domestic structure, and to make agreements dependent upon such a transformation would be counter-productive and raise tensions. American demands would be resisted, and this, in turn, would jeopardize accords on international issues which might otherwise have been resolvable. The United States was not omnipotent and had to abandon its habit of crusading to democratize adversaries. Negotiating with a Communist regime like Russia's was not a matter of morality which required an internal purification preceding discussions; it was a matter of dealing with a powerful state with which the United States had to discuss issues if peace was to be preserved. And in the nuclear age, maintaining the peace was itself a moral goal. In turn, peace could be kept only by a balance of power and that balance also, of course, protected democratic nations. Within the parameters of that balance, however, it was necessary to try and accommodate the legitimate needs of the principal disturber of that peace. Power neutralizes countervailing power, and satisfying the interests of other Great Powers would be more likely to produce acceptance of the present international system than continued frustration and hostility to an international system in which they had little vested interest. No state could be completely satisfied, but it could be relatively satisfied.

The focus of the Nixon- (and later, Ford-) Kissinger view, then, concentrated on the powerful actors. Although the rhetoric and style of American foreign policy were to be different and were to reflect more candidly and publicly the operational norms of the international system rather than domestic values and experience, there was to be an essential continuity in policy. The Russian-American balance remained the preoccupation; it was still Russia, as a Great Power, whose influence needed to be contained and behavior moderated. Indeed, this task had become more necessary than ever before, for by the beginning of the 1970's the Soviet Union had, like the United States, become a global power. Having acquired strategic parity and a sizable modern surface navy, it was no longer a continental power equipped with nuclear weapons but far inferior in nuclear strength to America; Moscow could now project its power on a global scale. A stable "structure of peace," to use the Administration's phrase, between the two nuclear superpowers of opposite political systems and philosophies would still rest on a bipolar balance, but one somewhat more complex and fluid than in the earlier cold war era. And it was here that the stylistic difference was to become more apparent. Nixon's predecessors, as we have argued, also pursued a balance of power policy but felt compelled to justify their policy in terms of the past crusading style; thus they—and especially Democratic Presidents—were frequently trapped by their own anti-Communist rhetoric and had to be more inflexible and interventionist than they would have been had they not had to pose as the guardians of the true faith against the barbarians from without. For twenty years the United States had therefore been unable to abandon the fiction that Taiwan was China and establish a formal diplomatic relationship with the real China on the mainland. The Nixon-Kissinger balance was to include Communist China. As Moscow's bitter rival, Peking could be used to provide the Soviets with an incentive to act with restraint and a greater willingness to compromise if it wished to avoid closer Sino-American relations and cooperation against the Soviet Union. The Nixon tripolarity was thus a tactic in order to make the superpower bipolarity work more smoothly and securely.

This balance was, furthermore, to be supplemented by a network of agreements and a set of rules of mutual restraint beneficial to both powers. Cold war bipolarity had been based on the fundamental assumption that what benefited one side would hurt the other and had, therefore, to be prevented by counteraction; this kind of bipolar competition, while still relevant on some issues, was, however, to be supplemented by agreements and rules profiting both, thereby presumably enhancing each country's stake in cooperation with the other. The Kissinger word was "interdependence." If a series of agreements and understandings cutting across the broad range of issues affecting American-Soviet relations could be arrived at, the Soviet Union, the more expansionist-minded state, would gain a vested interest in continuing stable and good relations with the United States. While Russia was to be faced with a continued balance and a strong American military that would provide an inducement for restraint in foreign policy, this "stick" was to be supplemented with enough "carrots" to make that restraint more appealing. There was another word: "linkage". This referred to the fact that the various issues would be linked together diplomatically. Progress on one front would be tied to progress on another; the Kremlin could not expect to make gains on one issue that interested it but refuse to meet American interests on other issues. If it did so there would presumably be a penalty exacted in the form of nonprogress on issues of interest to Russia. Cooperation and mutual concessions were, therefore, to be preferred. The adversary part of the relationship, then, was to be balanced by the partnership element in a new adversary-partnership. The over-all purposes were to lower tensions between the superpowers, to confront fewer crises, and to encourage diplomatic negotiations; it did not mean an end of American-Russian conflict and competition. A *détente* was not an *entente cordiale*.

Disengagement from Vietnam

Nixon's perception of power relations among the Great Powers heavily influenced his thinking about acceptable terms for the U.S. withdrawal from the war in Vietnam. An option he had upon becoming President, one that would have brought him much public acclaim, was to pull out all American forces immediately on the grounds that the United States had more than magnanimously fulfilled any obligations it had had to Saigon; that after many American deaths and immense amounts of American money, Saigon should stand on its own feet. But in President Nixon's view the central issue was, as he repeatedly pointed out, not getting out of Vietnam—that was a foregone conclusion—but *how* the country would get out. If the United States withdrew quickly, the events it had fought to prevent might well occur; if South Vietnam collapsed and Hanoi unified Vietnam under its control (and presumably eventually Laos and Cambodia as well), the credibility of the "imperial center's" commitments and power would be weakened, perhaps gravely so.

Thus the new Administration was from the beginning determined not to accept any settlement that was tantamount to a defeat, namely, a coalition government in Saigon controlled by the Communists. For it was Nixon's view that establishing a *détente* with Russia and a rapprochement with China would not be feasible if America's prestige—reputation for power—was badly impaired. It was the President's aim to modify U.S. relations with the two large Communist states, especially Russia, the more powerful of the two. Why should the Soviet Union, rapidly building up its strategic power, settle for parity and a mutually acceptable peaceful coexistence if she sensed that America was weak and could be pushed around? Why should China tone down its revolutionary rhetoric and conduct a more traditional state-to-state diplomacy, and indeed reorient its policy closer to the United States, if it could not count on American strength and determination to resist what it saw as Soviet attempts at hegemony in Asia? In short, the country had to "hang tough" in Vietnam in order to normalize relations with Russia and China.

Was this policy not contradictory, deciding on the one hand to improve relations with the giant Communist states while on the other hand fighting hard against a Communist pigmy which, unlike Russia and China potentially, could never constitute a threat to the U.S.? Nixon's answer, like Kennedy's in 1962, was no. For Kennedy too had won the Presidency determined to achieve what is now called *détente* with Russia. But it gradually had become clear to Kennedy that Khrushchev misread Kennedy's restraint in foreign policy for weakness and lack of resolve to defend American interests. The Missiles of October crisis had been only the latest and most agonizing of Khrushchev's challenges to Kennedy; to fail to meet this test and not disabuse the Soviet leader of his misperceptions of the President would therefore be extremely dangerous. Only if Khrushchev gained a healthy respect for Kennedy's will would there be an opportunity to negotiate fairly, compromise on outstanding issues, and relax international tensions.

President Nixon and Henry Kissinger, therefore, devised a twofold strategy. First, American ground troops were to be gradually withdrawn to cut the costs of the war and make further hostilities tolerable for the "silent majority," which Mr. Nixon felt was loyal, even though fatigued, and would support him in a search for an "honorable" ending of the war. Thus, in terms of domestic strategy, he would contain his critics. In terms of his Vietnam strategy, the continued involvement of United States forces, especially in the air while the army's participation in the ground fighting progressively diminished, would hopefully provide an incentive for Hanoi to negotiate an end to the war. This incentive would presumably be all the stronger if the President's strategy worked at home, for he would then remove Vietnam as a principal issue in the next election and presumably be re-elected. Thus Hanoi, confronted with the prospect of a lengthy war that might last longer than four more years, should have every reason to settle the war diplomatically.

The second part of the President's policy was the "Vietnamization" of the war. South Vietnam's forces were to be trained better and supplied with modern arms so that they could bit-by-bit take over the ground fighting and eventually acquire greater helicopter mobility and fighter support capacity. Assuming that the South Vietnamese Army could hold its own by 1972, although supported by American air and naval power as well as economic and arms aid, Hanoi's ability to win on the battlefield would dim as the cost of tenaciously pursuing the war increased. The offer of a negotiated settlement should therefore double its attractiveness.

But could Nixon win the time internally and persuade Hanoi externally? Criticisms and pressures remained strong in the United States. During Johnson's tenure the critics had focused their demands on cessation of the air war against the North to clear the way for what were anticipated to be fruitful negotiations to conclude hostilities; during Nixon's days these critics concentrated their arguments on the abandonment of the Thieu regime in Saigon, since Hanoi had made it clear that it was not willing to cease fighting unless Thieu was replaced. No coalition government with him was acceptable; indeed, no coalition government, even without Thieu, in which the Communists did not control the key positions appeared acceptable. Hanoi remained as adamant as ever in the belief that it was the rightful successor to French power in Vietnam, indeed Indochina. Thus in Congress, on campuses, and elsewhere, the calls for faster troop withdrawals and forsaking Saigon multiplied. But after the resistance to Nixon's policies climaxed in national moratoria in October and November, 1969, perhaps the most spontaneous and widespread demonstrations for peace in the nation's history, the President, by appealing to his silent majority, seemed to be quite successful in using Vietnamization to pull the sting out of the peace movement.

The danger inherent in the President's strategy was, however, that as American troops were withdrawn but before the South Vietnamese were ready to meet the enemy in battle, the North Vietnamese would attack. So, for example, in March,

1970, Cambodia's Prince Sihanouk, who had tolerated the Communist troops and supply lines in his country, was overthrown by a military regime that wanted Communist troops out of it. The President, aware of North Vietnamese activity in Cambodia and now dealing with a regime that was friendly toward an American presence, decided to expand the war. On April 30, 1970, American and South Vietnamese troops were given a six- to eight-week period and ordered to clean out the North Vietnamese sanctuaries in Cambodia–South Vietnam border areas. The President justified his move as necessary on the grounds that, as he pulled out of South Vietnam, the enemy could not be permitted to escalate with impunity; a major build-up only fifty miles from Saigon would endanger the lives of America's remaining men and, perhaps, the continued withdrawals. Thus the destruction of the opponent's supplies just before the monsoon season would set back his build-up and win more time for the training of South Vietnamese troops.

The critics were quick to dispute both the move and these arguments: The President had not consulted—or even informed—Congress before announcing his move into Cambodia. If the move was indeed short-term, the North Vietnamese could be expected to move right back into the sanctuaries after the troops had pulled out. The question at stake was not the credibility of American power but the wisdom of American policy. Dissension was, furthermore, widespread: within the President's Cabinet (the Secretaries of State and Defense reportedly had been among those opposed); within the State Department; in the Senate, members of which backed an amendment cutting off funds for military operations in Cambodia after June 30, 1970, as well as an "end of the war" amendment, which would cut off funds for all operations in Vietnam after June, 1971; and on the campuses, where demonstrations and riots erupted. In one such demonstration, four students were shot to death by the Ohio National Guard. The Cambodian invasion and the shootings at Kent State led to strikes on many campuses, with the complete shutdown of a number of colleges and universities. Protesters once again turned out for a peaceful mass demonstration in Washington.

In view of the domestic turmoil, it was debatable whether any alleged military advantages were worth the political price. The reaction to Cambodia made it clear that it would be foolhardy for the President to repeat such an action, unless he wished to revive the peace movement he had successfully iso- lated by his policy of troop withdrawals and appeals to his more patient countrymen. No further such uses of American troops were tried. One attempt to tackle enemy forces and supply lines in Laos was undertaken at a later time, but the operation was conducted by the South Vietnamese Army only. Its performance under fire was, to say the least, lamen- table.

Saigon's army was unfortunately, though, the key to the success of the President's strategy. In the spring of 1972 came its first real test. North Vietnam launched an attack unex- pected in locale and unexpected in form. The initial strike in a multifront offensive came across the DMZ (the demilitarized strip between North and South Vietnam) and it was a broad- scale conventional assault by almost all of North Vietnam's divisions supported by heavy weapons, including artillery and tanks. American commanders, experts in orthodox warfare, would have welcomed precisely such an enemy onslaught in the days of half a million American troops; but, with the ex- ception of Saigon's marines and paratroopers and a few other troops and local militia, the South Vietnamese Army per- formed poorly and, among other results, lost the northern provinces. Only American air support staved off even worse losses.

President Nixon was thus in quandary on the eve of his visit to Moscow. The Soviets had supplied Hanoi with its modern arms and, whether or not it had been informed of the date of the North Vietnamese offensive, it should—according to Nixon—have restrained its Asian ally if it wished the sum- mit conference to proceed. As a Great Power itself, it must have known that a major South Vietnamese defeat—and it looked momentarily as if that might happen—would be hu- miliating to its adversary on the eve of vital negotiations from which Moscow had as much to gain as Washington. The President was unwilling to negotiate under the shadow of defeat.

"Vietnamization" being in danger, he "re-Americanized" the war by once more initiating extensive bombing of the North—especially roads and railroads—and blockading North Vietnam's ports with mines. It was intimated but deliberately left ambiguous whether ships willing to try and sail into these harbors would be interdicted by the navy. This was also true for the possible use of Soviet minesweepers to clear the mines from the approaches to these harbors. The point was to stop the supplies from coming in; since the war was now a conventional one, dependent on oil and heavy weapons and large amounts of ammunition, air power might be more effective than during guerrilla operations in halting them.

Together with the promise of very heavy punishment for North Vietnam, and almost hidden by his new policy, President Nixon also appeared to offer Hanoi just about all it could reasonably expect to be given. He offered "the complete withdrawal of all American forces from Vietnam within four months"—that is, the end of blockade, bombing and all other American military activities in all of Indochina—if all prisoners of war were returned and an internationally supervised cease-fire were arranged. The Communists could, in other words, keep their forces in the South, a significant concession previously offered in secret talks. Equally important, the President did not insist on the survival of the Thieu government. Not only did he not mention Thieu, but he specifically said that the United States withdrawal "would allow negotiations and a political settlement between the Vietnamese themselves." Since Saigon would have to stand on its own feet after American military involvement had ended and the Communist forces in South Vietnam could presumably stay, the President seemed to be suggesting that, if Hanoi would let America withdraw gracefully, it would then be in a good bargaining position for the subsequent negotiations with Saigon for a new government. This new set of proposals was, at the very least, a concrete and serious basis for negotiations. But Hanoi rejected the offer. It appeared to want the President to do the one thing he refused to do—guarantee Communist control in Saigon. His proposal, in fact, had seemed to suggest that the North Vietnamese do this job for themselves, if they could do it.

The North Vietnamese thus confronted a dilemma. Despite the heavy bombing and blockade, the Soviet Union had gone ahead with its summit meeting with Nixon. Clearly, Russian interests were far more important to Moscow than North Vietnam's interests. For instance, the summit had not reached agreement on American credits and trade, which Russia wanted badly; Soviet help in ending the war would undoubtedly encourage Mr. Nixon and help him persuade American business and banks, Congress and public to extend the necessary credit. Communist China too was no longer the fervent advocate of continued revolutionary warfare and opponent of a negotiated cessation to the war that it had been earlier. Peking disapproved, in fact, of Hanoi's shift to conventional war and appeared to see the twin possibilities of obtaining an American withdrawal and a reduction of Soviet influence in Vietnam. Thus Hanoi was placed under great pressure to try Mr. Nixon's offer. Yet the North Vietnamese leaders had hung on to their goal of unifying Vietnam for so long, paid such a very high price for it, and been so often cheated out of the fulfillment of their dream by their adversaries that they were naturally suspicious of Mr. Nixon's offer and resentful of Russian and Chinese pressures. But suddenly in the middle of October, less than a month before the American Presidential election, Hanoi signaled its apparent willingness to accept something less than a total victory and by late October negotiated a tentative Indochina settlement. The terms included an internationally supervised cease-fire that would halt all American bombing and mining and bring about withdrawal of all U.S. forces within two months (two months less than the President's earlier proposal); separate future cease-fires were expected in Laos and Cambodia. Prisoners of war would be exchanged. A series of mixed political commissions, composed of elements from the Vietcong, the Saigon government, and neutralists, would then be estab-

lished to work out a new South Vietnamese political order leading to a new constitution and the election of a new
government.

Washington wanted assurance that the Communists could
not impose a government on Saigon by force so that neutral
and anti-Communist elements in South Vietnam would have
a reasonable opportunity to compete politically following the
end of the fighting. The Nixon Administration felt it had
achieved this goal, which it identified with an "honorable
peace," for the North Vietnamese, after having for years declared that the Thieu government would have to be dismantled as a precondition for a cease-fire, now accepted him as the
leader of the government faction; and Thieu remained in
control of a sizable army and large police forces with which
he administered most of the country and all the urban centers, leaving only minor areas and a small percentage of the
population under the control of the Vietcong and the approximately 145,000 North Vietnamese troops. Thus the
Thieu faction seemed to have a good chance to inherit a large
share of the power.

Hanoi and the Vietcong, in turn, were assured of the exit
of American power, and they would also gain a degree of political influence; how much would depend on how effectively
Thieu could compete politically, if not also militarily. The
sizable Northern forces left in the South would at the very
least strengthen the Communists' bargaining power in the
post-cease-fire negotiations; and if the fighting erupted once
more, it would give them an effective force with which to defend themselves and quite possibly inflict a series of defeats on
Saigon's army, which would now have to fight without massive U.S. air support. Not surprisingly, therefore, Thieu
stalled against the tentative October, 1972, settlement to
pressure the U.S. to demand the withdrawal of the Northern
army and recognize Saigon's authority over all of South Vietnam, including areas that Communist forces held. But President Nixon felt that Hanoi's willingness to allow Thieu to
administer the territory he now controlled was a crucial concession and that Hanoi, having fought for so long to unite

Vietnam and sacrificed so much, could not be expected to end the fighting without an opportunity to gain some political influence, even if it were less than the original goal; and militarily, he felt that even further prolonged fighting could not compel these forces to withdraw from South Vietnam. Thieu could thus procrastinate, but he held no veto. At the same time, a key element of the settlement which Nixon wanted was having a sufficient number of international cease-fire supervision teams in place early, giving them the authority and capability to manage effectively the cease-fire, and hopefully prevent further infiltration of North Vietnamese troops; anything less, Washington feared (correctly, it turned out in the end), might constitute a face-saving cover for a U.S. withdrawal and a disguised victory for the Communists. Another reportedly significant element (which was to turn out to be ineffective) was an American-Russian-Chinese understanding to restrain arms supplies to the two Vietnamese adversaries; in any event, they participated in a post-cease-fire conference guaranteeing the agreement ending the war.

One of the fascinating questions about the negotiations between Hanoi and Washington is why the former was willing to change its mind about Thieu after years of insistence that it would not do any business with him. One suspects that the North Vietnamese did not retreat from their earlier demand and agree to a settlement of the war to re-elect President Nixon; more likely, they too were familiar with American public opinion polls predicting a landslide victory for the President over his Democratic rival, Senator McGovern, and they feared that with four more years guaranteed Nixon would raise his demands. Therefore, it would be more profitable to reach a settlement, or at least the outlines of a settlement, before the election. Hanoi thus leaked the terms negotiated during October, thereby seeking to place the responsibility for the continuation of the war on Washington and Saigon; more significantly, it also elicited a public acceptance by the Nixon Administration of the basic outlines of a settlement. By the end of the second round of negotiations before Christmas the Administration's chief negotiator, Henry Kissinger, stated that

99 per cent of the settlement had been agreed upon, but on that 1 per cent the negotiations had broken down. Anxious to end the war, or at least American disengagement from the war, Nixon resorted to very heavy B-52 bombing of Hanoi partly to demonstrate to the South Vietnamese Government that despite its concerns about the Northern troops that would remain in the South the United States continued to support it and would maintain a hard line with Hanoi, partly to show the North Vietnamese the kind of heavy punishment they could expect if they did not sign a cease-fire and end the war, or at least the American involvement in the war. In late January, 1973, this American disengagement became possible as the war was formally concluded, although this was only a prelude to a continuing political military struggle among the Vietnamese themselves for control of South Vietnam. But for the Administration this disengagement from the war allowed it to concentrate more of its attention on its two large Communist adversaries.

Détente *with China and Russia*

When the Nixon Administration had come into office in January, 1969, Communist China was still outside of the bilateral relationship. The Chinese Communists were still adamantly opposed to resuming relations with the United States while the latter defended the Nationalist regime, rival to legitimate power over China, on Formosa, Chinese territory. But the new President recognized the changing circumstances and considered it vital to bring mainland China into the diplomatic constellation. Calling the regime by its chosen name, the People's Republic of China, ending regular patrolling of the Formosa Straits by the Seventh Fleet, lifting trade and visitation restrictions against China, Nixon opened the way for a visit to China. This visit served in part to symbolize to the American public and Congress, long hostile to dealing with Peking, the dramatic shift of American policy and in part to begin clearing away mutual misperceptions and defining the real nature of some of the more outstanding issues and problems impeding improved Sino-American relations. More important, it would also serve to bring pressure to bear upon Moscow to be more conciliatory on such prominent and substantial issues as arms control for offensive and defensive strategic missiles, *détente* in Central Europe, especially Berlin, and other key issues such as the continuing Arab-Israel hostilities to which the Kremlin had contributed by sending Soviet fighters and pilots, Soviet ground-to-air missiles with crews, and vast military supplies for the Egyptian military and military training mission.

For the United States, then, the Sino-Soviet split permitted Washington to bring pressure to bear upon Russia if the latter proved to be diplomatically inflexible and demanding; the clearly implied message to the Soviet leadership was that Soviet obstinacy would compel Washington to align itself more closely with Peking. To the Soviets, already fearful of China, such an alignment and the encouragement it would provide China to be more hostile, as well as renewed tension on Russia's other front in Europe, had to be a nightmare. Similarly, Peking had for years complained loudly about alleged American-Soviet collusion to isolate and contain China. But as the Soviet Union began to move huge numbers of troops eastward to defend its frontier with China, and on occasion let a rumor slip about the possibility of an attack on China, Peking—apparently convinced that Nixon was pulling out of Vietnam—was interested in detaching Washington from any possible cooperation with Moscow against China. Even more important, better relations with the United States would presumably restrain Russia from attacking China, especially with nuclear weapons, for the Kremlin could not be sure that Washington in such a contingency would not support Peking. In the communiqué released at the end of Mr. Nixon's historic visit, the United States and China declared their opposition to the hegemony of any power in Asia; it was clear that the power they meant was Russia. Thus Sino-American relations began despite Formosa, to which the United States reaffirmed its defense commitment. But it also declared that it would gradually remove all its forces and installations from the island and not interfere in a "peaceful settlement" between the Communists and Nationalists of their differences, including the future of Formosa, which the Administration acknowledged to be "part of China."

The stakes of both the Communist powers in their relationship with the United States were perhaps most evident when, after his visit to Peking and just before his visit to Moscow in the Spring of 1971, President Nixon ordered the mining of North Vietnam's harbors, particularly Haiphong, to stop Russian supplies of oil and tanks for the massive, successful conventional-style North Vietnamese Army invasion of South Vietnam. Both Peking and Moscow formally denounced the mining; but China continued to oppose shipments of Soviet arms across its territory, and Russia neither tried to break the "blockade" nor called off the President's visit. To prevent a closer Sino-American relations was the negative incentive for Moscow to go ahead with the summit conference: to move toward *détente* with the United States was the positive incentive. The most important benefit for Russia—as well as the United States—was to be a stabilization of the strategic balance upon which détente rested. Indeed, the Strategic Arms Limitation Talks (SALT) were to be the centerpiece of the *détente,* the label which both superpowers applied to their post-Vietnam relationship. Clearly, only a great degree of relaxation of tensions could provide the diplomatic atmosphere that would enable the two nuclear giants to arrive at an agreement that would leave them feeling secure, sanctify the strategic parity between them, and avoid another intensive and costly offensive and defensive "arms race"; by the same token, a failure to arrive at an agreement, or continue the SALT dialogue, was bound to have a deteriorating effect on their overall political relationship. SALT, in brief, became a symbol of *détente.* Without it, there would have been no SALT; but without SALT *détente* could not survive.

It was the bomb that had been largely responsible for this shift away from cold war. Bipolarity had been the most dangerous of all international systems, leading to continuous confrontations and crises; the possibility of a pre-emptive strike was ever present in a system in which to come in second was not to come in at all. But it was the enormity of the catastrophe that would occur if nuclear warfare broke out that had placed the emphasis on deterrence, limited war, and crisis management. Increasingly, the two superpowers felt the need for a mutual antisuicide pact, which took the form of a series of arms control agreements. But their relationship was subject to two opposing sets of pressures. On the one hand, the two superpowers remained in conflict and needed to assure themselves of protection; because both were highly industrialized and capable of applying great financial resources, scientific effort, and technical skills to their security needs, their great fear of a technological breakthrough that would upset the deterrent balance was well based. On the other hand, their equally compelling fear that a continuing arms race fueled by an ever changing technology would upset the balance and increase the possibility of nuclear war—which each strongly sought to avert—led them to attempt to negotiate a freeze of defensive and offensive weapons in the SALT talks. Such a freeze would allow each to acquire the arms necessary for its security while at the same time preserving a stable balance that would prevent either from acquiring a first-strike capacity.

By the late 1960's and early 1970's, military technology was rapidly changing. One matter of concern was that the antiballistic missile (ABM) system the Soviets had built around Moscow—as well as the more sophisticated ABM they were presumably working on—might be so effective it could shoot down enough incoming ICBM's to ensure that the damage inflicted on their territory would be held to an "acceptable level." Were this so, the Soviets could undermine the U.S. deterrent capacity. It was this fear that stimulated U.S. development of the Multiple Independent Re-entry Vehicle (the "space bus"). MIRV would carry multiple warheads that could separate in flight, change trajectory, and fly independently to assigned and dispersed targets. By sheer numbers, the next generation of strategic missiles—Minuteman III and Poseidon, with three and ten warheads on each, respectively—

would thus be able to penetrate any ABM defense. For their part, the Soviets had developed their own version of MIRV—the SS-9. Unlike its American counterpart, whose warheads were relatively small and could destroy vulnerable urban targets only (thereby, however, strengthening SAC's retaliatory capacity), the Soviet SS-9 reportedly could carry one 25-megaton or three 5-megaton warheads. It was on the basis of this information that the Nixon Administration concluded that the SS-9 was a first-strike weapon aimed at America's land-based missiles, endangering the Minuteman's survival. President Nixon therefore recommended development of a "thin" American ABM system that would protect enough missiles to ensure that U.S. retaliatory capacity could never be eliminated.

Technology, then, was about to upset the stability of the deterrent balance and threatened a new and very expensive defensive and offensive missile race that would, paradoxically, probably leave both superpowers less secure. The danger was twofold: one, that the United States would also develop a second generation of MIRV's that, fitted with larger warheads, would constitute a first-strike weapon; two, that once both powers possessed first-strike MIRV's, their mutual fear of a preventive war and, especially, of a pre-emptive strike during a crisis would make both jittery, possibly precipitating a nuclear war. Thus, the United States and the Soviet Union had arrived at a critical moment.

In May, 1972, in what was in this context probably the single most significant American-Soviet agreement of the post-war period, President Nixon and Soviet Communist Party leader Brezhnev signed two arms control accords that had taken two and a half years to negotiate. The first pact, a treaty, limited each nation's ABM's to 200 launchers (later to be reduced to 100 each; although the United States was to abandon the whole system, since such small ABM forces could not prevent a catastrophic strike by either side on the other); the second, a five-year interim agreement, essentially froze at the then present number the offensive missiles each side possessed. This meant 1,619 ICBM's plus 740 on nuclear submarines for the Soviet Union, 1,054 ICBM's for the United States plus 656 on nuclear submarines. Bombers, in which the United States had in 1972 a numerical superiority over Russia of 460 to 140, were not included in the accords. Given the American lead in MIRVing, the offensive accord meant that the larger size of the Russian arsenal was matched off against the technological superiority of the American arsenal. Each side had the right to make qualitative changes—to improve its weapons—within the over-all quantitative agreement, thus preserving a "parity" (or, perhaps better, a "sufficiency") of strategic arms acceptable to each adversary. While no on-site inspection to check against violations was decided upon, both sides pledged themselves not to interfere with each other's reconnaissance or spy satellites, which would be the principal means to check compliance with both accords. In addition, further negotiations were to be held in order to negotiate a final over-all offensive missile treaty; clearly, the nuclear warhead ratios, estimated to be 5,700 for the United States to 2,500 for the Soviet Union by the beginning of 1973, would change as the Soviets replaced their current missiles, including the SS-9, with an even larger missile capable of carrying up to twenty warheads.

SALT II would thus be crucial in the effort to give each side a sufficiency which it felt would be safe and which decreased each one's fear that the opponent had gained a significant enough advantage that he might risk a challenge because he believed his bargaining advantage in the consequent negotiations would compel his adversary to retreat. It was Nixon's successor who arrived at the guidelines for SALT II with Soviet leader Brezhnev at a Vladivostok meeting. For ten years each power would have an equal number of strategic weapons for each side: 2,400 missiles and bombers and, 1,320 of these delivery systems could be MIRVed. SALT I plus Vladivostok were thus important steps toward trying to stabilize the arms competition, unprecedented moves for powers whose differences were as wide-ranging and intense as those between the United States and the Soviet Union, but who needed to work together to avert the ultimate catastrophe that might be precipitated by their continuing rivalry and distrust. The length of these negotiations, that SALT II had still not been completed by early 1977, as the 1972 interim agreement was expiring, yet the fact that negotiations were continuing, reflected these contradictory pressures of conflict and cooperation. Militarily, the two superpowers had become interdependent. Admittedly, the levels of these strategic forces remained high; but hopefully, SALT III would focus on their reduction.

In 1972 and 1973 the two powers also underwrote their agreements and negotiations on arms control by setting down certain principles or standards of conduct to guide their relationship. The "structure of peace," in the American view, put a special obligation on the two nuclear giants. One principal summed it up:

> The U.S.A. and the U.S.S.R. attach major importance to preventing the development of situations capable of causing a dangerous exacerbation of their relations. Therefore, they will do their utmost to avoid military confrontations and to prevent the outbreak of nuclear war. They will always exercise restraint in their mutual relations, and will be prepared to negotiate and settle differences by peaceful means. Discussions and negotiations on outstanding issues will be conducted in a spirit of reciprocity, mutual accommodation and mutual benefit.
>
> Both sides recognize that efforts to obtain unilateral advantage at the expense of others, directly or indirectly, are inconsistent with these objectives.

The basis of peaceful coexistence, then, were: the necessity to avoid confrontations; the imperative of mutual restraint; and the rejection of efforts to gain unilateral advantages.

American policy-makers were willing to fortify the incentives for Soviet military restraint with economic help; the Soviet economy as it entered the decade of the 1970's seemed in serious trouble. The industrial growth rate had fallen off from 7 to 4.5 per cent in a ten-year period. The economic decline was particularly notable in those branches of industry associated with the Second Industrial Revolution: computers, electronics, and petrochemicals. In short, in those branches most important for the growth of industry in the last part of the twentieth century the Soviet Union was falling behind the West. The implication of this could hardly be ignored in terms of Russia's appeal as a Socialist state in the world in general, its power competition with the United States, and, not least, unrest within Russia at the continuing shortages of consumer goods. Even in agriculture the growth in production had fallen sharply below expectations and official plans. Workers on the land, like workers in the factory, fell quite a bit behind their American counterparts in per capita production. The problem of a superpower experiencing continued difficulties feeding itself bountifully—indeed, in some years just avoiding widespread hunger—was not just the result of weather conditions but the ideologically determined organization of an agrarian economy administered by a rigid bureaucracy.

The Soviet concern about falling behind in the scientifictechnological revolution led the Kremlin to look westward for a "technological fix" to help stimulate their economy. In the absence of basic structural reforms of the highly centralized and bureaucratic system, Western technology, industrial machinery, and credit to buy them with were the only recourse; and Russia particularly desired American assistance. In return, since it had little to sell the U.S., it offered to let the industrial nations develop and exploit the huge Soviet deposits of raw materials, especially in Siberia; the American capital to help finance this extraction would presumably be repaid in oil, natural gas, and other mineral resources in the future. Politically, the Administration thought that this was not a bad deal. Quite apart from profits for the American businesses involved, the Soviet need for American help would provide a powerful material reinforcement for the foreign policy of restraint and accommodation made necessary by the desire to prevent closer Sino-American "collusion" and achieve strategic arms agreements to stabilize mutual deterrence and recognize Soviet parity and equal status with the United States. As Henry Kissinger put it negatively: "Economic relations cannot be separated from the political context. Clearly, we cannot be asked to reward hostile conduct with economic benefits even if in the process we deny ourselves commercially profitable opportunities."

Détente: *Change or Tactic?*

The general mood of *détente* was soon to be questioned widely in the United States and other Western countries. A number of events were to occur which raised the central question whether the more moderate Soviet behavior in foreign policy was genuine or whether *détente* was more a tactical adaptation to a new international environment, but still part of an expansionist policy. Was *détente* for the Soviets merely a continuation of the cold war by other means? Did it reflect a Russian willingness to live and let live with the West on the basis of strategic parity, acceptance of the *status quo* (including the same nonintervention with regard to Western Europe that the West had practiced toward Eastern Europe, the Soviet sphere of influence) and mutual restraint? Or, having learned from experience that a hard line and fist tended to arouse and unite the West, was *détente* with its summits and smiles itself a way of relaxing the West's guard, shifting the balance, and gaining—slowly but surely—a superiority of power by lowering Western defense budgets, inducing withdrawals of American troops from Europe to weaken NATO, gaining legitimation of the *status quo* in Europe while confronting China, and acquiring Western technology and economic assistance? The great Russian writer Alexandr Solzhenitsyn, exiled from the Soviet Union for his dissidence, and the "father" of the Russian atomic bomb, Andrei Sakharov, another critic of the Soviet system, somberly warned the West that *détente* was a tactic: Soviet objectives remained expansionist, and when the Kremlin had gained new economic and military strength with Western help, it would once more confront the West, only from a position of superiority. Many Western critics of *détente* felt it was really a "selective *détente*" in which the Soviet Union reaped general benefits from the lowering of tensions while unilaterally and with impunity exploiting situations and opportunities that advanced its interests against the West and especially the United States.

The situation that first and most dramatically raised the above central question about *détente* was the Middle Eastern war of 1973. Only a few months after the second summit, which had reaffirmed the general rules of conduct between the two superpowers, Egypt and Syria attacked Israel on Yom Kippur, the highest of all Jewish religious holidays, the Day of Atonement. What shocked Washington and other Western capitals was the Soviet role immediately before and during the hostilities, even though the war may have seemed justifiable to the Arabs. Egypt was now ruled by Anwar Sadat, an Egyptian nationalist who had succeeded Nasser, an Arab nationalist or Pan-Arabist, upon his death. The country had become increasingly frustrated by Israel's continued occupation of Egyptian territory up to the East Bank of the Suez Canal. This territory, captured by Israel in the Six Day War in 1967, precipitated by Nasser, looked as if it might remain in Israeli hands for a long time since Israel had no incentives to surrender it. After the war in which it had established its independence, Israel had had to fight for survival again in 1956 and 1967. The Arab states continued to be hostile to its existence, and Nasser, the only Arab leader of stature who could have mobilized popular support throughout the Arab world for a compromise settlement recognizing Israel's right to exist, refused to play the role of peacemaker. Even after having lost the war of 1967, he refused to sit down with Israel and negotiate a settlement; Israel's victory did not therefore bring peace, only another cease-fire.

But Israel thought it was a peace of sorts. It was militarily superior and therefore not likely to be attacked. The American-Soviet *détente* also benefited Israel since the United States did not exercise any pressure on it to give up the captured Egyptian and Syrian territories. The Soviet Union, needing American technology, investments, and trade for its own ailing economy and wanting a SALT agreement, was also in no position to exert pressure upon Israel or to give active political and military support to the Arab states. Moscow, by limiting its support for North Vietnam despite the American blockade and bombing in the spring of 1972, had achieved better relations with Washington and was not about to permit Cairo to jeopardize these relations any more than it had allowed Hanoi to do so when the latter had launched its spring offensive. Indeed, having supplied North Vietnam with the arms that had helped it launch the offensive which had almost jeopardized better Soviet-American relations, Moscow made sure that the offensive arms Cairo wanted for an attack on Israel were not delivered; only Egypt's defenses were bolstered. The territorial *status quo* thus became frozen.

But Sadat was unwilling to live with this *status quo*. He was subject to domestic pressures, especially from the army and university students, to seek revenge against Israel; external pressures from the more militant Arab states, like Libya, and nonstate actors, such as the various Palestinian guerrilla movements, were also severe. Thus Sadat, an unglamorous figure succeeding the beloved and charismatic Nasser, was in danger of being overthrown; pro-Soviet Egyptian leaders were particularly anxious to replace him as Sadat first reduced and then eliminated their influence and undertook measures to attract foreign, including American, private capital to rescue Egypt's stagnate economy from Nasser's "Arab socialism." Above all, Sadat realized that if Israel was to be compelled to abandon the Arab territory captured in 1967 he had to look elsewhere than Moscow. Only the United States, Israel's friend, could help him achieve this goal; and this emphasis on the return of the 1967 territory suggested a reciprocal willingness to recognize Israel's existence. But Israel, skeptical after its previous bitter experiences, subject to constant guerrilla attacks, continuously denounced by Arab militants, did nothing; to Israel, Sadat was merely talking, wanting the return of territory that, once returned, would only strengthen him for yet another war. The United States, too, did nothing after Sadat in 1972 threw some Soviet military advisers out, thereby trying to entice Washington to take the initiative in seeking a peace agreement.

Sadat, frustrated, his power endangered, therefore launched

the Yom Kippur War, which took Israel by surprise and achieved initial success in crossing the Suez Canal and driving into the Sinai Desert. The Arab armies could not have achieved the successes without considerable Soviet arms shipments and bridging equipment. While it seems relatively clear that the Soviet Union did not wish to risk *détente* by helping to precipitate another Arab-Israeli War as it had done in 1967, it is also obvious that once informed of the Egyptian-Syrian determination to go to war it was unwilling to risk losing influence in the Arab world by opposing this move and withholding arms and advisers to train the Arab forces. Instead Moscow stepped up its delivery of arms; not only that, it supplied the most modern arms, including ground-to-air missiles and antitank missiles of great accuracy, which would inflict serious losses upon the Israeli Air Force and armor and greatly improve the chances of an Arab victory. When, indeed, the Egyptian and Syrian armies proved successful in the opening round of fighting, the Soviet Union began a huge airlift of war material and opposed any cease-fire calls that were not linked to a pullback by Israel to the 1967 frontiers; Moscow was proposing a settlement that the Arabs could achieve only by a major military victory, which they had not yet won. Moscow also called upon other Arab governments to join the war against Israel and approved the OPEC oil embargo against the United States. And when the United States finally began its massive airlift of military supplies (because the Soviet Union refused to match the American restraint) in the face of enormous Israeli fighter plane and tank losses, its denunciations of the United States were stepped up. There could be little question that despite the new code of conduct the Soviet Union was seeking energetically to exploit *détente* unilaterally in a favorable situation created by its client states.

Once Israel recovered from its shock and had driven the Syrians back from the Golan Heights, however, its forces concentrated on Egypt, crossed the Suez Canal to the West bank, and moved to cut off supplies to the Egyptian forces on the East bank and encircle them. At this point, the United States and Russia agreed upon a cease-fire resolution in the U.N. .

Security Council, the United States because it felt that no peace could be arranged if Egypt were again humiliated in war—indeed the psychological boost derived from its initial successes had to be preserved if it were expected to make any concessions in a peace settlement—and Russia to avoid an Egyptian defeat that might compel Moscow to enter the war to rescue its client state. But the shooting continued and the Israelis drove to encircle and destroy the Egyptian army on the Eastern side of the Suez Canal. Sadat now requested the United States and the Soviet Union to use their own forces to impose their cease-fire resolution. When the United States declined to intervene with its forces and Russia threatened to do so unilaterally, the two superpowers confronted one another as American military forces were placed on a worldwide alert. Thus Moscow had supplied the arms before the outbreak of the war; had not pressured the Egyptians and Syrians to abandon their plan for war; had not informed Washington that hostilities would occur; had opposed a cease-fire which did not reward the Arabs' initiation of the war; had called upon other Arab states to join the war; had begun a huge airlift of arms to exploit the initial Arab military successes; had endorsed the oil embargo against the United States (and after the war criticized moves for its removal); and had almost confronted the United States over the cease-fire when the Arabs were losing. None of these actions were compatible with the spirit of *détente.*

Nor was Moscow more helpful in the American attempt after the war to move forward a peace that would avoid future wars with their ever greater chance of a Soviet-American military clash. The Middle East with its unstable governments, militancy, and high emotions, and its ability to suck the superpowers into its regional quarrels, increasingly resembled the Balkans at the turn of the century. The Nixon (and later Ford) Administration resolved to avoid the past pattern in which the Israelis won the military victory but were unable to translate that victory into a political settlement, leaving the Arabs humiliated and resentful, more determined not to accept the right of Israel to exist and to prepare only for another round. The 1973 war had, in the American evaluation, shown a number of things: Israel could be caught by surprise; the ability of Arab armies to learn how to use modern weapons effectively; the intolerable cost in manpower losses to Israel of a war lasting longer than a few days; the grave difficulties for the Israeli economy when much of its manpower is mobilized; and the political isolation of Israel in a world in which even the Europeans (except the Dutch) were fearful of the Arab oil weapons and cowered before the people whom shortly before they had governed. All these factors spelled further trouble for Israel, whose only friend in the world was now the United States; and in the face of oil embargoes and ever higher energy costs, could Israel continue to count on American support—not for the existence of an Israel within its 1967 borders but for an Israel still holding the captured territories?

For the Administration with its Jewish National Security Assistant who had also become Secretary of State (which he had been in fact, if not in name, prior to his appointment), the urgency of attempting to reach a Middle East settlement was obvious. And the moment also seemed more favorable than at any earlier time. Sadat had declared his willingness to accept the existence of Israel and make peace with it on the basis of the 1967 frontiers. Sadat had also been able to organize Arab support for the Egyptian war effort from regimes spanning the spectrum from the ultra-conservative to the revolutionary left. Of the former, Saudi Arabia, even wealthier now that oil prices had quadrupled, was the most influential. Anti-Israeli but also anti-Communist and pro-American, the Saudis bankrolled the more moderate regimes like Egypt and made even militant regimes like Syria's more dependent upon Saudi money, especially for weapons. Egyptian leadership in the Arab world plus Saudi money made a potent combination, one that the Nixon Administration wished to exploit. Finally, the Arab armies for the first time had shown bravery and skill and recovered some Arab self-esteem; diplomatic concessions in these circumstances might be easier. Defeat had only led to inflexibility.

Kissinger's strategy was a step-by-step approach. These were too many issues to be settled. To attempt to solve these issues all at one time with all the parties present would be impossible. In a public conference to meet at Geneva, co-chaired by the United States and the Soviet Union, the most extreme Arabs would set the pace; to take a moderate position would in this atmosphere seem to betray the Arab cause. The presence of the Soviet Union was likely to lend support to the militants, because it profited from continued turmoil in the area; without turmoil the Arabs would perhaps not need Russia much. And such a conference would openly bring out Israeli-American differences. A step-by-step approach would start with the "easier" issues and proceed gradually to the hardest ones. The initial task was the disengagement of the Israeli forces and the Egyptians and Syrians after the war; next would be a further Israeli withdrawal in the Sinai and then on the Golan Heights; the last two issues would be the hardest and most emotional—the establishment of a Palestinian state, a cause espoused by the terrorist Palestine Liberation Organization (PLO), with whom the Israelis would not even talk directly, and the control of the old city of Jerusalem. By successfully resolving the initial issues, a momentum would be established to help resolve the more difficult ones; and success would divide the moderates from the more militant regimes, strengthening the former and weakening the latter.

Kissinger was successful in achieving two unprecedented interim agreements, the first the disengagement of the hostile forces on the Egyptian Sinai and Syrian Golan fronts, and later a further Sinai withdrawal by the Israelis from two strategic passes and an oil well. Throughout, the Russians denounced Kissinger. Becoming cooler toward the Egyptians to whom it was beginning to seem that the Americans could pressure the Israelis to withdraw and succeed where the Russians had failed, the Soviets increasingly threw their support behind the more militant Syrians and the PLO. As the Israeli Government, constantly subject to pressures from its own right, which opposed virtually any concessions to the Arabs, became increasingly inflexible, and Egypt more isolated in the Arab world for having signed the second interim agreement, this strategy seemed to permit the Soviets to recoup their prestige and influence. Egypt by its agreement had, as the Syrians saw it, left them to face Israel all by themselves; it had agreed to let Israeli-bound cargo on non-Israeli ships pass through the reopened Suez Canal, had permitted American technicians to monitor early-warning systems between Israeli and Egyptian forces, and had given general pledges to use diplomacy, not force, in the settlement of Egyptian and, more broadly, Arab-Israeli differences. (This also presumed that further steps toward a settlement would gradually occur since a freezing of the *status quo* short of Israel's 1967 borders was bound to lead to further violence eventually.) To many Arabs, these acts were tantamount to a betrayal of the Arab cause.

Syria and the PLO were the beneficiaries of this attitude; Damascus was increasingly looked to by other Arabs as the spokesman of Arab causes, as Cairo had been during Nasser's days. While Sadat in 1976 broke his fifteen-year treaty of friendship with Russia and became dependent on an America which, because of external Israeli and internal Jewish pressures, could hardly sell him six military transport craft—let alone other arms now that Egypt's Soviet arms were becoming obsolete—Syria's Assad repaired his relations with Jordan and established his influence in Lebanon as that country disintegrated in civil war between Christians and Moslems. The former, long the wealthier and politically the more influential, sought to retain their position by suppressing the Palestinians whose presence had become sizable since Jordan's King Hussein had driven them out of his country a few years earlier; sympathetic to their fellow Arabs and their aspirations for a greater say in Lebanese affairs and a better life, the Palestinians, heavily armed, constituted a threat to the integrity of Lebanon. They tended to upset the agreement of the Christians and Lebanese Moslems for a domestic redistribution of power because the more militant left-wing Moslems felt that they could militarily defeat the Christians with the help of the PLO and win all the political power in the fiercely fought civil war which had erupted in that country. Syria, however, was opposed to a solution which would probably lead to Christian secession from Lebanon and establishment of two states, one Christian and one Moslem. It therefore sought Lebanon's survival and political integrity, first through political mediation and, when that proved unsuccessful, through military intervention. Syria did so for several reasons: to boost its prestige; to prevent creation of a Moslem neighbor with a more radical and militant leadership than Syria's own; and to avoid being dragged into a war with Israel by such a leadership at a time of the latter's choosing.

Ironically, therefore, Assad who had sought to replace Nasser's successor as spokesman for the Arab causes and who had consequently aligned himself with the PLO, now found himself intervening in Lebanon in support of the Christians and against the left-wing Lebanese Moslem-PLO alliance. Moreover, since Moscow continued to support the latter, Syria's relations with Russia became strained as well. In addition, since the PLO feared that Syria, Like Jordan earlier, would seek to undermine its independence and seek to control it, the PLO now fought for its survival; and to enhance that possibility it improved its relationship with Sadat whom it had so recently vituperously denounced as a traitor to the Arab cause. (Sadat, in turn, sponsored the PLO to full membership of the Arab League, even though the PLO, unlike its other members, was not a state.) In this confusing, unstable Middle Eastern political situation with its intra-Arab conflicts and jockeying for leadership, persistent Arab-Israeli differences, American-Russian competition for influence, increasing American-Israeli bitterness as Israel became increasingly diplomatically inflexible, and Arab hopes dashed in the wake of 1973 as America seemed unable or unwilling to exert pressure on Israel for a peace based essentially upon the 1967 frontiers, the possibility of war remained an unfortunate possibility and a grave danger not only to regional peace but global stability.

A second test of *détente* came in Portugal. A year after a

military revolt had ended a half-century of a rightist dictatorship in 1974, radical officers led by a pro-Communist Premier
seized power and made the Communist Party the dominant
force in what had been a coalition government with the democratic Socialist Party and the left-of-center Popular Democrats. A general election of a Constituent Assembly to draft a
Constitution did occur, but the non-Communist parties were
compelled to agree that regardless of the election outcome
power would remain with the military. The election demonstrated a lack of support for the Communist Party; it could
muster only 12.5 per cent of the vote, whereas the Socialist received 38 per cent and the Popular Democrats 26 per cent for
a total of 64 per cent. Nevertheless, the Communists in cooperation with the radical officers seized many of the levels of
power in the army, government, municipal governments,
trade unions, press, and broadcasting. The Soviet Union reportedly funded and directed the Portuguese Communist
Party in its bid for power.

The struggle continued, however, as Catholics, townspeo-
ple, and peasants attacked Communist offices and halted Communist activities in the northern part of the country; the
Communists also lost some important trade union elections.
The country in the meantime suffered from increasing unemployment and inflation and an influx of refugees from Angola
(a Portuguese colony about to become independent). The
Common Market refused a loan to help out except to a democratic Portugal. Gradually over a period of months, the election results began to be reflected politically as the Socialists
led the popular struggle to isolate the Communists. Settlement of the unrest could come only if the Cabinet reflected
popular sentiment. The pro-Communist Premier was dismissed, the moderate officers deposed most of their radical
colleagues, and the Communists were limited to one Cabinet
post. But the Communist and their military supporters were
not yet ready to give up and used huge antigovernment demonstrations to try to paralyze and subvert the government;
radical military units refused to obey the government, openly
supporting the opposition. Loyal commando troops finally

went into action and resolved the issue of whether Portugal's new government would be democratically chosen or a radical dictatorship of the left. It had been touch and go.

What is remarkable about the Soviet role in this affair is its open support of a small minority's efforts to seize power in a country that was a NATO member. The whole point of the earlier cold war had been to draw lines or "frontiers" between the Western and Communist spheres of influence, which were to be off-limits to the other side. As perceived in the West, the basis of *détente's* peaceful coexistence was the mutual acceptance of this arrangement. This had already been American policy during the cold war. The United States had not interfered in Eastern Europe in 1953, 1956, or 1968. And the Soviet Union had certainly left no doubt that it expected the West to continue keeping its hands off this area. Yet Moscow, espousing *détente* and seeking to benefit from it, again saw an opportunity to extract a unilateral advantage in a key strategic area close to the mouth of the Mediterranean. For Moscow, *détente* again seemed to be a selective affair as it intervened in the domestic affairs of an American ally in a manner that it would not have stood for had the United States similarly interfered in Poland, Hungary, or Czechoslovakia.

The third example of selective *détente* came in Angola, as that African country became independent from Portugal. As the Portuguese withdrew, rival factions divided primarily by tribal and regional loyalties competed for power, and civil war erupted. Again, the Soviets intervened, this time with a sizable air- and sea-lift of jet fighters, mortars, rockets, armored cars, ground-to-air missiles, along with military advisers and a Cuban military force of over 10,000 men, reportedly costing Moscow $2 million per day, in support of a movement for the "national liberation" of Angola sympathetic to Moscow. Russia, which by late 1975 already held military facilities on Somalia on the northeastern coast of Africa, a strategic area for operations covering the entrances to the Persian Gulf (that is, Western oil supplies) and the Indian Ocean, as well as Guinea on the west coast, was thus seeking influence in a country with a 1,000-mile-long coastline; this would enhance the ability of the Russian navy and air force to operate effectively in the South Atlantic area should the Russians seek and be granted air and naval facilities. Angola, as well as neighboring states like Zaïre and Zambia, were also believed to be rich in oil and mineral resources. Angola was also where black Africa divided from "white supremacy" Africa, Rhodesia and South Africa, whose racial troubles were explosive and exploitable, particularly now that Portuguese colonialism no longer protected these racist states from black liberation movements. Another plus was that Russia, as the self-proclaimed supporter of "national liberation" movements and competitor with China for the title of the world's most revolutionary country, was presented by the Angolan situation with an opportunity to establish its credibility throughout the underdeveloped world. Undoubtedly, Russia was also seeking to increase the identification of the United States with South Africa, which sent some troops into Angola, and thus discredit its superpower rival in much of Africa while keeping its credentials flying high. Indeed, it appeared as if Russia were in a sure-win diplomatic situation in Southern Africa. Additional concern that Russia and Cuba would also actively support African guerrilla forces in Rhodesia led the United States to a more active diplomacy to explore whether it was possible to peacefully achieve black majority rule and white minority protection in Rhodesia, as well as independence for South African-controlled South-West Africa or Namibia, before intense racial violence and possible superpower intervention would erupt.

In any event, Soviet intervention in an African civil war for the first time since the Congo fifteen years earlier hardly constituted "national liberation," since that had occurred when Portuguese colonialism had ended. To the Ford Administration, the Soviet attempt to impose one of the three contending factions for power in Angola on that country smacked of "Soviet colonialism." The result was to reintroduce a measure of Great Power rivalry and possible confrontation into southern Africa. While rejecting any military reaction, Washington denounced the Kremlin's and Havana's acts but limited itself to covert arms aid, purportedly to strengthen the two rival factions, make it impossible for the Soviet-backed movement to win, and compel a negotiated settlement in which power would be shared. But this effort not only did not match that of Russia but further was cut off by the Senate, fearful of another Vietnam in an area that did not constitute a vital American interest. Rejecting the contention that Angola might become another Vietnam, Ford and Kissinger did agree that Angola as such was not a significant American interest. They emphasized, however, that Soviet behavior could not for this reason be ignored. Angola might be far away but, in their view, it was a test case of the superpower relationship. Soviet actions were simply incompatible with *détente;* it was another case of selective *détente,* of the Kremlin's seeking unilateral advantage from the general relaxation of tensions. The Secretary of State asserted that America could not be indifferent to Russia's attempt so far from home and so distant from traditional Russian interests to impose a government favorable to Soviet interests. The Soviet response was to defend its behavior by asserting that support of national liberation movements, including armed intervention, was not incompatible with *détente. Détente* did not mean the end of the antiimperialist struggle. "What's mine is mine, what's yours is negotiable," President Kennedy had once said in summing up the essence of Soviet foreign policy. Had things really changed, *détente* notwithstanding?

Allied Relationships

While Americans debated what *détente* meant and what its consequences were for the United States, in an atmosphere more skeptical and cynical than in the early and more euphoric days of 1972, America's relations with many of its allies and much of the Third World deteriorated significantly. Most worrisome before the Middle East Yom Kippur war of 1973 was the state of political health of the Atlantic community. The bonds of the NATO alliance had already been eroding at the time the Nixon Administration came into office. America's European allies were no longer willing to sub-ordinate themselves to Washington's direction. As noted ear-lier, they had become gravely concerned that an America which would have to sacrifice itself for the defense of Western Europe would become increasingly reluctant to defend them as Soviet strategic power grew; and they had watched the de-velopment of closer bilateral United States–Soviet diplo-matic relations with great anxiety and apprehension. The Nixon-Kissinger emphasis on this superpower relationship and its preoccupation with the creation of a "structure of peace" and negotiations with Moscow across a wide spectrum of issues were therefore guaranteed to arouse European suspi-cions and resentments. The SALT agreements, the definition of the code of conduct to govern superpower behavior, ar-rived at without genuine consultations within NATO, stirred not only European anger at this lack of concern by America for the views of its most important allies but also intensified the fear that the NATO commitments of the United States were no longer very credible. SALT I and strategic parity could only mean an implicit agreement by the nuclear giants that each other's territory would be off-limits and that, at best, Europe would be defended locally (and destroyed in the proc-ess probably); but the United States would no longer retaliate to Soviet aggression in Europe with an attack upon Russia.

It was in this context that another troublesome issue was raised. Economic relations between Europe and America were straining the alliance. Whereas in the immediate postwar era economic policy such as the Marshall Plan had clearly been consistent with and in support of American political-military policy, economic relations were now at odds with the other strands of policy. The enlarged Common Market was an in-creasingly strong economic competitor. European policies hurt in several ways: the decline of U.S. farm exports; the exten-sion of preferential tariffs by the Common Market to associ-ated members (mainly developing European states like Greece and former colonies); and the high price of American manu-factured goods, due to inflation, which made European goods more attractive, aggravated the situation by increasing the

U.S. deficit in the balance of trade. This in turn led to pressures to reduce the dollar drain by withdrawing a sizable contingent of the 310,000 American forces in Europe, of which the critical contingent was the 190,000-man army on the central front in Germany. This pressure, which was consistent with the new U.S. mood of retrenchment, nationalism, and economic protectionism, came from the Congress. The executive branch did not favor such a pullback of forces for political-psychological reasons: the further erosive impact this step would have on the credibility of American commitments in the capitals of Western Europe and Moscow. But Congressional and public pressures remained insistent. Such withdrawals, it was argued, would save the money which the American forces in Europe added to both the deficit in the balance of payments and the defense budget; the cold war was over; the large Russian forces were sizable in part because their function was to police Eastern Europe; furthermore, Europe, 250 million people strong with its very large industry and military tradition, could defend itself—if it wanted to do so. Twenty-five years after World War II it was still dependent upon America with a somewhat smaller population against a country of approximately the same population—in turn in conflict with a neighbor of 800 million people. Too long defended by the United States, Europe had become too used to being defended. It had the resources; it lacked but the will. Even after the devaluation of the dollar, when the trade balances improved once more, these arguments remained persuasive for many who felt that the Europeans ought to contribute more toward the maintenance of American forces in Europe.

The Nixon Administration sought to forestall the Congressional pressure in two ways. First, it sought discussions with the Russians for mutual and balanced force reductions (MBFR). Moscow had for a long time wanted a European security conference which, it hoped, would legitimate the postwar *status quo* in Central Europe. The Europeans, however, would not meet Russia without America, and Washington would not agree to the European security conference without

MBFR. So the two conferences were linked, and Nixon now could argue to Congress that a unilateral American withdrawal prior to an agreement with Russia would provide the latter with little incentive to negotiate; they could just wait for the withdrawal without reducing their own strength. The result would be an imbalance of conventional strength at a time of strategic parity, an imbalance which the Soviets might be tempted to exploit diplomatically in order to neutralize or "Finlandize" Western Europe. The MBFR talks did just what was expected: They relieved the pressure for American troop withdrawal. American proposals placed the emphasis on the word "balance" and sought to bring about an equality of troops and weapons, such as tanks, between NATO and Warsaw Pact forces. The Soviets omitted the B from MBFR and suggested mutual, meaning equal, force reductions across the board. Each side therefore rejected the other's proposals, the Americans because they were unwilling to accept reductions which would leave the Warsaw Pact forces, reinforced in numbers, already vastly superior in armor, in the same stronger position as before the reductions, the Russians because the American proposals amounted to a unilateral reduction of their alliance's strength while not really reducing NATO strength.

Second, the Administration tried to bring some coherence back to an alliance in disarray: 1973, the year of the American disengagement in Vietnam, as well as the year of the Common Market's enlargement, was also to be "the Year of Europe." In a major address, Henry Kissinger called for a "new Atlantic Charter" which would subordinate the diplomatic, military, and economic stresses dividing the alliance and reinforce its common purposes. In an era of *détente,* when fear could no longer cement Atlantic relationships, and with a new generation in the West which remembered neither Hitler nor Stalin, could Europe and the United States revive their partnership (which, Kissinger suggested, should include the other industrial democracy, Japan) by defining their common political interests in a changed world? Rather than leave the various issues to be discussed on a technical basis by experts and in terms of the narrow definitions of interest by government departments and pressure groups, this task ought to engage the top political leaders so that the negotiations would serve the larger collective purposes. Without an overriding sense of direction, Kissinger claimed, the economic rivalry would be carried on without restraint and would tear all the other strands of the alliance.

The response to Kissinger's call for a reaffirmation of unity showed how disunited NATO had become. In what was ironically the first success of the Common Market countries in arriving at a common foreign policy position, the Europeans reacted by stressing their "distinctive entity," urged cooperation on an equal basis, but refused to adopt the American-suggested words "interdependence" and "partnership" in a proposed joint declaration on American–Common Market relations. Above all, the Europeans were unwilling to deal with security, political, and economic issues in the same forum. Security was to be handled within the NATO framework, political-economic matters within the Common Market. There were to be two declarations! This twofold reaction only irritated United States–European relations further since Washington felt that all these issues were linked. The differences over trade and money played a major role in stimulating Congressional reluctance to continue stationing the same number of forces in Europe without sufficient offset costs being paid by the Europeans. The latter clearly wished to avoid this linkage between American troops on the Continent and possible European economic concessions. The United States wanted the Europeans to pay more for the American troops; the Europeans felt that these troops were in Europe also to protect American security interests, that they (Europeans) did contribute sufficiently to their own defense and already paid offset costs (bases provided by West Germany, American arms bought by the Europeans).

Perhaps the real question was whether an alliance can be expected to preserve its cohesion once the pressures dissipated that initially motivated the member states to unite. NATO was an "entangling alliance" when Soviet pressure was high, and only a return to the cold war could reunite it into a cohesive bloc. Once hostile pressures were relaxed, however, conflicts among the allies came to the fore; no longer was the commonly perceived security threat, once so primary, subordinated to other national issues. Indeed, the principal power within the alliance, close to its allies when the Soviet threat had been high, now communicated and negotiated directly with Moscow on the most important issues. NATO might be informed—or it might not—but it was not frequently consulted. Relations with the Kremlin had become far more important than the relations with NATO members.

The alliance was to receive one more major blow in 1973. The Yom Kippur War and its aftermath strained the alliance almost to the breaking point. The Europeans, almost totally dependent upon Arab oil for their well-being, were reluctant to antagonize the Arabs and bring an oil embargo upon themselves, as on the United States and the Netherlands. Thus although the Syrians and Egyptians initiated the hostilities, there was little backing for the United States in its support of Israel. Only then still right-wing Portugal permitted America to land its aircraft on its soil (the Azores islands) for refueling during the American airlift. Other NATO members, including Greece and Turkey, would not even grant fly-over rights and made initial supply operations to Israel from American military stocks in Europe, for example on Israeli ships, difficult. Washington, deeply angered, castigated its allies, and the Europeans responded by complaining about the lack of consultation, especially about the worldwide American alert for a possible confrontation with Russia without even warning them.

Worse was to come during this year when they were supposed to talk about improving the allied marriage but almost sued for divorce. The quadrupling of oil prices confronted all Western industrial societies, already suffering from inflation, with increased inflation because of the rise in price for gasoline, heating oil, and other oil derivatives such as fertilizer and plastic; it also caused a recession, as industries such as automobiles laid off workers as car sales plummeted, and the slackened consumer demand spread throughout the economy. Even with a lower oil demand, the possibility of bankruptcy confronted the European states as their oil bills mounted by tens of billions of dollars. OPEC's 1973 oil income rose from $23 billion to $110 billion, affecting an immense redistribution of wealth. Even if the industrial oil-importing countries avoided a runaway inflation or depression or bankruptcy, their bills would still amount to a huge debt even if they were able to borrow the "petrodollars," as they were called, from the Arabs who could not use all of their oil earnings and put the unspent money into Western banks. Had the OPEC countries been able to spend it all, they would have boosted Western employment and earnings and made it possible to absorb the oil price increase. Equally, if not more, important, Western social peace and the stability of political institutions were, in part, built upon a steadily growing economic pie and the ability to satisfy the various social groups in society with an increasing share of the wealth. The oil crisis might threaten this economic growth rate and the popular expectation of an ever higher standard of living, thereby perhaps endangering democracy itself.

American political strategy in these circumstances was two-fold: first, to conserve energy so that OPEC would find itself with a surplus of oil on its hands. Those countries which most wanted to earn petrodollars to invest and modernize themselves might then find their earnings cut back and could therefore perhaps be enticed to sell their oil at lower than OPEC prices. This would break the oil cartel's united front. Second, placing a high floor under oil and other energy sources would encourage the finding of non-OPEC oil and development of alternative sources of energy, old sources like coal or new ones such as nuclear energy. If this were successful, it would mean OPEC's current monopoly could be broken in about ten years, by the middle 1980's, even if the first part of the strategy were not successful. Or it would give OPEC the opportunity to avoid this rapid development of other sources by lowering its prices now, assuring itself of long-term markets, rather than a sharp reduction of markets in a few years.

It was the American feeling that this twofold strategy would work if the industrial democracies faced OPEC together. What happened initially, however, was that Britain, France, and West Germany struck out on their own, making long-term bilateral deals for arms and machines with various Arab states and ignoring the other Common Market countries. Such bilateral deals were likely to keep the price of oil high and hinder the resumption of economic growth in both the industrial and the underdeveloped countries. A common energy front for hard bargaining with OPEC remained difficult to attain as the United States too made a few deals of its own; agreement was, however, finally achieved within the framework of the larger International Energy Agency composed of the leading oil-importing nations.

These bilateral deals, and the fact that the other Common Market countries abandoned the Dutch as if they were lepers when the Arabs showed their displeasure at Dutch sympathy for Israel with an oil boycott, did not augur well for a community that presumably had just gained some momentum from its enlargement and the setting of a target date of 1980 for a union that promised closer political cooperation among the governments in formulating collective policies. Even though the oil crisis had dramatically shown Europe's weakness and the need for unity, the vision of Europe seemed to have faded. The threat from the East had waned, and the unique cold war circumstances in which the Europe of Six had been launched had passed. The European states looked increasingly inward. The Common Market's growing economic and financial strength, like Japan's, had not yet been translated into political and military terms that looked much beyond Europe. Admittedly, "Europe" was not dead. In 1975, among its signs of life were two symbolic decisions by its nine chiefs of government: to adopt a symbolic uniform passport system and hold elections in 1978 for the European Parliament, a move that might revive a united Europe and enhance the Parliament's rather limited present authority; but even the date of this election was almost immediately in doubt. Perhaps it is only fair to add that what is extraordinary is the

American expectation that nationalism could be quickly overcome in a complex and revolutionary attempt at transcending
nationalism by creating a supranational community, a task
immensely more difficult than building the United States
from thirteen colonies. The central question for Europe remains whether the nine member states will lose their belief
that community action cannot fulfill their purposes as well as
individual national action.

As if the increase of Soviet troop strength and modernization of their weapons and the continued conflicts of political
and economic interests dividing the alliance and the Common Market in its striving for greater political unity were not
enough, a new internal problem arose in the middle 1970's:
the possibility that a Western Communist party might receive
sufficient votes in an election that it would have to be included in a coalition government. This likelihood seemed
greater in Italy where both before and after the 1976 election
the Communists ran closely behind the Christian Democrats
who seemed after thirty odd years increasingly incapable of
governing, and in France where the Party too had great
strength. The implications of this eventuality were unclear;
opinion was deeply divided. On the one hand, the Western
European Communist leaders of Italy and France declared
that they would carry out their countries' obligations to the
Common Market and NATO and be faithful to the democratic traditions of social and political pluralism, ideological
diversity, and individual freedoms of their societies. They declared their autonomy and stated that their aims and tactics
were independent of Moscow; they were seeking their own
countries' "road to Socialism," consistent with their nation's
histories, which were inconsistent with the Soviet model. At
an East Berlin meeting of 29 Communist Parties from Eastern and Western Europe in 1967, this emphasis on nationalism Communism seemed confirmed when Soviet Party chief
Brezhnev publicly declared that each Party was responsible
for its actions first of all to the working class of its own country. The presence of Marshall Tito at the conference seemed
symbolic of a movement characterized increasingly by frag-

mentation and decreasing Soviet control over what in the West used to be called the "international Communist movement" and by Moscow "proletarian internationalism," two words Western European Communist leaders refused to use at the conference and which were not included in its final communiqué. Thus the consequences of including Communist parties in Western coalition governments did not seem fatal for democracy internally or security externally.

On the other hand, there were those who were more doubtful. Declaring national autonomy before achieving power was one thing, but once the Communist parties shared power would they really place their own countries' national interests first rather than act as Soviet agents, as so often in the past? Stating that they were committed to the continued existence of other parties and that they would allow themselves in democratic fashion to be voted out of office appeared to support their new image of parties committed to Western-style democracy, but were such statements tactical (since they were not yet in position to achieve a majority by themselves) rather than a matter of principle? How could parties that had always been organized on a Leninist authoritarian basis be committed to the preservation of democracy? If these parties were really dedicated to their own countries and to democracy, why did they still call themselves Communists rather than Social Democrats? Furthermore, if Communist parties did participate in governments of large Western states, would they not stress domestic social and economic tasks and deemphasize security commitments, even push for the abolition of NATO and the Warsaw Pact, and the withdrawal of U.S. forces from the continent? Indeed, if Communists came to power in countries like France and Italy, would not the United States itself pull back its forces since it could no longer justify their presence, or the alliance, to preserve democracy from Communism, which now was less an external threat than an internal one? For some, including Secretary of State Kissinger, these possibilities spelled disaster since its outcome would be an America which would be "an island in its own values."

Although the future of Western Europe remains somewhat cloudy, therefore, some of its past history seems at least to have been settled. Beginning with West Germany's Socialist Chancellor Brandt's efforts, something like a European peace treaty for Germany has been achieved. Brandt negotiated two treaties, one with Poland, the other with Russia, recognizing explicitly Poland's Oder-Neisse border (which included German territory seized by Poland at the end of war to compensate Poland for the Polish territory Russia took), as well as acknowledging Germany's continued division and the existence of East Germany. He also established diplomatic relations with Czechoslovakia, nullifying the 1938 Munich Treaty under which Hitler had annexed the Sudetenland. The American-British-French-Soviet-negotiated Berlin Settlement of 1971, ensuring unimpeded access to West Berlin, was the last link in this over-all settlement. The settlement accepted Moscow's demand for the recognition of the territorial *status quo,* in return for which Moscow was willing to make some concessions on Western access to West Berlin. This substitute peace was capped off symbolically with the 1975 Helsinki Conference attended by thirty-five states. The boundaries and the armistice lines which had hardened into boundaries between East and West, and had been accepted as *de facto* by the cold war adversaries, were now blessed with a *de jure* seal, even though Helsinki was not accompanied by any mutual force reductions on either side of the former Iron Curtain or any other Soviet concessions. (It was therefore heavily criticized by many in the United States for its one-sidedness.)

Greek-Turkish-American relations added a final touch and disrupted and gravely weakened NATO's southern flank because of a highly emotional and politically explosive situation on the island of Cyprus, an independent state, whose population was both Greek and Turkish. When the colonels then ruling Greece attempted to make the slogan "unity with Greece" into a reality by using the Cypriot National Guard, composed of Greeks and controlled by Athens, to overthrow Archbishop Makarios, who had preserved a fragile peace on the island for a number of years, Turkey became concerned for the Turkish minority on the island and invaded the island for the latter's protection from the Greeks. In the ensuing fighting, Turkey was victorious and the colonels, facing the possibility of a Greek-Turkish War, fell to be replaced by a democratic civilian government. But both Greece and Turkey were also upset with the United States. The Greeks were angry because Washington had not restrained Ankara from invading the island (this presumed the United States had such a capacity) or, after the Turks had protected the Turkish minority, from expanding their territorial control still further and displacing large numbers of Greeks. The Turks were mad because Washington had not used its influence with the military junta in Athens to head off the coup attempt or condemn it after it occurred and, because in retaliation against the extensive Turkish military push into the Greek areas of the island, Congress—strongly pushed by the Greek-American lobby—cut off all military assistance to Ankara until it would negotiate a political settlement for Cyprus with Athens. Turkey was now demanding about half the island for the less than 20 per cent Turkish minority; and it refused to budge diplomatically. The result was the closing of military bases in Greece and Turkey, of which the latter were the more important since they served intelligence functions, monitoring various activities in Russia. The whole southern flank of NATO seemed about to collapse, with Greeks and Turks embittered at each other and at the United States, the withdrawal of Greek forces from the NATO alliance and the closing of American bases in Turkey at the eastern end of the Mediterranean; the Soviet attempt to help the Communist Party control Portugal while neighboring Spain stood on the brink of Franco's death and a possible unstable political situation there too appeared to threaten the Western rim of NATO's southern flank as well, particularly because of the fear of the extension of Soviet naval activities to the Rock of Gilbraltar and beyond into the South Atlantic, as they had already been extended to the Indian Ocean to the east of Suez.

While this tension among three supposed allies was going on, SEATO collapsed completely. Actually in 1975 it formally dissolved itself after earlier in the year South Vietnam had unexpectedly disintegrated and the North Vietnamese had finally won power in the South. The collapse of Indochina began with another of the many military clashes between North and South Vietnamese troops, which had occurred since January, 1973. All expectations were that Hanoi would, as in 1968 and 1972, make its big push for victory in 1976 during the American Presidential campaign. But a rather routine fight turned into a rout as President Thieu of South Vietnam, allegedly short of military equipment and quickly depleting his stockpiles as a result of Congressional cutbacks of funds for South Vietnam, sought to withdraw troops from the northern part of South Vietnam and concentrate them in the more populated areas. This withdrawal, improperly prepared and hurriedly attempted by an undisciplined and not highly motivated army, spread panic among the civilians, who clogged the highways in their attempts to flee from the advancing Communist army. Hanoi, undoubtedly as surprised as Washington at the sudden collapse of Saigon's army, quickly sent its troops southward to help keep up with the retreating South Vietnamese. Saigon's fall in these circumstances was merely a matter of time. Thieu had made his decision to pull back in mid-March; Saigon fell April 30. The many leaders of the Saigon governments, who had inherited France's colonial legacy, had been too concerned with their own power and had relied too much on American assistance and forces instead of developing a social strategy to mobilize the morale and support of its population, now reaped their reward.

The war was finally over. The collapse of an ostensible ally in whom the United States had invested so much in energy and resources could not but fail to affect the politics of the area. Despite a show of force to recoup its perceived loss of prestige when the Cambodians seized the American merchantman, *Mayaguez,* leading to the recovery of the ship and its crew, there was no way to halt the erosion of American influence in Southeast Asia. In a sense, the original proponents of the war had been right to a degree when they had talked of a domino effect resulting from the loss of South Vietnam. Shortly after its victory, Hanoi announced plans for the early unification of Vietnam; Cambodian Communist troops also won in that country, and the Laotian Communists gained power politically shortly thereafter in their country, scrapping the monarchy in the process. Outside of Indochina, Thailand asked for the removal of all American forces; the Philippines stated that it would have to reconsider the future status of two big U.S. bases. Both countries established diplomatic relations with China. Formerly anti-Communist Malaysia had already done so. Everywhere in East Asia the result of what was seen as an American defeat in Vietnam was anxiety and nervousness and a move away from the United States toward Peking and Hanoi as a kind of insurance for a future in which not much hope for protection could be expected from the United States. South Korea was highly agitated as North Korea clearly wished to exploit the American humiliation by invading the South, but China and Russia reportedly discouraged such a plan. Japan too was apprehensive. The United States tried to reassure all these countries of its steadfastness, especially Japan, which, if it could ever define a political role for itself in Asia, ranked as a potentially very powerful American partner. In any case, it was in these circumstances that SEATO did the only thing it could do—bury itself. No one wept at the funeral. It had been an alliance that, unlike NATO, lacked the principal indigenous nations as its members; and it was organized against a threat that the countries of the area did not recognize. Its principal members were Western and white, two of whom had been colonial powers in the area, and the two Asian countries that joined did so for other than anti-Communist motives, the Philippines because of its traditional friendship with the United States and Pakistan to obtain American arms against India. At best, SEATO provided the United States with the justification for unilateral intervention, but the treaty forming the alliance had hardly proved itself to be what Secretary Dulles had once called it, the Monroe Doctrine for Asia. It had been another exercise in overstatement, so characteristic of the rhetoric of crusadism; unfortunately, it had also led the country into war. Vietnam had made a strong case for a more "limitationist" American foreign policy. But a world that would not leave the United States alone made that prescription hard to follow.

OPEC and the Fourth World

American foreign policy toward the Third World was already changing in some significant ways before the Nixon Administration came into office. First, the passing of bipolarity had lessened American fears that the competition with the Soviet Union for the loyalty and allegiance of the developing states might be decisive. Urgency over their modernization thus decreased as well. Second, in these circumstances there was less concern over whether these states aligned themselves with the United States. Their nonalignment was now acceptable. Third, it had become clear after two decades that the optimistic expectations of "instant development" had underestimated the difficulties and complexities of modernization. Aid seemed never ending. Fourth, aid had not even been particularly successful in winning friends and gaining influence. In the absence of traditional means of control, the friendship of aided countries was unreliable and frequently fluctuating. American aid, as a consequence of all these changes, had not only been reduced to its lowest point—less than half of 1 per cent of the gross national product, as already mentioned—but the emphasis had shifted from capital development to technical assistance. In 1971 the Senate even refused to pass any aid bill for a while, evidence that aid, which was felt by many senators to have been responsible for American military interventions such as Vietnam, had fallen into low repute. More fundamentally, the shift from bipolarity meant less attention and fewer resources from the two superpowers as their competition for the allegiance of the non-Western states (except a few strategically located and/or politically important ones) was increasingly replaced by direct American-Soviet dialogue on many significant international issues. Bipolarity had maximized the Third World's bargaining strength to elicit aid from the two principal contestants; it had also tended to transform local disputes into major big-power confrontations as their competition led them to intervene in small countries' quarrels. The new emerging multipolar system with its apparent American-Russian-Chinese core was likely to hurt the new nations, for as the Great Powers paid more attention to one another and sought agreements among themselves, their competition for the support and friendship of all but a handful of key underdeveloped nations would decline.

The view that the passing of bipolarity had reduced the underdeveloped countries to a status of only marginal significance exploded during 1973: First, in the Egyptian-Syrian-Israeli war stemming from the superpower *détente* which had frozen the post-1967 territorial *status quo,* precipitating Sadat's military action to call attention to his situation and the danger of procrastination; and second, OPEC's dramatic fourfold increase in oil prices. The oil companies, which, according to the imperialist interpretation, were supposed to be such powerful multinational corporations that they dominated the economies and countries in which they operated, were shown to be rather powerless and at the mercy of the governments of the territories under whose soil they operated. And the so-called imperialist states, whose governments are presumably controlled and directed by the capitalists, did not mobilize their military forces to squash the governments that were allegedly their puppet regimes. Confronting a vital threat to their security and well-being from countries that had no military power to speak of, the industrial democracies did not even debate the issue of military intervention. Had this event occurred a few decades earlier, they would not have hesitated to resort to force rather than face the possibility of being destroyed economically. In 1973 they talked of accommodation and acquiesced in this change in the rules of the game, at least in oil and temporarily.

For that was what the OPEC price change was: a change in the rules of the game. The underdeveloped countries had, as they saw it, for years been trying to lift themselves up by their own sandal-straps, but the problems they had faced in their attempts to modernize themselves were for many of them formidable. The hopes and expectations of the 1950's and early 1960's had turned into disappointment, even despair. The rules seemed stacked against them by the industrial nations, which, they felt, had long profited from their "cheap" raw materials and sold them high priced machinery. Therefore the rules had to be changed: Raise the prices so that earnings could be substantially raised and then try to link that price to the Western inflation (nothing was said about linking it to recession). This linkage was referred to as "indexing," which, should it be achieved, would in all likelihood stoke that inflation even higher. But how could the rules be changed? Follow OPEC's example: form producer-cartels, thereby controlling access and prices of raw materials. The assumption underlying this recourse was that the underdeveloped countries controlled their resources. In a 1974 U.N. General Assembly Declaration, they asserted that they had the "inalienable right" to sovereign control over their natural resources and economic activities. The end result would be what the Declaration called a New International Economic Order, an international system characterized by a major redistribution of wealth which would allow them to develop themselves and satisfy their revolutions of rising expectations. But there would not be just a reduction of the economic inequalities between the rich and poor nations; there would also be a parallel redistribution of power. The underdeveloped states felt that they possessed the resources the industrial states needed; without them, the latter would collapse.

The rich nations were, in brief, very vulnerable. The poor could place them in great jeopardy. The world had turned topsy-turvy. The weak were really powerful and the strong were really rather powerless in this new international economic order. To soften this argument based upon the power to hurt and injure, the underdeveloped nations added a moral layer whose purpose was to make this redistribution of wealth and power more palatable and acceptable to the Western industrial states. Colonial exploitation was invoked as the justification: Denied independence and the right to the ownership of their wealth (raw materials), they had been kept in poverty while the exploiting Western states grew rich. Thus the West was obligated to help them; the price rise of raw materials was, in the final analysis, not a question of supply and demand but reparations, a moral debt. The sins of colonialism were thus invoked to legitimate their demand for a redistribution of wealth and power; the memories of these sins would be used to exploit the Western democracies' sense of guilt for their past behavior.

The success of this strategy in terms of economic coercion remains debatable. In oil, it could work because oil was vital and, in a sense, irreplaceable; there were also only a few countries to organize into a cartel. For other resources this strategy might not, however, work for a number of reasons: the readier availability of substitutes (even the oil cartel could not last for this reason); recycling industrial scrap; conservation; stockpiling; new finds of resources, as under the sea beds. Even more debilitating for this strategy were the large numbers of raw material producing nations in most areas which would complicate the task of organizing a united front. However, the most difficult barrier to success remained the fact that the underdeveloped countries as the raw material suppliers for the industrial world was in part a myth. The Western countries produce most of the world's resources; so the cartel would have to include its adversaries. The ironic fact is that most underdeveloped countries are net importers of raw materials! Of the nonfood, nonfuel commodities, the Western industrial nations supply 60 per cent, the Communist states 10 per cent and the underdeveloped countries 30 per cent. And most of the world's food exports, as repeated Soviet imports of wheat and the recent threats of starvation in certain areas of the world like South Asia have shown, is from the rich countries, especially the United States.

Most underdeveloped countries have, indeed, been badly hurt—worse than the developed ones—by OPEC. This has led to a new distinction among the former: the Third World composed of resource-rich countries and the Fourth World composed of the resource-poor countries. For these nations the quadrupling of oil prices has seriously set back the development process, perhaps consigning many of them to stagnation. It is clear why this may be so: Recession in the West reduces the demand for raw materials, which lowers their prices, which in turn produces less foreign aid and increases the prices of Western machinery and other goods. With smaller earnings of foreign exchange, their ability to import high-priced oil goes down too. This means less capability to preserve the Green Revolution of miracle wheat, which is highly energy-dependent for fertilizer, irrigation, and transportation for the distribution of food. Thus a food crisis threatens many underdeveloped countries whose agricultural output has until now kept pace with the birth rate and which, in years of natural disasters, was helped by surplus grain reserves, largely in the United States; these reserves no longer exist, having been sold, given away or eaten up.

Yet, despite this enhanced suffering, the fourth world countries have not formed a coalition with the industrial states to lower oil prices. This is partly explainable by fear of irritating OPEC, partly by hope for promised but still largely undelivered OPEC economic help (most of it has gone to fellow Moslem nations, which have used much of it to buy arms) and partly, already noted, by the desire to imitate OPEC. But the basic reason is that the Fourth World identifies emotionally with OPEC. The latter's action, even though it hurt them the worst, was widely perceived by these countries as "getting even" for past exploitation; it gave them a good feeling that for once the weak had reversed the tables and made the strong suffer. The German word *Schadenfreude* says it best: pleasure received from seeing someone who deserves it really suffer, "get his." For this instance, material considerations, which perhaps should have moved them to align with the West against the Third World countries, were subordinated to far stronger emotional and psychological factors which aligned them with the resource-rich Third World countries against the West. OPEC has responded trying to maintain a united front by tying all negotiations on oil with the oil-importing countries to the discussion of all underdeveloped countries' raw material prices. Perhaps the five-year Lôme treaty between the Common Market and forty-six developing countries in Africa, Asia, and the Caribbean may point that way. It sought to stabilize these countries' earnings, mainly from agricultural commodities, in times of great price fluctuations by allowing them to borrow from a fund established by the Common Market in bad years when prices drop below a minimum set level, as well as giving them access duty free to the Market for most of their products. A fair response to the Fourth World countries' needs may yet produce a common front of the latter with the Western nations, especially if a continued lack of a generous response by OPEC to the resource-poorer countries aggravates their dismal economic lot; economics may yet triumph over *Schadenfreude*. Nevertheless, the Third-Fourth World alliance indicates, fairly or not from a Western point of view, the depth of resentment and feelings of anger and frustration against a system which they feel keeps them in an insubordinate and poverty-stricken status. Hence their outrage and sense of injustice exploded in delight as the powerful and rich quaked before "their kind" in OPEC.

In any event, OPEC had demonstrated rather dramatically that nations were "interdependent," to use a much-used phrase of the 1970's. A rise in oil prices stoked inflation and recession in the West, which reduced the demand for oil and slowed Western economic growth; the consequence was to blight many underdeveloped countries' hopes for development, enhance the problem of raising food production, and, to complete the circle, increase demands for Western economic and food help. Yet such help from the Western states, especially the United States, declined, as they bought fewer resources, could afford less foreign aid, and had to sell food in order to earn money to pay for the oil. But OPEC also showed another side to interdependence: the drive for greater national independence as the Western countries determined to reduce their dependence on OPEC for energy. Whatever the case for interdependence really is, the demonstration of energy interdependence had stirred a lot of ill-feeling. Moral denunciations about past and present exploitative practices by countries most of whom looked westward for help in their development plans hardly helped the situation. It was a bit annoying to be told repeatedly that the Western countries were rich because the non-Western countries were poor, as if plunder rather than hard work and discipline, technology and scientific inventiveness, political leadership, economic ideas, social organization, and generally an energetic, secularly oriented way of life had been the chief reasons for the West's industrialization and modernization.

Nevertheless, by 1974 confrontation between the developed and underdeveloped countries became an increasingly visible occurrence in the United Nations' General Assembly. Under Arab oil pressure, a majority of the underdeveloped nations invited the head of the Palestinian Liberation Organization, a nonstate actor whose acts of terrorism and hijacking the Assembly had debated only a few years earlier, to address it. Indicative of the Assembly's mood, it treated the PLO leader Arafat as a head of government and greeted him with sustained applause while limiting the time for Israel's reply, which was delivered to a virtually empty body. Simultaneously, the same Arab-African majority, supported by the Communist states, barred Israeli participation in the previously nonpolitical United Nations Educational, Scientific, and Cultural Organization. In addition to these actions, the Assembly ousted South Africa from its session for its racial practices after the Security Council, which exercises the ultimate suspension power, had refused to do so. In 1975 the Assembly passed a resolution condemning Zionism as racism, virtually giving its seal of approval to anti-Semitism. (So much for the one people who more than any other has been the victim of racism throughout history and probably done more to expose and condemn persecution of any kind.) UNESCO again followed suit, leading to a walkout of all Western members. The Assembly had also listened to Uganda's President, widely reported to have murdered thousands of his countrymen and cruelly expelled thousands of Indians who had lived for generations in Uganda and become citizens, attack the United States and Zionism in his role as spokesman for the Organization of African States; at the end of his speech, the Assembly had given him a standing ovation. These and other actions—such as ignoring the civil war in Angola, where Russia and Cuba were heavily involved— were all symptoms of an increasingly anti-Western pattern in the United Nations, not only in the General Assembly but also in the Security Council where in 1976 the PLO was allowed to participate in a debate on the Palestine Arab issue as if it were already a member state, as well as in specialized organizations such as UNESCO and World Food Conference. Paradoxically, these majorities insisting on their rights were composed overwhelmingly of nondemocratic states where the voice of the majority remained unheard.

The international organization had been founded to incorporate existing governments; other guerrilla leaders, including those of Algeria, were not invited to the organization or given observer status even where it appeared likely that they might someday establish a government. More important, governments were U.N. members because they in fact governed certain territory and population; they were not chosen to become members because they represented certain kinds of governments or practiced certain enlightened or virtuous policies. For instance, Uganda is a member, as well as democratic Israel; the former state is not excluded for its brutal internal practices. To exclude governments or limit their right of debate because a current majority of U.N. members objects would signify a radical transformation from the original and long-standing U.N. aim of including all governments so that their views may be represented and aired and formal and informal exchanges of different opinions occur. It would not only impede the Assembly's work. It would embitter states and either paralyze the Assembly's capacity to decide or render its resolutions, which are of an advisory nature only, useless. In the final analysis, it would alienate Western and especially American support, and intensify conflicts as in the

Middle East instead of helping to resolve them and preserve the peace.

Latin America and the United States

With the major exception of OPEC, the underdeveloped countries received Washington's attention only on a bilateral basis, particularly in Latin America, where cold war considerations continued to play a significant role despite the *détente* with Russia and China. American foreign policy, indeed showed a perhaps all too tenacious continuity with a policy that had historically considered Latin America to be in America's sphere of influence and continued to oppose what were perceived to be radical left-wing revolutions and regimes that might bring the principal adversary power, the Soviet Union, into America's so-called backyard. Thus when in 1970 Chile elected Marxist Salvador Allende to the Presidency, the Nixon Administration, while publicly acting correctly, sought first to prevent Allende from becoming President and, after that failed, to make life difficult for him and encourage the military to a *coup d'état*. Thus in a subtler way than Kennedy at the Bay of Pigs or Johnson in the Dominican Republic, the new Republican Administration used the Central Intelligence Agency for the same anti-Communist reason as preceding Administrations. Yet the reasons for the Chilean coup, when it came, stemmed essentially from Allende's own actions and the domestic reactions these precipitated. The CIA may have helped shorten the time until the coup occurred, but the causes of the crisis were internal; by 1973 Allende's end was merely a matter of time. Indeed, Chile provides a most persuasive example of why the United States should not intervene in this type of situation.

While not excusing the intervention, it is important to stress this point because Allende has become something of a martyr, frequently portrayed as the revolutionary who was fairly elected to seek reforms and better the lot of the poor and underprivileged, only to be blocked and finally overthrown by a fascist conspiracy on behalf of a reactionary ruling class in league with capitalist America. Had he in fact lived, Allende's reputation would have been stained by the failure of his political leadership; his suicide at the time of the coup elevated his reputation to a level he could have never have achieved had he lived and remained as leader of Chile's "road to socialism."

Allende came to power having won 36 per cent of the vote, two points ahead of his next competitor in a three-way race. In the runoff vote in the Congress, he received the support of the centrist Christian Democratic Party. At the start of his rule he possessed opposition support for much of his program, including the nationalization of the American-owned copper mines, banks, major industries, and land reform. While it thus seemed possible to work within Chile's constitutional norms with a democratic consensus, Allende believed in class struggle. He deliberately pursued a policy of polarizing Chileans, which did more to consolidate the professional middle and lower middle classes in opposition to him than to broaden his worker-peasant base of support. As he pursued his program, his vow to constitutional rule fell by the wayside. Representing a sizable minority, but hardly "the people," he could have governed only if he had gained the majority support in the Congress which he did not possess. In a Parliamentary system he would have fallen quickly; in Chile's Presidential system he survived by increasingly bypassing Congress and the courts. The Christian Democrats then joined the rightist opposition, and class polarity was then matched by executive-legislative polarity. Allende had eliminated the middle ground of Chilean politics and emasculated the spirit of the Constitution.

The nucleus of Allende's opposition came less from any privileged ruling class than from the lower middle class, which was deeply affected by an inflation over 300 per cent by 1973, shortages of all kinds in the shop (leading to marches by housewives with empty saucepans), and worries that their small businesses might be wiped out by inflation or government takeovers. In 1972 and especially in 1973, small truckers, who owned one or two trucks, went on strike and were joined by shopkeepers, doctors, lawyers, engineers, bus and taxi drivers, and airline pilots (between the strikes even the workers in the largest copper mine struck). It was this, the second truckers' strike, which was reportedly prolonged by the passing of CIA money to the truckers.

The military during this period became increasingly politicized. Asked by Allende at several points to participate in his Cabinet to reassure those worried about law and order in the midst of strikes, the street marches of Allende's supporters and opposition, and illegal seizures of land by the President's followers, the military initially served Allende as it had his predecessors (it even crushed one attempted revolt by some military units). What precipitated the military's intervention after forty years of staying out of Chilean politics was the rapid growth of paramilitary forces among Allende's extreme left-wing followers, who had always believed in armed confrontation with "reaction," and the public call for an insurrection in the navy by a close Allende friend and party co-leader; both events apparently occurred with Allende's complicity. The country was on the verge of civil war when the military struck. It did not need American urging.

Not that the United States had not been hostile to Allende from the start. After the expropriation of American property without compensation, Washington cut off American credit and pressured international financial institutions to follow suit. But Allende more than made up his American losses with credits from Communist states, other Latin American countries, and West European countries. Chile also had rich copper mines. Had Allende been a Nasser, he would have survived American pressure and hostility by arousing his people's nationalist ardor. But that was why Allende did not survive; he rejected a role as President of all Chileans. He declared himself to be President of only some Chileans—against other Chileans. Such polarization of society, a galloping inflation plus increasingly unconstitutional rule, were hardly recipes for political success. Had the CIA practiced abstinence, responsibility for the Chilean group would properly have fallen on Allende; he destroyed himself politically before he did so physically. The CIA meddling drew attention from this and reaped the blame for Allende's difficulties and fall for the United States. Whatever it says for or against American intervention in its sphere of influence—if such a sphere can still be considered important and relevant in areas far beyond the nearer Caribbean area in this intercontinental age—Chile stands as a persuasive case for nonintervention. Even the Bay of Pigs operation in the Caribbean should have made a few points for nonintervention, covert or overt. Americans, perhaps because of the democratic nature of their society, seem on the whole rather clumsy at this sort of thing and feel morally uneasy about it. Perhaps most reprehensible and in some ways symbolic were the several attempts to assassinate Castro, involving the Kennedy Administration, the CIA, and Mafia figures—certainly an immoral alliance to murder in the name of national security. And, unlike in a television play, this unholy alliance failed in all of their attempts. In Chile, a country as far away from the United States as the Middle East, the question is surely whether the United States had the right to try to upset the election of any political figure who was elected according to the constitutional processes either in the name of American national security or for the broader consideration of the preservation of democratic values—values Washington did not insist on in Chile after Allende or in other parts of this increasingly nondemocratic globe.

In an increasingly nationalistic world the limits of even America's enormous power had become increasingly clear. The United States could still exercise great influence, but its power could not always bring about preferred solutions. Sometimes it was best perhaps not to interfere, to learn to live with unpleasant realities and let events take their course or seek to influence them with a less heavy hand and only in proportion to the degree of vital interest to the country. Vietnam had shown dramatically the high material and moral costs of intervening against a militarily weaker regime which could mobilize the support and morale of its people on a basis of nationalism; even if the war could have been won militarily, the price for a democracy seems to have been prohibitive. For the weak can resort to guerrilla war and gain victory by attrition, as the Algerian nationalists and Vietnamese Communists did over the French and American armies with all of their superior technology and firepower. Military attacks or economic pressures against smaller, weaker, underdeveloped, nonwhite countries are no longer considered legitimate except perhaps in extreme circumstances; they tend to be politically counterproductive for the Western, industrial, former colonial, white nation seeking to do so. Perhaps this is why there has been so little discussion of military retaliation against OPEC, short of its attempting to strangle the West by a long total oil embargo (by the rule that nations have a right to defend themselves when their survival is at stake, the use of military force in such an unlikely circumstance is a foregone conclusion).

It is also perhaps why, in the wake of Vietnam and Chile, the United States had to rethink its attitudes toward nationalism in this hemisphere and has made some moves toward accommodating itself to this phenomenon, thereby preserving a degree of influence in a continent where anti-Americanism is rife and some ugly political clashes are possible. Hesitatingly, Washington has at least tolerated new nationalist regimes, often military, which may be leftist but which, like that in Peru, have not hesitated to expropriate American property like Standard Oil or seized American fishing vessels up to 200 miles off their coasts. And some very tentative moves have been made, largely in response to the desires of other Latin American states, to improve relations with Castro's Cuba, although Cuba's Angolan intervention set this effort back. But perhaps the most important sign of a change in American attitudes would be the acceptance of a change in the status of the Panama Canal Zone.

For Latin America, the disposition of this issue was critical. This was not a strictly American-Panamanian issue. For all of the Latin American states—left, centrist, and right—supported Panama in its determination to assert its control over a piece of territory that America treated as if it were America's.

Would the United States seek to preserve its control of the Zone, which would lead to violence between the American forces in the Zone and the Panamanians, or would it accommodate itself to the nationalism of not only Panama but all the states to its south? Theodore Roosevelt had created Panama in order to build the canal for the growing American navy at the turn of the century; the 1903 treaty between the two countries had granted the United States "in perpetuity the use, occupation, and control" of a ten-mile-wide zone to build, run and protect the canal, although the sovereignty of this territory was to remain vested in Panama. The result was a virtual colonial situation. The American role in that small country became dominant. The Canal Zone cuts Panama in two and is run by the U.S. Army. Panamanians in the Zone are subject to American law administered by American courts. All business enterprises are operated by the United States; Panamanians are denied the opportunity to compete. And the American government holds large tracts of zonal land and water needed by Panama's rapidly growing population. What all this amounts to is that the United States acts as if it were sovereign in the Zone when in fact it only possesses certain treaty rights over a piece of Panamanian territory. And to make matters worse, Panamanians felt that they had received rather scanty economic benefits from the Canal; fair or not, the contrast between the standards of living in the Zone and outside it was grating and humiliating. Political discontent had become so high by 1964 that nationalist frustrations burst into riots when Panamanian students tried to fly their country's flag next to the American one at the zonal high school. American students resisted, and twenty-one Panamanian and three American students were killed in the subsequent explosion. The confrontation had been a symbolic one and a sample on a minor scale of what faced the United States should it seek to preserve its control "in perpetuity."

Time was running out. The Canal's economic benefits to the United States were declining with shifting world trade patterns and the increasing use of supertankers and container ships too large to pass through the Canal; even its military value was being reduced by a two-ocean navy with huge air-craft carriers, which could not go through the Canal, and nuclear submarines, which would have to surface to pass from one ocean to the other (providing intelligence to the Russians of their whereabouts). The Canal Zone issue, like the flag issue, had become primarily symbolic. American liberals recognized the need for change to meet Panama's aspirations for territorial integrity and real instead of nominal sovereign control; if denied, Panama might become "another Vietnam." But American conservatives, very strong in Congress, bitterly resisted a new treaty, which would restore the Zone to Panama by the end of the century while ensuring America's right to continued use of and protection for the waterway; if granted, Panama would become "another Suez," an indication of a retreat of American power, another instance of a once-powerful America groveling before a tiny country. Common sense may yet prevail, although not without a struggle in Washington.

The Canal could obviously be better protected with the Panamanians' consent than without—or against—it; the latter would produce sabotage and violence, which would compel the United States to send large military forces to the Zone to protect it from "the natives." The pictures of American troops shooting Panamanians would make ugly headlines. So would the public confrontation in the United Nations, an international forum where Panama has said it will take the issue rather than to the Organization of American States, which it considered an appendage of the United States. In the universal organization, the United States would stand virtually alone against a solid bloc of underdeveloped countries. Thus the symbolism of the issue was domestic and international. While for many Americans, and not just some in Congress, the Canal Zone was "American," anything less than eventual Panamanian control over its own territory was equally unthinkable. A new treaty would therefore be a symptom of a change in American attitudes toward the nationalist aspirations of its Southern neighbors; it would also constitute a recognition of an American reassessment of its formerly dominant position in this hemisphere. Already Peru, Venezuela, Bolivia, Argentina had asserted themselves strongly against the United States and American influence throughout Latin-America was clearly on the wane. The area was less and less of an American "sphere of influence." The real stake in Panama, in brief, was America's new global image and role.

Détente: *An Evaluation*

How can *détente* be evaluated? Did the United States benefit by it, or was it advantageous primarily for the Soviet Union? Was *détente* primarily a tactic or was it a symptom of a more moderate Soviet Union in international politics? The critics of *détente* have argued that it was essentially a continuation of the cold war by other means, that the Soviet Union remained an expansionist power but that it had realized that the payoff from smiling was greater than from shaking the fist. *Détente* was thus a tactical change seeking to put the West off its guard and exploiting the resulting relaxation of tensions in order to attain a position of superior power—hegemony, as the Chinese called it. Once achieved, this would lead again to more direct, crude pressures and a renewal of the cold war, only this time the Soviet Union would be the stronger power.

The critics have attributed the Soviet desire for *détente* primarily to Russia's economic needs. They therefore argued that the West must use its economic tools—as well as other tools—to bargain harder for such things as strategic arms stabilization and reductions, Red Army withdrawals from Central Europe, freer Jewish emigration, and access for Western publications and ideas to the Soviet sphere. If Russia wanted a legitimation of the *status quo* in Europe, it should have to pay a price for it as, for instance, some force reduction of the huge number of tanks facing NATO. Otherwise, no deals. According to the critics, Russia's economic troubles are in large part due to the excessive investment in the arms area. American technology and credits would thus be subsidizing this effort unless such assistance were tied in to arms reduction talks. Furthermore, some of the critics have asserted that arms limitations by themselves do not suffice; more fundamental domestic reforms must be demanded. For Russia will evolve into a state that other states can live with in confidence and trust only if its government becomes more responsive to popular needs and expectations. In the words of an English Sovietologist, "Since Peter the Great, that country's rulers have sought the technology of the West with the purpose of arming and equipping a political culture based on totally anti-Western standards." Internal liberalization was thus critical. Then Russia's leaders would be preoccupied with domestic issues and satisfying their people's aspirations and have less time and fewer resources for foreign adventures.

Whether the United States can, in fact, use trade and technology to extract such significant political concessions remains a debatable issue. American machinery and know-how will undoubtedly help the Soviet economy, but Russia has alternative sources of credit, capital goods, and skills in the European industrial countries and Japan. Food may be a better instrument for bargaining. The question really revolves around the kind of political expectations the United States harbors beyond those of a straight and profitable commercial deal. No Soviet leader, especially during a period of *détente,* is likely to make deals on the free access of Western ideas which he believes will weaken the regime's authority and threaten the security of the Soviet sphere's frontiers. Brezhnev did in fact reject a commercial agreement which included a Senate-attached provision about Jewish emigration (thus removing a bargaining chip from the Administration and reducing, rather than increasing, Jewish emigration). Few, if any, governments, especially not those of Great Powers, will sign agreements on the condition that they virtually admit publicly that they are mistreating their citizens, and few will admit that they will amend their ways under foreign pressure. Secretary Kissinger has argued that to make foreign policy agreements with Russia dependent upon domestic changes within Russia will, indeed, be counter-productive, compelling Soviet leaders to take firmer stands on international issues and possibly endangering their tenure because they may be accused of "coddling capitalism" instead of a vigorous defense of "socialist interests." The Soviets have also demonstrated that, despite their burdensome defense budget, they have been willing to make the necessary sacrifices to attain strategic parity and modernize their conventional forces. Once they achieved this parity they did show an interest in strategic arms stabilization, partly no doubt to save some money but in large part because of the increasing Soviet awareness of the dangers of continued offensive and defensive arms competition.

It is, of course, true that Soviet power, strategic and conventional, has grown immensely in the last decade and that the Soviet Union sought to exploit the Middle Eastern war in 1973, the Portuguese upheaval after the collapse of the dictatorship, and Angolan independence after the Portuguese withdrew. But it did not do much to take advantage of the bitter Greek-Turkish dispute over Cyprus, which weakened NATO's southern flank, or the general economic crisis of the West. It remained rather mild in its denunciations of the United States throughout the Vietnam war, in which a fraternal socialist state was being attacked; indeed, it continued to seek a relaxation of tensions and negotiated with the United States, including at the summit meeting right after Nixon's heavy bombing and blockading of North Vietnam. Presumably Moscow placed pressure on Hanoi to permit the American disengagement from the war; and it could be no more sure than in 1954 that Hanoi would later be able to pick up the South. For *détente* Moscow was quite willing to "sell out" Hanoi, as it had Cairo by not supplying it arms until the Egyptians made it plain in 1973 that they were going to go to war anyway and that Moscow had the choice of either supporting its friends or losing its influence in the Arab world. Moreover, does *détente* really look as good to the Soviets as some Westerners suggest? The American strategic arsenal remains awesome, American troops are still in Europe, Soviet influence in the Middle East is down, and the American economic connection has not yet proved to be as bountiful as might have been hoped.

In any event, it is fair to ask whether *détente* was ever

meant to be a set of self-denying ordinances. If the Soviet Union is faced with unexpected but favorable situations to exploit, should it shun this opportunity? Self-denial as a policy is asking a lot of any Great Power. The United States itself did not forgo the opportunity, especially since 1973, to take advantage of Sadat's westward turn to enhance American influence and reduce Soviet influence in the Middle East. If the United States does not or cannot use countervailing power in instances where the Soviet Union seeks to take advantage—as in Angola where the Senate cut off funds for the arms the Administration was sending to the anti-Communist factions—or when it fails to bargain hard when it has a strong hand—as with wheat when the Administration may be reluctant to withhold sales because the farmers wish to maximize their earnings and the President does not want to alienate a sizable vote—the consequences are in part the responsibility of the United States. Should the Soviet Union be held accountable for American default? In the Middle East in 1973 the United States was willing to act and compel Russia to desist and behave responsibly. If an Administration is unable or unwilling to exert pressure on Russia or withhold items the Russians want, be they strategic agreements, industrial equipment, or wheat, it holds no incentives for Soviet moderation; but it has only itself to blame.

What, then, is the balance sheet for *détente?* For the United States—as for the Soviet Union undoubtedly—*détente* has had mixed results. Perhaps the most important benefit of *détente* is the reduction of the ideological zeal which had marked the cold war and raised so many issues to conflicts of good and evil. Differences were now viewed as differences of interests which were resolvable through negotiations, not a clash of moral absolutes to be inflexibly defended lest one compromise with—and be tainted by—evil. Indeed, one criticism in the United States of *détente* was that Nixon and Kissinger were too chummy and comfortable with Brezhnev; another was that they were compromising too much and getting too little in return! Both of these criticisms were a far cry from the days when even the slightest signs of an administration's desire to negotiate with the Russians and Chinese were subject to accusations of treachery, sell-outs and "coddling Communism." Soviet and Chinese proposals were then generally rejected out of hand as mere propaganda or tricks to deceive; they were rarely examined for merit or seen as a reflection of legitimate interests.

A second benefit of *détente* has been the attempts to stabilize deterrence, slow down the quantitative buildup and qualitative improvement of strategic offensive forces and virtually eliminate the defensive forces. Dangers, admittedly, remain. The strategic ceiling of 2,400 delivery systems is so high that to reach it the United States will have to add missiles or bombers; the 1,320 MIRV's under this ceiling, moreover, may be dangerous, possibly destabilizing deterrence. No agreement was reached during SALT on the number of warheads a missile could carry. The far greater "payload" that the bigger Russian missiles can carry means that they may end up with a considerably larger number of warheads which, if accurate, may give the Soviets a first-strike capability. Future negotiations about reductions in numbers of weapons and unilateral restraint in the development of destabilizing weapons will be necessary if renewed arms competition and rising political tensions are to be avoided. Still, given the general scope of the American-Soviet conflict and the distrust which had grown up over two and a half decades, what is remarkable is that SALT produced any achievements at all. In a critical way, then, SALT remains the barometer of *détente:* Agreements are an indicator that *détente* is, on the whole, healthy; inability to agree reflects not only the difficulties of arriving at an accord but that *détente* may be in trouble. SALT symbolizes both superpower cooperation and common interests on the one hand and continuing superpower competition and distrust on the other hand; such attitudes are bound to affect the whole range of American-Soviet relations.

A third achievement which *détente* produced was what might be called a German peace settlement. The four-power Berlin settlement, West Germany's treaties with Poland and Russia, the treaty between the two Germanys plus their admission to the United Nations, all capped by the 1975 Helsinki Conference, legitimated the *status quo* that had existed since 1945. Two world wars in this century had broken out in Europe. It was the German issue that had precipitated these conflicts, and it was the same issue that had contributed to the eruption and intensification of the cold war. While the Russians and East Germans could some day reopen the issue of Western access to West Berlin, if Moscow should feel that a favorable shift of power to it has occurred, or America's will and determination to play a great power role has become questionable, the German question seemed largely resolved.

A fourth benefit of *détente* has been the opening to the People's Republic of China. President Nixon's trip to Peking in 1972 symbolized a dramatic change in Sino-American relations and, once and for all, ended the irrationality of a situation in which the United States for almost a quarter-century seemed to ignore the existence of the world's most populated country, a nation with great potential power, a significant stake in Asia's future, and an ideological rival of the Soviet Union. And just as Washington, during the 1950's, had feared the Sino-Soviet coalition, and Peking, during the 1960's, had frequently pointed to an alleged Russian-American collusion in an attempt to isolate China, so Moscow now became apprehensive of closer Sino-American relations since, among other things, it gave the United States a persuasive lever—if skillfully used—in its negotiations with the Kremlin. The American shift of policy from Taiwan to Peking was long overdue; domestic politics had too long blocked a rational adjustment and exploitation of the Sino-Soviet conflict, a conflict whose tensions may rise or lower from time to time but one which is likely to continue despite changes of leaders in both countries for their quarrels reflect differences of interest more profound than merely differences of personalities, as the death of Mao in 1976 has already shown.

On the negative side is the further erosion of NATO. But the bonds of this alliance had been weakening even before *détente* set in. *Détente* only weakened them further and posed the central question of how an alliance, forged in a period of danger when all the partners perceived the security threat as paramount, can survive a relaxation of tension when the danger has seemingly passed and other issues—often divisive ones, especially of an economic nature—appear more important. The way to unite NATO once more would be to regenerate the cold war. In the absence of this eventuality other bases than fear and insecurity can perhaps be found to regenerate the cohesion of the Western alliance. One such possibility may be the necessity for greater economic cooperation made essential by the new awareness among the industrial democracies (including Japan) of their interdependence as a result of the mutually interacting simultaneous recession and inflation of the early middle 1970's. Another possibility of establishing a closer relationship among countries who, after all, share common values, political organization and level of economic development, would be to collectively develop a more constructive relationship with the third and fourth worlds and build an international system in which the less developed countries can play a positive and responsible role. But it remains to be seen whether either course can replace external threat as cement for the NATO alliance.

Détente has certainly led to the neglect of the less developed countries. Partly it was a matter of priorities. Nixon and Kissinger concentrated on, first, ending the Vietnam War, second, relations with Russia and China, and third, Europe and the Atlantic alliance. Relations with the underdeveloped countries appeared less urgent at a time the superpowers were dealing with one another and negotiating on key issues; the need to compete for the loyalties and support of the underdeveloped countries seemed, with some exceptions, no longer very important. The Middle East remained on the back burner until in 1973 the United States could no longer afford not to get involved. In the war between India and Pakistan over Bangladesh the Administration sided with Pakistan when China, which Nixon was about to visit, supported Pakistan. Angola became important because of the large-scale Russian effort there and Kissinger's feeling that Moscow would misread a lack of an American response to a Soviet

effort to dominate a country 8,000 miles away from the Soviet Union as an indication of a lack of American will. If
correct, this might lead to other challenges, perhaps including violations of SALT agreements. Chile too was seen in the
context of the American-Soviet competition. The new states,
then, received American attention largely when they intruded
on Great Power politics.

In 1973 they, therefore, placed themselves in the picture.
Yet the global problem of the gross inequalities of wealth,
and more broadly, the human condition remains. The Third
and Fourth World's growing frustration with their underdeveloped status, their sense that the international system is
structured against them and that they wish to play a larger
role in decisions affecting them, their desire to use the price
of the resources they export to the rich countries to enhance
their earnings for their modernization, the difficulties many
of them experience feeding their rapidly growing populations
a balanced diet—all spill over into the international arena and
affect other states in significant and sometimes disturbing
ways. In 1973 the Western world learned the meaning of the
word "interdependence"; resources, especially energy, population, and food, were not issues likely to disappear soon. And
confrontation between the First World (the industrial democracies) and the Third and Fourth Worlds was not a way to resolve these problems; that could only benefit the Second or
Soviet World. A more sympathetic response is required if the
system is not to be strained to the breaking point, however
provocative and radical the underdeveloped countries' rhetoric sometimes becomes and however annoying this becomes to
the Western nations; this is probably all the more true, since,
if the United States had the will to develop its own many
resources, the underdeveloped countries' attempts to economically coerce the West will, with the exception of a few resources, probably have only a limited effect. The more fundamental questions for America are: can it, as a democracy, live
with good conscience in a world in which it is in a minority,
in which the majority will grow hostile if basic political and
economic changes do not occur; and can it, as a great power,

cope with the consequences of the "revolution of rising frustration": on the international system in which it has such an immense stake and in which on the sidelines stands a rival only too willing to pick up the pieces and become the hegemonic power? In short, the American-Soviet "game" is no longer the only game in the state system, although it cannot but help affect the superpower relationship.

The results of *détente* are thus mixed. It is not an entente with which it is often confused. *Détente* refers to the relaxation of tensions between the superpowers; it suggests the continued presence, not absence, of tensions. Entente refers to a more cordial state of relationship. A better phrase for *détente,* one more apt and descriptive of the nature of the relationship, would be "adversary-partnership." Both elements are and will in the future remain present in this relationship; *détente* does not therefore signify the arrival of the millennium and superpower harmony. As we know, some of the critics of *détente,* citing continued American-Soviet conflicts of interest on some issues, have argued that *détente* has benefitted the Soviet Union more than the United States and have suggested that tougher American bargaining would have compelled the Soviet Union to comply more with American preferences. The assumption behind this assertion seemed to be that Washington could afford to sacrifice *détente* while Moscow could not. This is a dubious assumption: the United States also needed *détente* as it sought to stabilize the arms race, slow rapidly rising defense costs, reduce risks of confrontation and crises, and lower international tensions while the country was experiencing a post-Vietnam period of disillusionment with foreign policy and mood of retrenchment from extensive overseas commitments plus a desire to reorder the priorities between foreign and domestic policies. In that short-term tactical sense, *détente* for the Nixon-Ford Administration was a holding operation until the country's mood changed once more so the United States could continue to play a major role in the world. Whether that role would be less extensive than during the cold war, as Americans overwhelmingly preferred, remained to be seen. Racial problems in South Africa, nuclear proliferation, instability in the Middle East were just some of the problems in addition to continued concerns about Soviet intentions, and capabilities, which questioned whether America could reduce its own role in a world that would not leave it alone, whose problems impinged upon every facet of American life, and many of whose leaders looked to the United States for help and answers. The United States, it would seem, remained the one indispensable power in the world.

Yet a beginning has been made on the longer-term and more basic building of a "structure of peace" which, on the one hand, seeks to prevent the Soviet Union from using its military power to enhance its political influence and, on the other, seeks to resolve conflicts and differences through negotiations while trying to fortify the incentives for moderation by expanding areas of common cooperation. Nevertheless, although American-Soviet *détente* and Sino-American rapprochement constitute the basic building blocks of a more stable and peaceful state system, they are by themselves not enough since they cannot deal effectively with the global problems presented by the less developed countries whose modernization is so closely linked politically, economically and even morally to the future security and well-being of Western societies. At the very minimum, it would be expecting too much for the Soviet Union under these circumstances to help shape the international system; the confrontation of the industrial and underdeveloped worlds, the mutually interacting "stagflation" among the Western democracies, have all revived Soviet hopes of a "general crisis of capitalism" and expectations for revolutionary changes and an increase of Soviet influence not just in the less developed world but in the Western world itself, the "citadel of capitalism." Thus, more than ever, the containment of Soviet power is not merely a matter of the military balance but, as importantly, a matter of constructing an international order which nations—especially those of the developing world—tend to perceive as just and feel convinced that they have a stake in. As George Kennan said more than thirty years ago in his article explaining the need for containment: "The issue of Soviet-American relations is in essence a test of the over-all worth of the United States as a nation among nations. . . . Surely, there was never a fairer test of national quality than this." This is as true as the United States enters her third century under the Carter Administration, as it was when it became actively involved in world affairs after World War II.

A SELECTIVE BIBLIOGRAPHY

American Society

ALMOND, GABRIEL A. *The American People and Foreign Policy.** New York: Praeger Publishers, 1960. This is a first-class analysis relating the "American character" to foreign policy.

BOORSTIN, DANIEL J. *The Genius of American Politics.** Chicago: Phoenix Books, 1953. As Hartz (see below) does, Boorstin emphasizes the unique nature and conformity of American society.

HARTZ, LOUIS. *The Liberal Tradition in America.** New York: Harvest Books, 1955. This is a brilliant analysis of America as a liberal society; it stresses heavily the absolutism of the American value system.

HERBERG, WILL. *Protestant, Catholic, and Jew.** Rev. ed. New York: Anchor Books, 1960. This excellent and stimulating book clarifies beyond any doubt that "Americanism" is this country's real religion, and that Protestantism, Catholicism, and Judaism are merely three different expressions of the "American way of life."

HOFSTADTER, RICHARD. *The Paranoid Style in American Politics.** New York: Vintage Books, 1967. A detailed analysis of the conspiratorial explanations sometimes invoked to explain domestic and foreign policy, especially by such men as the late Senator McCarthy and Presidential candidate Goldwater.

POTTER, DAVID M. *The People of Plenty.** Chicago: Phoenix Books, 1954. A penetrating analysis of the concept of national character and of the impact of American abundance on American character and foreign policy.

* Asterisked titles are available in paperback editions.

American Foreign Policy

ALPEROVITZ, GAR. *Atomic Diplomacy: Hiroshima and Potsdam.** New York: Vintage Books, 1967. This is one of the more important revisionist books. Its thesis is that, upon Roosevelt's death, Truman's tough line, which sought to exploit America's new atomic power in order to push the Soviet Union out of Europe and back behind its prewar frontiers, precipitated the cold war. For an evaluation of this thesis, see Arthur M. Schlesinger, Jr., "The Origins of the Cold War," *Foreign Affairs,* October, 1967, pp. 22–52. Two books that analyze contemporary American foreign policy in some detail and from opposite perspectives are George Liska, *Imperial America,** and Robert Tucker, *Nation or Empire,** both published by The Johns Hopkins University Press in 1967 and 1968 respectively.

ARON, RAYMOND. *The Imperial Republic.** Cambridge, Mass.: Winthrop Publishers, 1974. A sympathetic French observer of American policy, especially trenchant on revisionist interpretations.

BARNET, RICHARD J. *Roots of War.* New York: Atheneum, 1972. Vietnam, and the cold war preceding it, is seen as the product of certain domestic forces: the national security managers, capitalists, and America's leaders' manipulation of public opinion.

BLOOMFIELD, LINCOLN P. *In Search of American Foreign Policy.** New York: Oxford University Press, 1974. An attempt to combine realism with American democratic values for a "humane use of power." Detailing the author's own anguish at M.I.T. during the Vietnam War, its prescriptions are broad and perhaps not always relevant for specific policies in complex and ambiguous circumstances.

COMPTON, JAMES V. (ed.). *America and the Origins of the Cold War.* Boston: Houghton Mifflin, 1972. A good, if necessarily brief, set of selections, primarily summing up the revisionist attacks.

FLEMING, D. F. *The Cold War and Its Origins, 1917–1960.* 2 vols. Garden City, N.Y.: Doubleday, 1961. Fleming places particular stress on Truman's anti-Communism in this lengthy and rambling book.

FULBRIGHT, J. WILLIAM. *The Arrogance of Power.** New York: Vintage Books, 1967.

———. *Old Myths and New Realities.** New York: Vintage Books, 1964.

———. *The Crippled Giant.** New York: Vintage Books, 1972.

These three books are among the most influential and readable of the liberal critiques of America's postwar foreign-policy role. The former Senator particularly stresses American policymakers' false perceptions of the world, as well as their tendency to cling to cold war dogmas and to commit the United States beyond its power to uphold these commitments. Two excellent responses to these views may be found in Lionel Gelber, "The American Role and World Order," *Yale Review,* October, 1967, and J. H. Huizinga, "America's Lost Innocence," *The New York Times Magazine,* January 26, 1969.

GADDIS, JOHN L. *The United States and the Origins of the Cold War, 1941–1947.** New York: Columbia University Press, 1972. A balanced, detailed, careful refutation of the various revisionist interpretations and a good introduction to the post-1945 period.

GILBERT, FELIX. *To the Farewell Address.* Princeton, N.J.: Princeton University Press, 1961. A discerning commentary on the conflict between utopianism and realism in early American foreign policy.

HALLE, LOUIS J. *The Cold War as History.** New York: Harper & Row, 1967. While critically examining more orthodox interpretations, Halle sees the cold war as essentially a tragedy because both superpowers were trapped by the state system.

HILSMAN, ROGER. *To Move a Nation.* New York: Doubleday, 1967. A memoir by a Kennedy Administration participant, focusing on the nature of governmental decision-making.

KENNAN, GEORGE F. *American Diplomacy, 1900–1950.** New York: Mentor Books, 1952. A brief analysis of this period in terms of what Kennan calls our "moral-legalistic" approach to foreign policy. The book contains Kennan's famous "Mr. X" article, "The Sources of Soviet Conduct" (originally published in *Foreign Affairs*), which was the basis for the containment policy.

———. *Memoirs.* Boston: Little, Brown, 1967. Kennan's retrospective views on postwar U.S. policy.

———. *Russia and the West under Lenin and Stalin.** New York: Mentor Books, 1961. A beautifully written book with incisive comments and frequent indictments of Western, and especially American, policy toward the Soviet Union.

KOLKO, GABRIEL. *The Roots of American Foreign Policy.* Boston: Beacon Press, 1969.

——— and JOYCE KOLKO. *The Limits of Power.* New York: Harper & Row, 1972. The Kolko thesis in both books is that American capitalism is by its very nature expansionistic. Others, the U.S.S.R. or North Korea for example, are its innocent victims.

MAY, ERNEST R. *Lessons of the Past.** New York: Oxford University Press, 1973. Suggesting that those who remember the past may misapply it in different contemporary circumstances, the author makes a good point but overstates his case.

MORGENTHAU, HANS J. *In Defense of the National Interest.* New York: Knopf, 1951. A critique of early U.S. postwar policy, particularly good for the barrage it levels against American "moralism," sentimentalism," "utopianism," and "legalism" in foreign policy.

——. *A New Foreign Policy for the United States.** New York: Praeger Publishers, 1969. A sharp critique of the modes of thought underlying two decades of American foreign policy that led the country into Vietnam.

OGLESBY, CARL, and RICHARD SCHAULL. *Containment and Change.* New York: Macmillan, 1967. A well-written New Left interpretation of past and present U.S. foreign policy.

STEEL, RONALD. *Pax Americana.** New York: Viking, 1967. Perhaps the best over-all liberal critique of U.S. policy and very readable.

WILLIAMS, WILLIAM A. *The Tragedy of American Diplomacy.* Rev. ed. New York: World, 1962. This book, with its focus on U.S. capitalism's expansion, is written by the man who has trained most of the contemporary revisionists.

American Military Strategy

ABEL, ELIE. *The Missile Crisis.** New York: Bantam Books, 1966. An exciting account.

BRODIE, BERNARD. *Strategy in the Missile Age.** Princeton, N.J.: Princeton University Press, 1959. Like all the author's writings, outstanding for the incisiveness of its thought and the freshness and candor of its insights into such problems as total war and limited nuclear war.

BUCHAN, ALASTAIR. *NATO in the 1960's.* Rev. ed. New York: Praeger Publishers, 1963. A good brief analysis of NATO's nuclear crisis.

—— (ed.). *A World of Nuclear Powers?** New York: Spectrum Books, 1967. A series of analyses of the impact of nuclear proliferation. Buchan's introduction and Stanley Hoffman's essays are especially valuable.

GEORGE, ALEXANDER L. *The Limits of Coercive Diplomacy.** Boston: Little, Brown, 1971. A fine analysis of the American use of coercion in Laos, Cuba during the 1962 missile crisis, and the beginning of the Vietnam intervention.

—— and RICHARD SMOKE. *Deterrence in American Foreign Policy.** New York: Columbia University Press, 1974. An excellent detailed historical analysis of deterrence of limited challenges: Berlin, Korea, Quemoy-Matsu, Indochina, the Middle East, and Cuba.

HORELICK, ARNOLD L. "The Cuban Missile Crisis: An Analysis of Soviet Calculations and Behavior," *World Politics,* April, 1964, pp. 363–89. Definitive treatment.

—— and MYRON RUSH. *Strategic Power and Soviet Foreign Policy.*

Chicago: University of Chicago Press, 1966. A very able analysis of Soviet nuclear blackmail tactics from 1957 to 1962.

KAHN, HERMAN. *On Escalation: Metaphors and Scenarios.* New York: Praeger Publishers, 1965. An analysis of the dynamics of escalation involved in limited conflicts.

————. *Thinking About the Unthinkable.** New York: Avon, 1964. A much condensed and more readable version of the author's famous *On Thermonuclear War.* Some of the topics covered are the different types of nuclear war, civil defense, and various types of deterrence.

KAUFMANN, WILLIAM W. (ed.). *Military Policy and National Security.* Princeton, N.J.: Princeton University Press, 1956. Contains Kaufmann's own perceptive analysis of American total- and limited-war strategy.

KISSINGER, HENRY A. *The Necessity for Choice.** New York: Anchor Books, 1961. A critical analysis of American military policy during the 1950's, plus superb sections dealing with American attitudes toward negotiations, the underdeveloped nations, and the problems of policy formulation.

————. *Nuclear Weapons and Foreign Policy.** New York: Harper & Brothers, 1957; abr. ed. New York: Anchor Books, 1958. A trenchant critique of America's all-or-nothing strategy, this volume includes a controversial chapter on the use of tactical atomic weapons in limited wars.

————. *The Troubled Partnership.** New York: Anchor Books, 1966. A good presentation and critique of the U.S. position in the NATO crisis of the mid-1960's.

OSGOOD, ROBERT E. *Limited War.* Chicago: University of Chicago Press, 1957. Excellent in its analysis of American post-war military policies up to the end of the 1954 Indochina war and of the political and social conditions that prior to the twentieth century kept wars limited.

————. *NATO.* Chicago: University of Chicago Press, 1962. The best detailed historical analysis of the alliance since its inception. It stresses, particularly, the changing strategic and political factors that threaten to disentangle the cohesive bonds of NATO.

PARET, PETER, and JOHN W. SHY. *Guerrillas in the 1960's.* Rev. ed. New York: Praeger Publishers, 1962. A concise analysis of guerrilla warfare.

QUESTER, GEORGE H. *Nuclear Diplomacy.* New York: Dunellen, 1970. An historical analysis of post-war U.S. foreign policy as influenced by nuclear arms deployment.

SCHELLING, THOMAS C. *Arms and Influence.** New Haven: Yale University Press, 1966. A detailed analysis of deterrence by one of the most influential thinkers in this field.

THAYER, CHARLES W. *Guerrilla.** New York: New American Library, 1963. The best and most readable analysis of guerrilla warfare.

WOLFERS, ARNOLD (ed.). *Alliance Policy in the Cold War.* Baltimore, Md.: Johns Hopkins Press, 1959. An analysis of the manifold problems inherent in the relationship between American strategy and alliance systems during the first decade of containment.

American Policy in Postwar Europe

CALLEO, DAVID P. *The Atlantic Fantasy.* Baltimore, Md.: The Johns Hopkins Press, 1970. While somewhat revisionist in its examination of past NATO policy, Calleo argues for a more independent Europe with its own nuclear force.

————. *Europe's Future.** New York: Norton, 1967. A good examination of the alternatives: the Common Market's Federalist Europe, De Gaulle's Nationalist Europe, and America's Atlantic Europe.

COTTRELL, ALVIN J., and JAMES E. DOUGHERTY. *The Politics of the Atlantic Alliance.** New York: Praeger Publishers, 1964. A good analysis of the military, political, and economic aspects of the alliance.

DAVISON, W. PHILLIPS. *The Berlin Blockade.* Princeton, N.J.: Princeton University Press, 1958. A detailed account of the first Berlin crisis.

HOFFMAN, STANLEY. *Gulliver's Troubles or the Setting of American Foreign Policy.** New York: McGraw-Hill, 1968. A lengthy analysis of the international system and of U.S. political culture and institutions and how they bore on the NATO alliance at the time.

HOLBORN, HAJO. *The Political Collapse of Europe.* New York: Knopf, 1951. This is a masterpiece of brevity and lucid analysis of the main political and social currents that have affected Europe's development since 1815.

JONES, JOSEPH. *The Fifteen Weeks.* New York: Viking, 1955. This is the definitive account—and a very exciting one at that—of the formulation of the Truman Doctrine and the Marshall Plan.

KLEIMAN, ROBERT. *Atlantic Crisis.** New York: Norton, 1964. An excellent analysis and indictment of the Kennedy Administration's inept attempts to implement its plan for Atlantic partnership.

KRAFT, JOSEPH. *The Grand Design.* New York: Harper & Row, 1962. A fine presentation of the problems that the new Europe posed for the United States in the early 1960's and the response of the Kennedy Administration in terms of an Atlantic partnership.

MANDER, JOHN. *Berlin, Hostage for the West.** Baltimore, Md.: Penguin Books, 1962. A first-rate brief analysis of the post-1958 Berlin crisis and Soviet nuclear-blackmail tactics.

NEWHOUSE, JOHN (ed.). *U.S. Troops in Europe.* Washington: The Brookings Institution, 1971. A balanced analysis of various facets of the proposed withdrawal of a sizable contingent of U.S. troops from Europe.

PFALTZGRAFF, ROBERT L., JR. *The Atlantic Community.* New York: Van Nostrand Reinhold, 1969. Perhaps the best brief over-all analysis of the political, economic, military, and psychological problems besetting the alliance in the 1970's.

PLANCK, CHARLES R. *The Changing Status of German Reunification in Western Diplomacy, 1955–1966.* Baltimore, Md.: Johns Hopkins Press, 1967. A brief Washington Center of Foreign Policy Research study.

SPEIER, HANS. *Divided Berlin.* New York: Praeger Publishers, 1961. A blow-by-blow account of the Berlin negotiations under the Soviet threat of war after 1958.

STEEL, RONALD. *The End of Alliance.* New York: Delta Books, 1966. An excellent analysis of the impact of Europe's resurgence on European-American relations.

WHITE, THEODORE H. *Fire in the Ashes.* New York: William Sloane Associates, 1953. This sympathetic and beautifully written book remains by far the best general introduction to Europe after 1945 and to the role of the United States in rekindling the fire of the Old World.

American Policy in Asia

BARNETT, A. DOAK. *A New U.S. Policy Toward China.* Washington: The Brookings Institution, 1971. A thoughtful analysis proposing what its title suggests. Written before Nixon's visit to Peking.

CLOUGH, RALPH N. *East Asia and U.S. Security.* Washington, D.C.: The Brookings Institution, 1975. A thorough and balanced analysis of the changing relationships of the United States in this key area with Japan, Russia, Communist China, and other countries from Korea to Southeast Asia in which containment is replaced by a more complex set of problems and policies.

CLUBB, O. EDMUND. *China and Russia.* New York: Columbia University Press, 1971. A very detailed historical account concluding, somewhat surprisingly, that the possibility of Sino-Soviet reconciliation after Mao's death exists.

COHEN, WARREN I. *America's Response to China.* New York: Wiley, 1971. A knowledgeable and useful interpretive history of Sino-American relations over the last 100 years.

DRAPER, THEODORE. *Abuse of Power.* New York: Viking, 1967. A highly critical analysis of American policies toward Cuba, the

Dominican Republic, and Vietnam, particularly the resort to force instead of handling problems politically.

FALL, BERNARD B. *The Two Viet-Nams.* 2d rev. ed. New York: Praeger Publishers, 1967. The single best analysis of the guerrilla war, especially since 1957. Fall shows particularly well the difficulties confronting the United States in fighting anti-guerrilla warfare.

FEIS, HERBERT. *China Tangle.** Princeton, N.J.: Princeton University Press, 1953. A good account of American policy toward China during World War II.

GURTOV, MELVIN. *The First Vietnam Crisis.** New York: Columbia University Press, 1967. A definitive analysis of the decision-making process within the Eisenhower Administration on the issue of whether the United States should have intervened or not in 1954.

HALPERIN, MORTON H. *China and the New Bomb.* New York: Praeger Publishers, 1965. A fine analysis focusing upon Peking's objectives, its perception of the role of force, and the role that the bomb might therefore play.

HAMMER, ELLEN J. *The Struggle for Indochina, 1940–1955.** Stanford, Calif.: Stanford University Press, 1966. The best volume on French policy in this area, providing background for the later American involvement.

HELLMANN, DONALD C. *Japan and East Asia.** New York: Praeger Publishers, 1972. A good introduction to the problems, external and domestic, Japan confronts in a changing post-Vietnam Asia and world.

HINTON, HAROLD C. *Three and a Half Powers.** Bloomington: Indiana University Press, 1975. A good historical analysis of the changing balance of power in Asia since World War II.

HOOPES, TOWNSEND. *The Limits of Intervention.** New York: McKay, 1969. A fine insider's account of the increasing opposition among the Pentagon's civilians to the bombing of North Vietnam, resulting in President Johnson's suspension of bombing.

LACOUTURE, JEAN. *Vietnam: Between Two Truces.** New York: Vintage Books, 1966. An interesting analysis, especially of the nature of the Vietcong movement and its relationship to Hanoi.

OBERDORFER, DON. *Tet.* New York: Doubleday, 1971. A good reconstruction of America's Dien Bien Phu.

*The Pentagon Papers.** New York: Bantam Books, 1971. A fairly full, but by no means complete, analysis of the U.S. involvement and conduct of the Vietnam war.

RASKIN, MARCUS G., and BERNARD B. FALL (eds.). *The Vietnam Reader.** Rev. ed. New York: Vintage Books, 1968. The pros and cons of the Vietnamese war.

REISCHAUER, EDWIN O. *Beyond Vietnam.** New York: Vintage Books,

1967. A good analysis of America's alternatives in Vietnam and a rather general postwar prescription for a Far Eastern policy.

SALISBURY, HARRISON E. *War Between Russia and China.* New York: Norton, 1969. A journalistic account suggesting that the deep mutual hatreds may well precipitate war.

SCHLESINGER, ARTHUR M., JR. *The Bitter Heritage.** New York: Crest Books, 1967. A bitter critique of Johnson's policy and an apologia for Kennedy's handling of Vietnam policy.

SPANIER, JOHN W. *The Truman-MacArthur Controversy and the Korean War.** Rev. ed. New York: Norton, 1965. A full-length study and analysis of the policies and events during this war that had such an overwhelming impact upon the United States after 1952.

STAVINS, RALPH, RICHARD J. BARNET, and MARCUS G. RASKIN. *Washington Plans an Aggressive War.* New York: Vintage Books, 1971. The title tells the story.

TANHAM, GEORGE K. *Communist Revolutionary Warfare: From the Viet-Minh to the Viet-Cong.* Rev. ed. New York: Praeger Publishers, 1967. An analysis of the successful Vietminh guerrilla war against the French; updated to include comparative analyses of Vietcong strategy and tactics.

TSOU, TANG. *America's Failure in China, 1941–50.** 2 vols. Chicago: Phoenix Books, 1963. The definitive analysis of this controversial subject.

THOMPSON, SIR ROBERT. *No Exit from Vietnam.* New York: McKay, 1969. A leading British expert on counterguerrilla warfare and special consultant to former President Nixon gives his own tough-minded analysis of Vietnam. Well worth reading.

VINACKE, HAROLD M. *The United States and the Far East, 1945–51.* Stanford, Calif.: Stanford University Press, 1952. Very good and, also to its advantage, quite short.

Memoirs and Biographies of American Statesmen and Administrations

ACHESON, DEAN. *Present at the Creation.* New York: Norton, 1969. The lucid, beautifully written memoirs of the former Secretary of State.

BUNDY, MCGEORGE (ed.). *The Pattern of Responsibility.* Boston: Houghton Mifflin, 1952. A compilation of Secretary Acheson's speeches and Congressional testimony.

BYRNES, JAMES F. *Speaking Frankly.* New York: Harper & Brothers, 1947.

DONOVAN, ROBERT J. *Eisenhower: The Inside Story.* New York: Harper

& Brothers, 1956. Apparently an "inside" account. (For a very fine evaluation of the Eisenhower Administration—one that is likely to stand for a long time—see William V. Shannon, "Eisenhower as President," *Commentary*, November, 1958.)

EISENHOWER, DWIGHT D. *Mandate for Change.** New York: New American Library, 1965.

————. *Waging Peace.* New York: Doubleday, 1965. Eisenhower's narrative of his Presidential years.

FERRELL, ROBERT H. *George C. Marshall.* New York: Cooper Square Publishers, 1966. A volume in the U.S. Secretaries of State series.

GERSON, LOUIS. *John Foster Dulles.* New York: Cooper Square Publishers, 1967. A volume in the U.S. Secretaries of State series.

GUHIN, MICHAEL. *John Foster Dulles.* New York: Columbia University Press, 1972. Guhin suggests that Dulles was neither a moralist nor an idealist in foreign policy, but a realist.

HARRIMAN, W. AVERELL. *Special Envoy to Churchill and Stalin, 1941–1946.* New York: Random House, 1975. A personal memoir and commentary on the origins of the cold war from an eminent presidential advisor.

HOOPES, TOWNSEND. *The Devil and John Foster Dulles.** Boston: Atlantic-Little, Brown, 1975. A most comprehensive Dulles biography, very critical of the Republican Secretary of State's moralistic-ideological approach to foreign policy.

JOHNSON, LYNDON B. *The Vantage Point.** New York: Popular Library, 1971. The late President's perception of his domestic and foreign policies, especially Vietnam.

KENNEDY, ROBERT F. *Thirteen Days.** New York: Norton, 1971. A personal memoir of decision-making at the highest level during the 1962 Cuban missile crisis.

PARMET, HERBERT S. *Eisenhower and the American Crusades.* New York: Macmillan, 1972. A lengthy assessment of President Eisenhower, notable for its presentation of Eisenhower as a shrewd and rather clever leader and maneuverer.

SCHLESINGER, ARTHUR M., JR. *A Thousand Days.** New York: Crest Books, 1967. A compelling analysis of the Kennedy Administration in office.

SMITH, GADDIS. *Dean Acheson.* New York: Cooper Square Publishers, 1972. A volume in the U.S. Secretaries of State series.

SORENSEN, THEODORE C. *Kennedy.** New York: Bantam Books, 1966. An eloquent and sensitive account by a close friend of President Kennedy.

TRUMAN, HARRY S. *Memoirs.** 2 vols. New York: New American Library, 1965. The late President's account of the events that occurred during his stewardship.

INDEX

JOHN SPANIER, Professor of Political Science at the University of Florida, is the author of *Games Nations Play, The Truman-MacArthur Controversy and the Korean War,* and *World Politics in an Age of Revolution.* He is a co-author of *The Politics of Disarmament, Analyzing American Politics,* and, most recently, *How American Foreign Policy Is Made.*